FOURTH EDITION

Managing Classroom Behavior

A Reflective Case-Based Approach

James M. Kauffman

University of Virginia

Mark P. Mostert

Regent University

Stanley C. Trent

University of Virginia

Patricia L. Pullen

University of Virginia

Boston   New York   San Francisco
Mexico City   Montreal   Toronto   London   Madrid   Munich   Paris
Hong Kong   Singapore   Tokyo   Cape Town   Sydney

Executive Editor: *Virginia Lanigan*
Editorial Assistant: *Scott Blaszak*
Marketing Manager: *Kris Ellis-Levy*
Manufacturing Buyer: *Andrew Turso*
Production Coordinator: *Pat Torelli Publishing Services*
Cover Coordinator: *Kristina Mose-Libon*
Editorial-Production Service: *Lynda Griffiths*
Electronic Composition: *TKM Productions*

For related titles and support materials, visit our online catalog at www.ablongman.com.

Between the time Website information is gathered and then published, it is not unusual for some sites to have closed. Also, the transcription of URLs can result in typographical errors. The publisher would appreciate notification where these occur so that they may be corrected in subsequent editions.

Library of Congress Cataloging-in-Publication Data

Managing classroom behavior: a reflective case-based approach / James M. Kauffman...
  [et al.].
     p. cm.
   Includes bibliographical references and index.
   ISBN 0-205-44881-X
     1. Classroom management. 2. Classroom management--Case studies. 3. Case method. I.
Kauffman, James M.

LB3013.M326 2006
371.102'4-dc22   2005043000

Printed in the United States of America

10 9 8 7 6 5 4   09 08

CONTENTS

PREFACE

When teachers are not successful in helping students learn and enjoy school, the reason is likely to be, in large measure, the difficulty they experience in managing classroom behavior. Many teachers who become discouraged, feel "burned out," or leave the profession attribute their unhappiness in teaching to their difficulty in managing students' behavior. Managing students' behavior has always been a demanding task, but it has become much more exacting during the past decade. What experienced teachers tell us, what we read, and what we see in schools—every reliable indicator—tell us that disruption, aggression, disinterest in school, social withdrawal, and other forms of undesirable behavior are increasingly common in nearly all schools. The federal No Child Left Behind law has made teaching even more demanding, and demands for higher academic performance have not made students more tractable. Without effective strategies for dealing with unacceptable and troublesome behavior, teachers are unlikely to seek a career in teaching and even less likely to enjoy and be successful in their chosen profession. Furthermore, students are very unlikely to learn what they should when their teachers are unhappy and feel defeated.

We understand both the immensity of the challenge of dealing with students' behavior in today's schools and the importance of preparing teachers for that challenge. This book represents our efforts to help prospective and in-service teachers meet that challenge as reflective practitioners of the profession of teaching. Our experience in working with students of teaching, whether in preservice training programs or in the field, has led us to the conclusion that the typical expository style of textbooks and the typical lecture-discussion format of courses are inadequate.

In the late 1980s, we began experimenting with a different approach—the case method of teaching, which has been used for decades in schools of business and law. We found much in the case method to recommend it, and we became convinced that it could become the model for some, but not all, of the courses we teach in education. The case-based approach, it seemed to us, was a "natural" for an applied course in classroom behavior management because successful management requires the kind of reflection and analytical skills case analysis demands. Nevertheless, we discovered that teaching cases without readings that provide a foundation of basic concepts about reflection on behavior management issues was also unsatisfactory. For a course in classroom behavior management, we found no texts that presented the information we found most pertinent in a manner designed to encourage reflective analysis of teaching practices. This book was born, in our minds, of necessity. Over a period of several years, we have collected and written cases of our own and used them in our teaching. The cases included in this book are stories we have found useful in helping teachers think through the complexities of dealing effectively with troublesome classroom behavior.

In Part I, we provide an overview of basic concepts that our experience leads us to believe are essential to classroom behavior management. Each chapter begins with an advance organizer—an outline of the major headings, giving the reader a preview of the questions we will be addressing. The body of each chapter is organized around a common framework: (1) an opening statement about the topic of the chapter, (2) one or more vignettes (except in the opening chapter) illustrating problems of the type we will be discussing, (3) the major questions on which we are asking the reader to reflect, (4) consideration of the questions for reflection, and (5) a brief chapter summary. At the end of each chapter, we list references that provided the basis for many of our statements, as well as resources for further study.

Our intention is not only to present basic concepts succinctly but also to induce in readers a process of self-questioning that carries forward from the first chapter to the eighth and that is intimately connected to how one analyzes cases. We have not prepared a "cookbook" or behavior management manual. Rather, our approach is based on the assumptions that asking good questions is a prerequisite for finding good answers and that the preparation of reflective professionals requires primary attention to question asking. Thus, although we make some specific suggestions regarding behavior management, we raise more questions than we answer. Our writing style, we hope, is both readable and conducive to reflection. We have deliberately written without the usual number of reference citations and used reference notes to indicate specific sources that are especially pertinent to our statements. We hope you will pursue the concepts, strategies, or issues we address by consulting the references and resources at the end of the chapter.

In Part II, we offer cases for analysis. Some are cases we wrote following interviews with teachers, others were written by teachers or intern teachers themselves or by parents. All the cases are factual—they are not hypothetical—and the only changes in the facts of the cases are those necessary to protect the identities of the individuals about whom they are written. Each case suggests problems and analyses to which most or all of the chapters in Part I are relevant. One aspect of the case-based approach that is frustrating, yet that makes case-based teaching and learning particularly challenging and exciting, is the multitude of perspectives from which one can view any given case and the multiple problems each case presents. That is also one of the strengths of the case-based approach—it reflects the real-life complexities we do not ordinarily encounter in brief vignettes, hypothetical examples, and the straightforward exposition of principles.

Case-based teaching is relatively new in teacher education. Consequently, you may not have any prior experience in case analysis. The process of case analysis is one you can learn only by doing it. Your instructor will lead you and your fellow students through the analysis of cases by asking you to prepare study questions and by guiding your discussion of various aspects of the cases. Some of our cases are divided into parts: Part A and Part B. For these cases, Part A is included in this book. Part B, a continuation of the cases (found in the instructor's manual), will be provided by your instructor after you have discussed Part A and tried to predict what might happen next.

If your experience is anything like that of the students with whom we have used these materials, you will find case-based learning highly intriguing and rewarding. We hope you enjoy both parts of this book and find them useful in thinking about how you manage students' behavior.

New to the Fourth Edition

Although the fourth edition follows the same structure as the first three editions, we have added some new features. Specifically, new to the fourth edition are:

- A new opening chapter (Chapter 1) about how to analyze cases
- A rewritten chapter (Chapter 7) on working with other educators
- A rewritten chapter (Chapter 8) on working with parents and families
- A rewritten instructor's manual with case analyses paralleling Chapter 1
- Suggested links in the instructor's manual between chapters in Part I and specific cases
- Several new cases in Part II, two of which involve secondary-level teachers
- Revisions of all chapters for improved readability
- Updated references in all chapters included in previous editions

We wrote several of the cases included in this book based on our own experiences. However, we are indebted to many teachers and parents for writing their own cases or telling us their stories, some of which are included in Part II.

We acknowledge with thanks the assistance of our wonderful editor at Allyn and Bacon, Virginia Lanigan, who encouraged us to prepare this revision, and her able assistant, Scott Blaszak. We also thank our fine copyeditor, Lynda Griffiths. In addition we thank the reviewers: Kate Mitchem, West Virginia University; Karen Pukys, Arizona State University; and Melody Tankersley, Kent State University.

J. M. K.
M. P. M.
S. C. T.
P. L. P.

PART ONE

Developing a Reflective Approach to Problems

CHAPTER

1

Analyzing Cases

Case-based teaching has certain advantages, but only if you have an orientation to analyzing cases. Consequently, we start with some questions and suggestions about case
analysis. After all, this is a *case-based book*, and we want you to get in the habit of reflecting on what you read. We want you to be able to apply the principles you read about in
subsequent chapters to the cases in this book and to your own practices as a teacher. You
will likely be able to do that only if you have a systematic way of trying to make sense of
the circumstances teachers face. We provide illustrations of some of these circumstances throughout the chapters. However, we describe such circumstances more
extensively in the cases in Part II.

Questions for Reflection

As you encounter cases in your reading and study, we suggest that you ask yourself some
important questions about cases. You might start with these:

1. How will analyzing cases help me in the classroom?
2. How should I analyze a case?
3. What are the issues that I should attend to first?
4. What actions should I take to resolve the issues?
5. What knowledge will I need to formulate an action to resolve the issues?
6. What are the perspectives of the people involved in the plan, and what can I predict about their behavior?
7. What might be the consequences of my actions?

How will analyzing cases help me in the classroom?

Studying cases has been part of university programs in business, law, and medical schools for decades. These professions have long understood the benefits of analyzing real-life problems on paper before heading into the real world. All of the cases in this book are real—none is fictitious—and some are daunting in their scope and depth of problems. They are all real-life problems of teachers.

Many if not most of the problems encountered in the cases that students study are common problems that appear daily in given professions, which means that the resolutions students find in cases often generalize into the real world. This generalization helps them to make better decisions quicker when they obtain a job.

How should I analyze a case?

So, case analysis might help you make better decisions. But how do you analyze a case? Where do you begin? Are some *issues* more important than others? What *knowledge* is most important? Will some *actions* have better *consequences* than others? And why should you be concerned about the consequences? Why is understanding of the *perspectives* of those in the case important, and why would you worry about an administrator's or a parent's perspectives on your plan?

There are many ways to analyze a case. The following method was developed by Joanne McNergney, who constructed a system consisting of five parts.[1] Even though we delineate the five parts of a case here, it is important to understand that these parts are interdependent and sometimes difficult to see separately. When you analyze the cases, it's helpful to ask the following questions:

1. What are the *issues* in this case, and which issue is the most important?
2. What are the *actions* I could take to resolve this issue?
3. What *knowledge* do I need to implement my action?
4. What are the *perspectives* of the people involved in the implementation of my plan?
5. What might be the *consequences* of my actions?

Always read a case and obtain the facts first. Without all the facts, you can't accomplish the rest of the case analysis. Ask yourself questions like these (and read for the answers):

- Who is in the case?
- What happens in the case?
- Where does the problem occur? During reading? At recess?
- Is there an important *sequence* of events in the case? If so, can you determine the antecedents and the consequences of the behavior?
- If several teachers are involved in the case, how much teaching experience do the main characters have?
- Is the students' culture different from your culture?

Carefully determining the facts should lead you to the *issues*. *Roget's Thesaurus* gives synonyms for the word *issue: a situation that presents difficulty, uncertainty, or perplexity*. There are many difficult situations in the cases and in our classrooms that perplex us, ranging from suspicion of child abuse, threats of suicide, poor academic achievement, and noncompliance, to lack of parental involvement or a distrustful parent who watches every move in the classroom.

What are the issues that I should attend to first?

Safety and legal issues are always the first concerns. Is there a safety issue presented in the case? Is either the student's or the teacher's safety in jeopardy? Is child abuse suspected? Has the student threatened suicide? Suspected child abuse could be both a safety and a legal issue because in most states, teachers are considered "reporters" of child abuse and are legally bound to report *suspected* child abuse to the child protective services. Consider the following vignette:

> Adrian's mother, Mrs. Beckett, never answered my notes home, and was barely polite the few times I phoned her. It was clear that she was not going to be part of any home/school behavior management plan, so I garnered the principal to mentor Adrian, give him stickers for good work, and compliment him for good behavior. But because I believed so strongly in collaboration with parents, and because I wanted to develop rapport with this parent, I scheduled a home visit to explain the results of the educational assessment for Adrian's approaching triennial evaluation.
>
> The speech-language pathologist, Susan, accompanied me to explain her testing results also. Our first impression when Ms. Beckett let us in was how spotless and ordered the apartment was. As Susan said, "It was uncomfortably clean. You would never have guessed that children lived there." Mrs. Beckett asked us to sit at the dining room table, and then pointed to Adrian and his younger brother, and yelled, "Sit on the sofa! Now!" They sat.
>
> During the explanations of the assessments, I said, "I'm so proud of Adrian. He has worked very hard lately and is completing all of his work neatly and accurately." When I mentioned his name, Adrian approached his mother with one of his assignments. Before Adrian could show his mother his paper, Mrs. Beckett slapped the table close to Adrian with a cut-off razor strap attached to her wrist with a leather thong, and yelled, "Sit down!"

Susan, Adrian, and I jumped, and Adrian backed away, apologizing, "I'm sorry, Mamma. I'm sorry." Susan and I were amazed that we had not seen the razor strap attached to Mrs. Beckett before she banged it on the table. But as Susan later observed, "I guess you don't expect a mother to have a razor strap around her arm when you go for a home visit."

If Mrs. Beckett would wear her razor strap when school faculty visited, Susan and I suspected that she wore it all the time and that she probably thumped her children and not the table when no one else was around. Susan and I were also amazed that Mrs. Beckett was so volatile. We thought this was definitely a safety issue; a mother with a short fuse and a ready razor strap. We involved Child Protective Services (CPS).

One of the cases in this book involves a mother who wants her son tested for what she considered "learning problems." After many pleading letters from the mother, the school finally tested the son, but only when an advocate became involved 18 months after the initial request. The school was not in compliance with the special education law, which was clearly a legal issue.

Usually there are multiple issues in a case. Most children do not present one problem but a cluster of problems, and we are compelled to determine which issue to work on first. Always remember, safety first, for the kids as well as for yourself.

What actions should I take to resolve the issues?

Actions are the plans you implement to resolve the *issue*. What *actions* could you take in a case to *prevent* problems in similar situations? For example, the action the speech-language pathologist and I took about Mrs. Beckett's suspected abuse of her children was to call CPS. Consider the following vignette:

I'm a single mother, and I have to work, but I think I'd rather dig ditches than continue teaching. Even though I'm a speech-language pathologist and have no training in teaching, I am desperate to move my children away from the crime in the big city. So I've accepted the only available job in the small school system in which I was educated.

I foolishly thought that a classroom of 12 students with mild mental retardation in a middle school wouldn't be so hard. What a doofus I am! There are *no* materials appropriate for my class. Even though all the texts are too hard for them, there is no money to purchase any new texts. When I asked the principal what reading program the previous teacher used with the class, he said, "Don't worry much about actually teaching these kids anything. They're retarded and probably won't amount to much. And anyway, we don't have any money to buy any new reading material." (He actually said this!) And if there were money, would I know which texts to purchase? Nope. And these kids are bad! They fight and hit each other on a daily basis, curse each other and me, and won't pay attention in class or complete the few assignments that I give them. And I have no idea how to get them to behave.

Last week, two of the girls got into a knock-down-hair-pulling-scratching cat fight, and when I tried to separate them, I got hit. One of the boys in the class grabbed me and shoved me under the desk, and said, "Now you stay there, you crazy little white woman, 'til I get help." Seemed like a good plan to me! But I can't spend every day hiding under my desk. All I can do is hold on until spring while I search the want adds for another job—*any* job, as long as it's not in the classroom. So far, I can't seem to find anything that offers the same benefits as my miserable teaching job, and I definitely need insurance for my children and me. It's going to be a long winter.

There are lots of issues in the preceding, including the following:

1. An unsafe, out-of-control classroom where children are physically and verbally aggressive
2. No behavior management plan
3. Teaching out-of-field—teacher is a speech-language pathologist, not a classroom teacher
4. Inappropriate curriculum—texts seem too hard
5. No funds to provide another curriculum

The action the teacher would implement for the preceding would depend on which of the issues she chose to remediate. For example, if the teacher decided that teaching out-of-field is the most pressing issue, she could ask for reassignment as a speech-language pathologist, and if there were no such jobs available, she could resign. But she has already said that leaving the classroom without another job that provided benefits is not an option. She has to teach, even though she is miserable. The physical and verbal aggression presents a safety issue and should be addressed immediately. Because many educators say that the best behavior management tool teachers have is good instruction, she should address this issue first, along with the violence. But if you consider the last issue, no funding, how would she do this? The following might be actions to consider:

1. Obtain appropriate texts by pleading for funds from an advocacy organization (e.g., the ARC, formerly known as the Association for Retarded Citizens).
2. Contact parents for collaboration in obtaining appropriate texts.
3. Develop and implement a behavior management plan that reinforces nonaggressive behaviors, attention to teacher presentations, and correctly completed assignments.
4. Enroll in education courses that will help the teacher manage academic and social behavior competently.

If she is already stressed, taking a night class might be the last straw, so enrolling in a course may not be an option—particularly if the school system won't pay for the course. If she decides to plead with the ARC and parents to help her acquire appropriate texts, she needs to know two important facts: (1) the academic achievement of the students and (2) what texts or commercial programs would best serve the needs of her students. The teacher knows how to test and interpret the language and articulation deficits of her students and could develop a speech and language program, but she does not know where her students are in their academic or social skills or how to determine these skill deficits. She needs more knowledge if she is to implement an appropriate action.

What knowledge will I need to formulate an action to resolve the issues?

Let's assume that this benighted soul decides to press for better texts and to develop a behavior management plan. She needs to know where her students are in their academic skills because, as she already knows, if the texts are too hard, the students won't complete tasks or attend during instruction—a clear path for chaos in the classroom. However, if the texts are too easy, the students will be bored and will find inappropriate ways to ease the boredom. The child study committee is a logical place to ask for help, but before she pleads for help from the child study committee, she needs to consult the following for information:

1. *Student cumulative folders*, including the individualized education programs (IEPs), where she can possibly determine her students' academic levels, previous behavior problems and how they were handled, and names of faculty who have worked with the students before.
2. *Personnel* who have worked with the students in the past, and who might be able to elaborate on successful academic and social skills programs.
3. *Parents* who could possibly provide more information about academic and social skills problems and how they handle these issues at home. Even if the parents have little information to share, she should develop rapport with them. The parents could also petition the school board for more funding.
4. *The school psychologist* who may have tested the students, and who also may have time to help her develop a behavior management plan.

In this case, the teacher determined that 10 of her 12 middle school students had been retained two years, were reading on first-grade or primer level, and had been notorious troublemakers their entire academic careers. Eight students were from single-parent families, and grandparents were raising two. Most of the parents or guardians blamed the school for their children's behavior problems, and as one grandmother said, "The schools don't teach my grandson, and so he finds something to do. Ain't always what's best for him, though." Indeed. This teacher also discovered that the texts she was asked to use were on fifth-grade level—clearly too hard for her students.

Armed with the knowledge that reading texts were too difficult for her class, this teacher may now take the following actions:

1. Contact the special education supervisor and other administrators to ask for appropriate texts, and to investigate programs that the students had used successfully in the past.

2. Contact the parents and ask for help to obtain appropriate texts.
3. Contact ARC and ask for funding.
4. Present this information to the child study committee that might have more appropriate texts available.
5. Ask the child study committee to help her make a behavior management plan.

What are the perspectives of the people involved in the plan, and what can I predict about their behavior?

Perspectives are the values of the people involved in the case. Teachers, students, parents, and administrators might view situations depicted in the case differently. How do the values of the characters in the case determine how they will react? Are some of their actions predictable? There are some cases when you will probably say out loud to a character in the case, "No, don't do that!" because you can see what the predictable reaction of the child or parent will be. If you know the perspectives of the characters, you may be able to *predict* how these folks will behave in a given situation. The predictive quality of knowing how a person will react in a situation helps you formulate a better plan of action. In the preceding case about the speech-language pathologist teaching out-of-field, the principal stated his perspective about children with mental retardation. He said, "Don't worry much about actually teaching these kids anything. They're retarded and probably won't amount to much. And anyway, we don't have any money to buy any new reading material."

From his stated perspective on students with mild mental retardation—that they won't amount to much anyway, and that there is not money for new material—the speech-language pathologist could predict that it would be a waste of her time to ask the principal for money to purchase new materials. She could also predict that he won't invest much time or effort in searching for funds from parents, community leaders, or the school board. The teacher will have to hunt for money to purchase appropriate texts. We might hope that the principal will support her efforts, but he is not going to start any campaigns to purchase appropriate curriculum materials for this class.

The grandmother who was a guardian of one of the boys in the class said, "The schools don't teach my grandson, and so he finds something to do. Ain't always what's best for him, though." Her stated perspective is that her grandson is a behavior problem in school because the school doesn't teach him, and that if he were involved in academics in school, he might not find inappropriate ways to amuse himself. What can the teacher predict from the grandmother's statements that would influence her actions? Would the grandmother be supportive of petitioning the school board for appropriate texts? She might. She also might be more supportive of the teacher and more willing to collaborate with school personnel if she knows that the teacher is working hard to obtain materials so that she really can teach her students.

People often do not consider the perspectives of the characters involved in problems they encounter, and they loose valuable time formulating actions that won't work because of the values of the folks in the case. Consider the following true story about Raymond, married two weeks to a divorcee with a 4-year-old girl, Katy:

Raymond's new wife, Betty, met him at the door when he came home from work and said, "You have to spank Katy right now."

Raymond was startled. Katy had always been a model child around him, and there had never been any reason to do more than ask her to sit down and be quiet. He and Betty had never discussed behavior or discipline problems because there didn't seem to be any.

He said, "Betty, I don't believe in spanking children. There is never a good enough reason to hit a child."

"Well, there is this time, and you have to spank her."

"What in the world did she do, Betty?"

"She called me a bitch."

"Well, you spank her. You were the one she called a bitch."

"I would, except she crawled under the porch, and I can't reach her. You have to go get her, bring her out here, and spank her."

Betty insisted that Raymond fetch Katy, so he changed clothes, and armed with a flashlight, he crawled through spiders, mice feces, and dirt to reach Katy, who was in the farthermost corner under the house. When he was about six inches from Katy's face, he opened his mouth to say he-knew-not-what—how was he to persuade her to leave her safe haven of spiders and rat feces so her mother could spank her?—when she said, "Did that bitch run you up under beneath the porch too?" Raymond collapsed laughing, and he and Katy held onto each other howling with laughter. Katy escaped a spanking. Betty was just glad "for those howling idiots to come from under the porch."

Betty predicted from Raymond's stated perception—"There is never a good enough reason to hit a child"—that Raymond would probably never spank his children. If Katy warranted a spanking, then Betty would have to do it. Katy is now 45 years old, and Raymond never spanked her or her two younger siblings. Understanding the perspectives of the people involved in your cases can save you time when you plan your actions.

What might be the consequences of my actions?

All actions have *consequences*—some good, some bad. You must determine what the consequences of your action *might* be. Suppose that the speech-language pathologist/teacher in the earlier case decides to ask her supervisor for help. The teacher hopes that after explaining the academic skill level of her class and the inappropriateness of the texts the class is expected to use, the supervisor will try to find the funds for new materials. However, a bad consequence might be that the supervisor not only doesn't have the funds and doesn't know how to obtain them but she would also be angry with the teacher for asking for something that she can't have.

The consequences of asking the child study committee for help in developing a behavior management plan might be that the committee would make a plan and help the teacher implement the plan, and that this would significantly reduce the aggressive behaviors in class. Or the committee might dismiss the teacher's pleas as whining. Or the committee might be too busy to help her. It might be better to take the chance on the more positive consequence.

Sometimes, the bad consequence that might occur far outweighs the positive one, and school personnel revise their actions. Consider the following:

I had been on the child study committee for 10 years, and I felt that we had had a positive effect at the school—until Mrs. Randolph. Gerry Randolph was a first-grader who was absent 3 to 4 days a week, and his teacher was a bit frantic trying to keep up Gerry's skills. The teacher said, "He's not God's brightest light, but he certainly is average, and he wants to come to school. But I can't teach him if he's not here!" On the days that Mrs. Randolph allowed Gerry to attend school, she sat in her car in the school parking lot all day and waited for Gerry. The first-grade teacher, the visiting teacher, and the principal made separate visits to Mrs. Randolph's home and explained to her why Gerry should attend school regularly, and that she could be held legally responsible if she did not see that Gerry came to school every day unless he was ill. Gerry often expressed how much he liked school, and how much he wanted to come to school. He even volunteered that he could get himself ready every day if someone would pick him up. But Mrs. Randolph just wouldn't allow him to come to school. On several mornings, the visiting teacher, Anne Gregory, had tried to persuade Mrs. Randolph to allow her to drive Gerry to school, but Mrs. Randolph would hold Gerry tightly in her arms and refuse to allow him to leave, even when Gerry reached his arms toward Anne and begged his mother to allow him to go with the visiting teacher.[2]

During a child study meeting, the committee decided to send the visiting teacher and the school system's lawyer to the house and physically remove the student from the home. The committee felt that after a couple of visits, Mrs. Randolph might be more amenable to having her son come to school. "She can sit in the parking lot, or we can bring her to school with Gerry and allow her to sit in the classroom. But Gerry must come to school."

Thank goodness that Mrs. Randolph's Department of Social Services (DSS) case worker was present at the meeting when we discussed forcibly taking Gerry from his mother. She said, "Mrs. Randolph is receiving treatment for a serious mental illness, and if you drag her child from her, she is likely to commit suicide before Gerry gets to school."

The principal was visibly shaken by this news, and promised the DSS worker that we would not follow this action. The committee thought that Gerry's safety was another issue, which we had not considered carefully enough, and asked the DSS worker to look into foster placement for Gerry.

Later, when committee members discussed this plan with the school lawyer, he asked, "Are you nuts? School personnel can't pull children from their mother's arms!"

Sometimes, there may be drastic and terrible consequences for implementing certain actions—consequences that would render your action useless or even dangerous. No evaluation of a case, no plan of action is complete until both *good* and *bad* consequences are considered.

Summary

Studying cases will help you make better decisions more quickly. Case analysis should follow a systematic pattern. Every case can be analyzed for the following elements:

- *Issues:*   Problems encountered in a case; safety and legal issues should be the first considerations
- *Actions:*   Plans formulated to resolve the *issues*
- *Knowledge:*   Information teachers need from theory, other professionals, practice, texts, or experience to formulate a plan of *action*
- *Perspectives*:   Understanding of the values of the people involved in the case gives predictability to how they will react to your *actions*
- *Consequences*:   Understanding the *good* and *bad* effects of your plan of *action*

Case analysis requires addressing each of these elements of a case.

REFERENCES AND RESOURCES FOR FURTHER STUDY

The following references provided the basis for many of our statements in this chapter. You may wish to consult selected references for additional information on specific topics.

Goor, M. B., & Santos, K. E. (2002). *To think like a teacher: Cases for special education interns and novice teachers*. Boston: Allyn and Bacon.

Kauffman. J. M. (2005). *Cases in emotional and behavioral disorders of children and youth*. Upper Saddle River, NJ: Prentice-Hall.

Kolodner, J. L. (2003). Case-based reasoning. In J. W. Guthrie (Ed.), *Encyclopedia of education* (2nd ed.) (pp. 1154–1159). New York: Macmillan Reference.

Mostert, M. P. (1998). *Interprofessional collaboration in schools*. Boston: Allyn and Bacon.

Silverman, R., Welty, W. M., & Lyon, S. (1992). *Case studies for teacher problem solving*. New York: McGraw-Hill.

Sudzina, M. R. (Ed.). (1998). *Case study applications for teacher education*. Boston: Allyn and Bacon.

Sudzina, M. R. (Ed.). (1999). *Case study applications for teacher education: Cases of teaching and learning in the content areas*. Boston: Allyn and Bacon.

ENDNOTES

1. Joanne McNergney, personal communication. We are grateful to Joanne McNergney and Robert F. McNergney for information related to case analysis.
2. The professional called "visiting teacher" in Virginia is called "school social worker" in some states.

2 Identifying Behavior Problems

Questions for Reflection

Could this problem be a result of inappropriate curriculum or teaching strategies?

What do I demand and prohibit, and what should I?

Demands

Prohibitions

Why do certain behaviors bother me, and what should I do about them?

Is this behavior developmentally significant?

Academic Failure

Aggression

Depression

Problems with Peers

A Note about Multiple Problems

Should I focus on a behavioral excess or a deficiency?

Will resolution of the problem solve anything else?

Summary

References and Resources for Further Study

Reference Notes

Managing classroom behavior is a complex task requiring self-questioning and careful reflection that even the best teachers must work to acquire and maintain. This self-questioning and reflection should begin as soon as a teacher becomes concerned about the behavior of a student or group. First impressions about a problem can be misleading. Our experiences in classrooms with children and youth lead us to believe that even outstanding teachers sometimes jump to conclusions about what the problem is rather than taking a more reflective, analytic approach to identifying it. As a consequence of not being sufficiently reflective and analytical, a teacher can waste a lot of time and energy dealing with an issue that is not the most important while neglecting a more significant problem. In the following vignette, consider two teachers' reflections on their initial mistakes in identifying problems.

Effective teaching requires much more than keeping students' behavior under control. Yet, without reasonable control over students' classroom behavior, a teacher will have no chance of being effective. Behavior management skills are necessary but not sufficient for good teaching. Because behavior management skills are necessary, some educators and parents make the mistake of judging the competence of a teacher solely on the basis of how well the class is controlled. Because these skills are not sufficient, other educators and parents misjudge a well-managed class as an indication that the teacher is more concerned about control than teaching. We hope that as you study issues in behavior management you will carefully examine your own concerns and values about controlling the students you teach.

Sally

Kevin was a first-grader who drove me nuts by doing all kinds of things that were not just irritating but kept me from being able to teach effectively. It seemed he was always out of his seat when he was supposed to be working. He grabbed things from other kids and pestered them when they were working. He yelled out things to me when I was across the room. He whined. At first, I thought if I could only keep him in his seat I'd be making a lot of progress. So I devised a plan for rewarding him for working at his desk—at first, you know, for just a couple of minutes at a time, then for gradually longer periods. And he began staying in his seat more. But I realized after a while that the other problems weren't getting any better and that there was a bigger problem. The bigger problem was noncompliance. Kevin just about never did what I told or asked him to do, and staying in his seat to do his work was just one of those things. When I finally figured out that getting him to be reasonably obedient was the real problem, I started teaching compliance as a skill in short lessons. Then I really saw a change in all these things that at first I saw as separate problems. I wish I'd gotten the bigger picture right away, before I spent a couple of weeks on just keeping Kevin in his seat.

Sam

A couple of years ago, the kids in the high school where I taught often wore hats. A lot of the boys wore baseball hats or painters' hats just about everywhere they went. The school administration didn't have any rules about wearing hats, so I had to make my own. I have this "thing" about wearing hats in homes, restaurants, schools, and so on. It seems impertinent to me. The way I was raised, you just don't do it. I think it's disrespectful, and I just want to grab these guys' hats and tell them to keep them off until they get outside. So I spent a lot of my time and psychic energy on hats. I made a strict no-hats rule in my classroom, and I enforced it successfully most of the time. But I ended up having some serious conflicts with kids, too, especially because I was the only teacher in the school who strictly prohibited hats. I wish I'd been able to see at the time that the real problem was my intolerance for a cultural custom that differs from mine. Sure, I have a right to my feelings, but the real issue was how I could exercise control of myself, not a custom of these kids that many see as harmless.

- How much control is enough?
- How do I judge the amount of control necessary in a given circumstance?
- What means of control are legitimate?
- How do I learn to relinquish and regain control?

To a large extent, these and similar questions cannot be answered for you. They are matters that you must address for yourself—as a teacher exercising informed, professional judgment.

Questions for Reflection

We suggest that when you believe a behavior problem in your classroom needs attention and correction, you begin at the beginning—by asking yourself questions that will help you focus on what the problem really is. Only after you have identified it accurately can you feel secure in analyzing the problem and planning ways to manage it. The questions you need to ask yourself include the following:

1. Could this problem be a result of inappropriate curriculum or teaching strategies?
2. What do I demand and prohibit, and what should I?
3. Why do certain behaviors bother me, and what should I do about them?
4. Is this behavior developmentally significant?
5. Should I focus on a behavioral excess or a deficiency?
6. Will resolution of the problem solve anything else?

Could this problem be a result of inappropriate curriculum or teaching strategies?

As teachers, we have a tendency to overlook the fact that what and how we teach can contribute directly to our students behaving in ways that we find irritating, perplexing, or unacceptable. This tendency comes, in part, from the difficulty of keeping the student's perspective in mind while concentrating on teaching. It is easy to forget how frightening new tasks can be, how overwhelming assignments and expectations can look, how boring and mindless requirements can seem, how devastating criticism can be, or how irritating it is to be unengaged in activity and spend long periods simply waiting. It is easy to fall into the trap of assuming that because most students learn what we are trying to teach, *all* students can, or that all students will respond similarly to our teaching methods.

Consider life in the classroom as a student might experience it. For example, imagine yourself as a student who sees no point in what she or he is being asked to learn, one who finds the materials or instructions utterly confusing, one who sincerely believes that she or he cannot do what is expected, one who is expected to repeat again and again a lesson already mastered, one who is expected to listen attentively once more to instructions he or she has heard and comprehended and followed many times already, one who often hears criticism but seldom receives recognition for work well done. Under these circumstances, students are prone to misbehave—to talk to and distract their neighbors, daydream, become irritable, make hostile remarks, and so on. Adults, including teachers themselves, respond in like manner to these conditions. Think of your own behavior, or the behavior of some of your colleagues, in poorly taught classes, at "boring" faculty meetings, or "useless" in-service sessions. Adults, too, are vulnerable to inappropriate behavior, given certain conditions. Before assuming that there is more to the problem, reflect on questions such as these:

- How relevant to or functional in the student's life is the curriculum?
- Do I have the option of teaching something more relevant and functional?
- To what extent could I individualize instruction?
- How successfully is this student or group performing in the curriculum?
- Am I using an approach to teaching that provides too little structure, too much direction, too little positive feedback, or too much criticism?

- How frequently do my students have an opportunity to respond to academic tasks?
- What percentage of time are my students actually actively engaged in learning?
- How and how much could I change the teaching strategies I use?

Behavior problems are not always a result of poor choices of curriculum or teaching strategies, but these must be the first factors you examine. No other questions are appropriate until you can conclude that the *what* and *how* of instruction are not the likely source of the problem. That is, you should not proceed until you are satisfied that what you are asking students to learn is important to their lives, that they are being challenged by assignments but not overwhelmed by failure, that they have frequent opportunities to respond as well as listen, and that they are performing with a high degree of success and receiving frequent positive feedback about their performance. These are essential elements of effective instruction. If they do not characterize what happens in your classroom, then the first order of business is to put them into practice.

We are aware of the difficulties teachers can encounter in using effective teaching practices. The best efforts of excellent teachers sometimes fail to convince students of the importance or relevance of the subject matter. Sometimes teachers are given little or no control over what they are to teach, the materials they are to use, or the instructional methods they are to employ. In such cases, it may be difficult to resist pressures from administrators or supervisors who impose curricula and methods on a wide or schoolwide basis. Sometimes teachers are faced with overwhelming problems in being able to meet the instructional needs of individual students. They may have too many or too diverse a group of students to be able to serve them all adequately, or they may be told not to expect relief or assistance. Advocacy for additional resources to meet students' needs may be ignored or receive hostile responses. Teaching is not an easy profession. It sometimes demands taking risks, sometimes dictates compromise, and always requires struggling with dilemmas. You might ask yourself other questions:

- If I am uncertain about whether my teaching strategies or curriculum are contributing to behavior management problems, what steps could I take to resolve my uncertainty?
- How might I evaluate whether my teaching approximates best practice?

Best instructional practices are summarized by the descriptions in Figure 2.1. Note that we have arranged the characteristics in order so that the first letters can be used as a mnemonic—CLOCS-RAM. Mnemonic devices are helpful for most learners, and there is good evidence supporting their use.[1] You may want to compare your own practice to the characteristics we list in Figure 2.1. We do not assume that there are no other characteristics of best instructional practices that could be listed. However, we do consider these to be the most basic features of best instructional practices. Without any of them, a teacher is likely to be less than optimally successful and to create a classroom environment in which misbehavior is likely to occur.

FIGURE 2.1   **Characteristics of Best Instructional Practices**

Keys to offering effective instruction:
1. *Clarity:*   The student must know exactly what to do (i.e., have no doubt about what is expected).
2. *Level:*   The student must be able to do the task with a high degree of accuracy (i.e., be able to get at least 80 percent correct), but the task must be challenging (i.e., the student should not easily get 100 percent correct repeatedly).
3. *Opportunities:*   The student must have frequent opportunities to respond (i.e., be actively engaged in the task a high percentage of the time).
4. *Consequences:*   The student must receive a meaningful reward for correct performance (i.e., the consequences of correct performance must be frequent and perceived as desirable by the student).
5. *Sequence:*   The tasks must be presented in logical sequence so that the student gets the big idea (i.e., steps must be presented and learned in order that the knowledge or skill is built on a logical progression or framework of ideas, which is a systematic curriculum).
6. *Relevance:*   The task is relevant to the student's life and, if possible, the student understands how and why it is useful (i.e., the teacher attempts to help the student see why in his or her culture the task is important).
7. *Application:*   The teacher helps the student learn how to learn and remember by teaching memory and learning strategies and applying knowledge and skills to everyday problems (i.e., teaches generalizations, not just isolated skills, and honors the student's culture).
8. *Monitoring:*   The teacher continuously monitors student progress (i.e., records and charts progress, always knows and can show what the student has mastered and the student's place or level in a curriculum or sequence of tasks).

What do I demand and prohibit, and what should I?

Assuming that you are satisfied with the what and how of your academic instruction, and that they do not set up circumstances under which students' misbehavior is predictable, you should next consider your expectations for students' behavior. You will need to consider what you demand of your students and what you will not tolerate in two areas: academic performance and social behavior. You will also need to question your expectations for both the class as a group and for individual students. The specific behavior demanded and prohibited varies considerably from teacher to teacher. Some teachers have very different expectations for individual children, compared to those they hold for the class as a whole. In some cases, management problems are not so much a result of students' behavior as they are a result of teachers' inappropriate expectations.

There is much greater agreement among teachers about what behavior is prohibited than about what is demanded. That is, teachers find it easier to specify what they will not tolerate than to specify the appropriate behavior they demand. Perhaps this is a result of our culture's focus on punishment as the primary means of behavior control. Yet, knowing what to demand of students—and therefore what to reward with recognition and praise—is a key to good behavior management. Adults' expectations for children are matters of constant debate in U.S. culture, and teachers' expectations for their students are a central point of controversy.

- How do teachers arrive at their expectations for their students?
- To what extent are expectations biased by labels or stereotypes?
- Are expectations based on cultural standards that discriminate unfairly against some students?
- Are expectations based on cultural traditions that are not necessary for, or are even inconsistent with, effective teaching?

With these questions in mind, we consider the kinds of academic and social behavior most teachers demand and prohibit.

Demands.   Most teachers demand a set of academic and social behaviors that describe a good or "teachable" student.[2] For example, most teachers indicate that the following types of behavior are critical for success in their classrooms: following their established classroom rules, listening to their instructions, following their written instructions and directions, complying with their commands, doing in-class assignments as directed, avoiding breaking classroom rules even when encouraged to do so by peers, producing work of acceptable quality for the student's skill level, and having good work habits (e.g., making efficient use of class time, being organized, staying on task). Far less agreement is found regarding demands for behaviors such as these: using social conventions appropriately (e.g., saying "thank you," "please"), volunteering for classroom activities, working on projects with other students, sharing materials with others in a work situation, and initiating conversations with peers in informal situations.

Prohibitions.   Teachers generally agree that they will not tolerate certain types of behavior in their classrooms. Among those behaviors considered intolerable by the vast majority of teachers are the following: inappropriate sexual behavior, stealing, physical aggression, destruction of property, behaving inappropriately to correction, refusing to obey classroom rules, disturbing or disrupting the activities of others, self-injury, lewd or obscene gestures, ignoring teacher warnings or reprimands, creating disturbance during class activities, cheating, and being verbally aggressive toward others. Considerably less consistency among teachers is found in teachers' intolerance of behaviors such as the following: pouting and sulking, asking irrelevant questions or making irrelevant remarks, refusing to play games with others, ignoring the social initiations of others, and refusing to share.

Opinions about teachers' expectations—what they demand and prohibit—vary widely among educators and the public. One commonly heard criticism of teachers' expectations are that they are too low, that teachers get about what they expect from students and they expect too little. Another criticism is that teachers' expectations are too traditional and self-serving. According to this criticism, teachers set expectations for their students based primarily on the way they themselves were taught. Furthermore, their expectations are designed primarily to make their jobs more comfortable rather than to create effective environments for learning, and to avoid criticism in a system that places a high value on conformity. This stifles innovation and maintains the status quo in schools. Another criticism is that teachers' expectations are not sensitive to cultural and ethnic differences in behavioral styles or norms; thus, they are unnecessarily restrictive and oppressive. In any given situation, every teacher must consider the extent to which these criticisms are justified.

A major concern of educators is that teachers' expectations should not be too high or too low. Expectations that are too high are problematic because students and teachers are too frequently confronted with failure. Students become demoralized because they almost never are able to measure up to the teachers' standards. Teachers, too, become demoralized and drop all expectations because they lose confidence that their students can succeed. Expectations that are too low do not challenge students, convey to students the idea that they are not capable of meeting higher standards, and result in low achievement and frequent misbehavior. Low expectations become self-fulfilling prophesies.

High expectations for some students will be too low for others, depending on what the students have experienced and learned. Getting the expectations just right requires a high degree of knowledge of, and sensitivity to, students' abilities and histories of success and failure. "The same high expectations for all students" may sound egalitarian and be consistent with some educators' philosophies. The problem with this philosophy, however, is that individual differences are ignored.

Nearly every teacher insists on some basic classroom rules that apply to all students. It is as if the teacher has said, "If you want to be a part of this classroom, then there are certain things you have to do and certain things you must not do." Yet, most teachers have more specific expectations for one or more individuals in the class. For certain students, the teacher may interpret the standard expectations differently or articulate a different set of demands and prohibitions. Having different expectations for different students presents a dilemma, however; on the one hand, having the same expectations for everyone ignores individual differences, and on the other hand, individual expectations could be based on favoritism or negative bias. This is not an easy dilemma to resolve. It is part of the extremely difficult task of creating classrooms and schools that are both sensitive to individual differences and consistently enculturating.

Another major concern is that expectations must be communicated clearly and consistently. Sometimes behavior problems arise because the teacher has not articulated clearly and frequently what is demanded and prohibited in the classroom. The teacher may feel that her or his expectations have been communicated, but if the students are asked, they cannot state what their teacher expects. Perhaps the teacher has never discussed, posted, or reviewed any classroom rules. Some teachers and administrators have so many rules that students cannot reasonably be expected to remember them all. We have been in schools in which the rules were several single-spaced typewritten pages in length and in classrooms where 20 or more rules were posted. This kind of rule "overkill" does not result in effective communication of expectations.

Sometimes teachers state one set of expectations verbally but in subtle ways convey a different set of expectations through their nonverbal behavior. For example, a teacher might state that students need to raise their hands and wait to be called on before speaking, yet respond to students who call out answers. A teacher might also say that showing respect for others in the class is expected, but respond to some students with sarcasm. Teachers may also fall into a pattern of changing expectations from day to day so that students are never quite certain which rules are in effect or how they will be enforced.

Very likely, you will be able to state what you demand and prohibit in your classroom. Once you have done so, however, you will need to reflect on several questions about those expectations:

- Are my expectations justifiable, and if so, on what grounds?
- Have I clearly, repeatedly, and consistently communicated those expectations?
- Are my expectations biased against certain groups of students?
- Do I hold the same expectations for everyone, or do I make exceptions for certain individuals?
- If I make exceptions, how do I justify and communicate them?

Why do certain behaviors bother me, and what should I do about them?

We have been discussing expectations as if they are somehow objectively determined with little reference to teachers as individuals with highly personal, emotional responses to children's behavior. This is because to a great extent teachers must be able to take a detached, objective view of their behavior and that of students. Nevertheless, teachers must maintain a high level of self-awareness and understanding of how their personal responses to behavior affect their interactions with students.

One's expectations for behavior—what one considers polite, proper, crass, threatening, profane, annoying, unacceptable, and so on—are a result of one's upbringing in a particular culture and family; one's exposure to other cultures, groups, and individuals, and one's personal values, biases, preferences, and sensitivities. Some teachers' expectations are based on what they believe children need to learn if they are to have friends, be employable, and avoid incarceration or institutionalization. These expectations might be considered universal in our culture. Other expectations, however, are based primarily on more limited social conventions or personal preferences. Sometimes it is difficult to judge whether an expectation is based primarily on broad social or cultural norms or on personal preferences. Consequently, all teachers need to be aware of multicultural issues in education.

Student teachers and those new to the profession are sometimes unprepared for the "tacky" or "trashy" behavior many children may exhibit in the classroom. Many children engage in behavior that may seem intended to challenge, threaten, badger, humiliate, irritate, agitate, or disgust others, including their teachers. Behavior of this type may indicate that a child has serious emotional problems, but often it does not. Furthermore, some individuals may find certain behaviors annoying, offensive, or threatening, whereas others do not. The language children use at school, particularly certain forms of address and various words that some consider vulgar, is a type of behavior about which teachers often have very different opinions. One teacher may bristle at a student's use of the word *nerd* or *dork* (or any other word describing someone unfavorably), whereas another may feel these words are a legitimate part of all youngsters' vocabulary. The mannerisms of certain children may elicit excruciating tension in one teacher but be easily tolerated by another. The way you respond to a given type of behavior may say a lot about how you were reared and enculturated in school yourself. It may also say a lot about how secure and competent you feel as a teacher. Sometimes it merely indicates a hypersensitivity to certain characteristic behaviors of an individual child.

Given that certain behavioral characteristics may "set us off," how should we deal with them as professional educators? All of us find certain idiosyncrasies of others particularly grating and have our pet peeves, and it is legitimate to have especially intense reactions to some types of behavior that others may be able to tolerate far more easily. But teachers must be very careful not to foist their personal standards on their students and not to become peevish or tyrannical in response to personal irritations. They must also be aware of how certain types of behavior may make them defensive and distract attention from important issues. Behavioral standards and personal preferences raise issues of the rights of students and teachers, teachers' responsibility to exercise self-control, and the recognition of developmental risk.

- When do you have a right to impose your personal standards on your students?
- When do your students have a right to behave as they wish?
- How do you determine whether your expectations are consistent with broad social or cultural demands or are primarily idiosyncratic?
- How do you recognize that you react intensely to a particular student's behavioral characteristics, yet avoid treating this student unfairly?

These are not easy questions to answer, and they frequently demand careful reflection. You may need to solicit the opinions and suggestions of other teachers, an administrator, a parent, or others more detached from the situation to help you weigh these issues.

Imagine that you have become aware that a behavior irritates you primarily because it offends your personal values or sensitivities. You consider it inappropriate or bothersome, but you realize that in the broader social context it is trivial. You consider it "tacky" and grating, but you know that it is essentially harmless. It might be wearing a hat indoors, as Sam described in an earlier vignette, or it might be a child's tone of voice that you consider grating or disrespectful. What should you do about it? You might try to change it. On the other hand, you might try to learn to live with it. Perhaps it isn't worth trying to change; maybe it isn't something you feel you can learn to tolerate. In either case, considerable self-control might be required on your part to deal effectively with the situation. Sometimes teachers find that managing their own behavior—learning techniques of self-control—is the better solution to dealing with irritating student behavior. Unfortunately, some teachers seem not to learn to ignore irritating but unimportant misbehavior, and they become embroiled in conflicts about trivia.

Also unfortunately, some teachers learn to ignore or tolerate behaviors that they should not. They allow students to behave in ways that have serious consequences.

Some types of behavior should not be ignored or tolerated because they entail developmental risk for students. That is, these behaviors are signs that students have serious problems that are likely to become worse without effective intervention.

Is this behavior developmentally significant?

Developmentally significant behavior problems are those that have serious long-term consequences for children. That is, if the problems are not resolved, it is highly likely that the children who exhibit them will have increasing difficulties in becoming self-sufficient, reasonably well-adjusted adults. Many of these behaviors are seen by teachers at school. It is extremely important that teachers recognize the seriousness of these behaviors and intervene as early and effectively as possible to change them. Although there may be other types of developmentally significant behavior, most of them fall into one of four primary categories: academic failure, aggression, depression, and problems with peers.

Academic Failure.   Children who fail to acquire basic academic skills in the early grades, those who fail grades or earn failing grades in courses, and those who drop out of school are at high risk for social and economic difficulties. In fact, failure to learn basic skills in reading and math in the early grades is likely to lead to later failure and dropping out. At least a moderate level of success in academics is necessary for most children to develop a healthy self-image. Students who are not academically competent are often shunned or rejected by their peers. Thus, identifying that a student's skills lag seriously behind grade level and taking steps to bring them up to grade expectations is critically important.[3]

At first thought, identifying and remediating deficient academic skills as early as possible seems a straightforward task. A little reflection, however, will bring out some of the persistent problems in defining and dealing with academic failure.

- How do I establish performance expectations for a particular grade level or age of student?
- How far behind grade expectation is far enough to merit special attention? That is, how much failure does a child have to experience or how far behind the rest of the class must a child fall before I become seriously concerned?
- If I perceive that a student is falling significantly behind, how should I intervene?
- How can I tell whether my efforts to help are merely making matters worse?
- When I've exhausted my own knowledge in trying to improve the student's performance, whom should I consult?
- Under what conditions should I conclude that I don't have, and can't acquire quickly enough, the skills or resources necessary to address the problem effectively?

These are only a few of the questions you must consider in dealing with academic failure. Questions such as these have sparked much controversy among educators for many decades, and the answers are not obvious. Nearly all educators agree that a teacher has an obligation to see that every child in her or his class experiences frequent success and achieves at the highest level possible. Nevertheless, nearly everyone who has been a teacher has experienced failure in dealing with a student's failure—despite his or her best efforts, the teacher has not been able to help a student experience an acceptable level of success in the classroom and approximate the achievement of the peer group. The way teachers assess their limitations and deal with their failures as teachers is extremely important for the education profession, and even more important for the futures of the students they have been assigned to teach.

Academic failure usually brings with it a variety of behavior problems. Children who do not keep up with their peers in academics seldom have a strong sense of personal worth and dignity. They have little to lose, and sometimes much to gain in the way of attention from peers and adults, by getting into trouble. If they do not become persistently annoying to others, they may withdraw from social interaction and become morose. In either case, such students are laying the groundwork for further academic failure, which leads to an increasing tendency toward aggression, depression, or both. Breaking the vicious cycle of academic failure and maladaptive behavior may require attention to multiple aspects of the problem. Besides academic remediation, the teacher needs to be ready to intervene in other developmentally significant behavior problems.

Aggression.   Numerous writers have noted that aggression is endemic in the United States—"as American as apple pie," as some have put it. Violence is the primary active ingredient in the popular media. Hostile aggression and other antisocial behavior, both physical and verbal, is pervasive in many neighborhoods and schools. Homicide is one of the leading causes of death among adolescents and young adults. Because of its pervasiveness in U.S. culture, and because of the long-held misconception that it is not a highly significant indicator of mental illness, hostile aggression is often ignored. We are not referring here to the adaptive assertiveness that is necessary for survival in a humane society. We are referring to hyperaggressive behavior that harms others or destroys property, drives others away by threats or intimidation, prompts counteraggression, and is incompatible with learning prosocial behavior or academic skills. It is behavior that is inappropriate for one's age and the social circumstances in which it occurs.

Extremely aggressive behavior carries an extremely high risk of other developmental problems. The earlier in life a child's behavior is highly aggressive (compared to other children of the same age), the longer a child's history of aggressive acts, the greater the variety of settings in which a child is aggressive (e.g., playground, classroom, bus, home, neighborhood), and the more varied a child's aggressive acts (e.g., hitting, kicking, biting, pinching, scratching, throwing things, threatening, extorting), the worse the prognosis is for later adjustment and achievement.[4] Thus, early intervention to stop aggression and teach more prosocial behavioral alternatives is critically important.

If a child stands out from his or her peers as being highly aggressive, teachers are doing the child and society no favor by ignoring it, assuming that the child will outgrow it, or justifying it on grounds that the expression of aggression may help to reduce it. Engaging in aggressive antisocial acts is not good for children; it does not help them develop appropriate behavior, but increases the likelihood of further aggression, maladjustment, and social and academic failure. Effective means must be sought to stop it and replace it with more adaptive, self-enhancing behavior.

As is the case with the other topics we've discussed, easy answers to most of the questions raised by students' aggression are not to be found. Following are questions every teacher must consider.

- What aggressive acts fall within the developmentally appropriate range for youngsters of a particular age, social background, and gender?
- When is aggressive behavior acceptable because it falls within the student's cultural norms, although it violates the teacher's expectations?
- How much aggression should be tolerated in a regular classroom, given the teacher's best efforts to reduce it, before the student is excluded from the regular class?

Questions such as these will likely stir controversy among educators for many decades to come.

Nevertheless, we feel confident in stating that hyperaggression is a developmentally significant type of behavior that teachers must take seriously. The more clearly a child is verbally and physically more aggressive than the norm for his or her age, the more teachers should be concerned for the child's future. We also feel confident in stating that educators' responses to students' aggression must not be counteraggressive. That is, truly effective interventions in aggression do not involve adults' aggression against students. The response to aggression must be, to the greatest extent possible, nonviolent and instructive. We discuss this matter further in subsequent chapters (see especially Chapter 4).

Depression.   Only within the past couple of decades have developmental psychologists, mental health professionals, and educators begun to understand the nature and extent of the problem of depression among children.[5] Suicide and suicide attempts by children and adolescents have increased dramatically during the past 20 years, and suicide is now one of the leading causes of death among adolescents and young adults. Furthermore, studies of the thoughts and feelings of children and adolescents have revealed that they become depressed in much the same way adults do and that depression is a far more frequent problem among minors than previously thought. Depression is often a problem related to aggressive behavior, social withdrawal, hyperactive and inattentive behavior, and academic failure.

The signs of depression in children and adolescents may be similar to those in adults. Any radical change in behavior should be taken as a signal that the student may be experiencing depression. If a student exhibits one or more of the following characteristics over a period of weeks, he or she should be evaluated for depression by a mental health professional:

- Inability to experience pleasure, or depressed mood
- Sudden change in appetite or weight
- Disturbance of sleep (insomnia or constant drowsiness)

- Exaggerated, excessive, or retarded physical movement
- Loss of energy, feelings of fatigue
- Feelings of worthlessness, self-reproach, excessive guilt
- Inability to think, concentrate, or make decisions
- Talk about suicide

Signs of depression are often ignored by teachers. Frequently, depressed students do not disrupt the class (although this is not always the case), so it is easier for the teacher not to become involved with their behavior. Ignoring depressed students may compound their problems, however, because depressed students often feel isolated, neglected, or "invisible." They often have given up on themselves and see themselves as unworthy of other people's concern.

How should you respond to students whom you suspect are depressed? Perhaps the most important thing you can do is persist in attempts to establish communication with these students, to reach out to them and let them know you have noticed them and are not going to give up on them. You should also ask others to help; a school psychologist or counselor, for example, can evaluate students and, if necessary, make referrals to mental health professionals. In some cases, you may encounter problems that call for difficult personal or professional judgments. Some depressed individuals are extremely manipulative and are masters at getting others entangled in their problems in ways that are not helpful. If possible, seek the advice of a mental health professional who is familiar with the student.

Problems With Peers.   Children and adolescents who do not have friends their own age or who are in frequent conflict with members of their peer group are at high risk for other developmental problems. Those who have serious academic problems are not typically popular among their peers. Those who are aggressive are, understandably, typically rejected by their classmates. Those who are depressed often cut themselves off from social interaction with others. Whatever the reason, the student who ends up a loner is not headed down a developmental path likely to lead to personal fulfillment and satisfactory adult adjustment.

Healthy psychological and social development depends on friendships—close, mutually gratifying relationships that involve giving and receiving support in dealing with life's vicissitudes. Teachers frequently overlook or downplay the importance of peer relationships in school. The focus in schools tends to be on individual achievement and deportment, with social relationships relegated to a secondary or even minor role. When thinking about a student who is exhibiting problem behavior, you should inquire about his or her friendship patterns and social interactions:[6]

- To what extent is this student accepted or rejected by peers?
- Does this student have friends, including a best friend?
- When this student interacts with others, who initiates the interaction?
- How sensitive is this student to influence, positive and negative, from the peer group?
- If this student has friends, who are they and what are they like?

The last question is one that research has shown is particularly important to ask in the case of antisocial students. Some students whose behavior is developmentally dangerous do have friends, but they are the wrong kinds of friends—other antisocial students. The fact that a student is enmeshed in a social group does not mean that he or she does not have peer-related problems. Running with the wrong crowd, admiring and imitating the behavior of deviant peers, and choosing to associate primarily with those who exhibit significant problematic behavior are risk factors for a variety of negative outcomes.

These and more specific questions should help you assess the extent to which peer problems are an issue, a topic to which we return in Chapter 6.

A Note about Multiple Problems

Finally, we note that academic failure, aggression, depression, and problems with peers are not mutually exclusive categories of behavior. Academic failure often is accompanied by aggressive behavior, depression, poor peer relations, or all of these. Not all depressed students are socially withdrawn; a substantial percentage manifest aggressive behavior as part of their depression. The prognosis usually is worse for an individual with multiple, interrelated problems. Students who fail academically and are aggressive and depressed are at particularly high risk for severe and protracted personal problems. The co-occurrence of problems is sometimes referred to in the literature as *comorbidity*. Regardless of the term used to refer to multiple problems, the meaning and implications are essentially the same: Students with multiple problems are typically at higher risk than those who have a single problem.[7]

Should I focus on a behavioral excess or a deficiency?

When we think of behavior management, we typically think first of things we want students to stop doing—behavioral excesses. Just as important, however, are the things students do not do but should—behavioral deficiencies. The aggressive student needs to learn alternative nonaggressive ways of interacting with others. Trying to reduce excessive behavior without at the same time increasing deficient behavior is a common tactical blunder that contributes to many teachers' behavior management difficulties.

Because it is so easy to focus on getting rid of maladaptive behavior and forget the importance of teaching alternative adaptive behavior, some have suggested always thinking of "behavior pairs." A behavior pair includes both a behavior that should be increased and one that should be decreased. For example, completing schoolwork might be paired with not paying attention to work. This pairing would help the teacher focus on what is desired and what should be rewarded (completing work), not just on what is undesirable (inattention). The pairs chosen must be opposites—things that are very difficult or impossible to do simultaneously—so that increasing the desirable behavior is virtually certain to decrease the undesirable behavior.

The pairing of behaviors to be increased and decreased helps the teacher avoid thinking only of the negative side of the student's behavior. This is critically important because effective and humane behavior management relies very little on punishment and is primarily a matter of supporting desirable behavior.

Before assuming that you have identified a behavior management problem with sufficient clarity, ask yourself these questions:

- How do I want this student to behave?
- Can I describe in positive terms what I want the student to do?
- For each behavior I want the student to stop or decrease, have I identified an alternative behavior that I want the student to learn or exhibit more often?

Will resolution of the problem solve anything else?

Some behavior management problems seem overwhelming because there are so many things that need changing. It is hard to know where to begin. Some problems seem insurmountable because the behavior is so extreme. It is hard to know how much change is reasonable to expect. When faced with such problems, teachers can easily become hopeless or adopt strategies that are self-defeating. They may begin attacking problems at random or choose to work on trivial behaviors, or they may reach the unfortunate conclusion that unless they can resolve a problem completely their efforts will be wasted. An important skill in behavior management is identifying problems in ways that help one know where to begin and how to judge progress. We offer two caveats about managing difficult behavior problems. First, you should not expect to solve all problems at once. Second, you should not expect to resolve all problems entirely.

The more difficult the management problem, the more important it is to address first things first—to look for key behaviors that, if changed, will make the greatest difference overall. People who are very experienced in managing difficult children are able to identify the behavior in a constellation of problems that holds the key to generalized improvement. For example, Patterson and his colleagues,[8] who have helped hundreds of families achieve better control of aggressive children, have found that not minding (disobedience to parents and teachers) is a key behavior. Rather than starting with other aggressive acts, Patterson and others have found that it is often better to start dealing with an aggressive child by working on compliance or obedience. Furthermore, experience shows that it is wise to begin a behavior management program by concentrating on one important behavior and dealing with it very consistently. The temptation to deal with multiple problems at once must be resisted. Thus, if you are confronted by a child or class with multiple problems, you should ask yourself the following:

- Can I identify one behavior that seems likely to be the key to general improvement?
- If I resolve this one problem, what else is likely to change?
- How can I develop a consistent, effective plan for attacking this key behavior?

Teachers typically are judged harshly by others, and they sometimes fall prey to harsh self-judgment. And teachers, like most other people, are impatient with behavioral change that is slow or incomplete. Sometimes it is difficult to know whether the amount of change achieved in a behavior is worth the teacher's effort, or whether change is occurring rapidly enough to meet a reasonable goal. Teachers may benefit from asking themselves the following questions:

- Has the change in behavior made a significant difference in the classroom, even if the change is not total and complete?
- Is the change worth my investment of time and energy?
- How much more change should I try to accomplish?
- What is a reasonable goal?

Teachers vary considerably in what they see as worthwhile progress. Too often, in our judgment, teachers devalue progress or behavioral change because they expect themselves to accomplish a radical and permanent transformation of a pupil or their class.

Summary

Skillful classroom behavior management requires that teachers first engage in careful reflection about the nature of the problem. Before attempting to analyze a management problem in detail or develop a management strategy, teachers must consider their own behavior, values, sensitivities, and knowledge about pupil behavior. The behavior management problem may be a consequence of inappropriate curriculum or teaching strategies. Teachers' demands and prohibitions may be poorly communicated or overly lax, strict, or inappropriate for the class or for certain students. They must examine the reasons that certain behaviors of their pupils are bothersome and decide whether self-control (personal tolerance) or intervention to change the pupil's behavior is more appropriate. Teachers must be particularly concerned about academic failure, aggression, depression, and problems with peers, as these behaviors carry particularly high risk for continuing developmental problems. They also must take care to give at least as much concern to what they want students to do as they give to what they want students not to do. In dealing with multiple behavior problems, teachers must begin with a single key behavior which, if changed, will likely produce more generalized improvements. Teachers must also weigh carefully their goals and standards for judging success.

REFERENCES AND RESOURCES FOR FURTHER STUDY

The following references provided the basis for many of our statements in this chapter. You may wish to consult selected references for additional information on specific topics. Our reference notes for this chapter refer to sources in this list.

Curriculum and Teaching Strategies

Bateman, B. D. (2004). *Elements of successful teaching: General and special education students.* Verona, WI: IEP Resources.
Carnine, D. W., Silbert, J., & Kameenui, E. J. (1997). *Direct instruction reading* (3rd ed.). Upper Saddle River, NJ: Prentice-Hall.
Engelmann, S. (1997). Theory of mastery and acceleration. In J. W. Lloyd, E. J. Kameenui, & D. Chard (Eds.), *Issues in educating students with disabilities* (pp. 177–195). Mahwah, NJ: Lawrence Erlbaum.
Forness, S. R., Kavale, K. A., Blum, I. M., & Lloyd, J. W. (1997). What works in special education and related services: Using meta-analysis to guide practice. *Teaching Exceptional Children, 29*(6), 4–9.
Lloyd, J. W., Forness, S. R., & Kavale, K. A. (1998). Some methods are more effective. *Intervention in School and Clinic, 33*(1), 195–200.
Rosenshine, B. (1997). Advances in research on instruction. In J. W. Lloyd, E. J. Kameenui, & D. Chard (Eds.), *Issues in educating students with disabilities* (pp. 197–220). Mahwah, NJ: Lawrence Erlbaum.
Walker, H. M., Ramsey, E., & Gresham, F. M. (2004). *Antisocial behavior in school: Strategies and best practices* (2nd ed.). Pacific Grove, CA: Brooks/Cole.

Teachers' Demands and Prohibitions

Kauffman, J. M. (2005). *Characteristics of emotional and behavioral disorders of children and youth* (8th ed.). Upper Saddle River, NJ: Prentice-Hall.
Walker, H. M. (1995). *The acting-out child: Coping with classroom disruption* (2nd ed.). Longmont, CO. Sopris West.

Developmentally Significant Behavior

Forness, S. R., Kavale, K. A., & Walker, H. M. (1999). Identifying children at risk for antisocial behavior: The case for comorbidity. In R. Gallimore, L. P. Bernheimer, D. L. MacMillan, D. L. Speece, & S. Vaughn (Eds.), *Developmental perspectives on children with high-incidence disabilities* (pp. 135–155). Mahwah, NJ: Lawrence Erlbaum.
Gresham, F. M., Lane, K. L., McIntyre, L. L., MacMillan, D. M., Lambros, K. M., & Bocain, K. (2001). Risk factors associated with the co-occurrence of hyperactivity-impulsivity-inattention and conduct problems. *Behavioral Disorders, 26,* 189–199.
Gresham, F. M., MacMillan, D. L., Bocain, K. M., & Ward, S. L. (1998). Comorbidity of hyperactivity-impulsivity-inattention and conduct problems: Risk factors in social, affective, and academic domains. *Journal of Abnormal Child Psychology, 26,* 393–406.
Kaslow, N. J., Morris, M. K., & Rehm, L. P. (1998). Childhood depression. In R. J. Morris & T. R. Kratochwill (Eds.), *The practice of child therapy* (3rd ed.) (pp. 48–90). Boston: Allyn and Bacon.
Kauffman, J. M. (2005). *Characteristics of emotional and behavioral disorders of children and youth* (8th ed.). Upper Saddle River, NJ: Prentice-Hall.
Kazdin, A. E. (1998). Conduct disorder. In R. J. Morris & T. R. Kratochwill (Eds.), *The practice of child therapy* (3rd ed.) (pp. 199–230). Boston: Allyn and Bacon.
Kerr, M. M., & Nelson, C. M. (2002). *Strategies for managing behavior problems in the classroom* (4th ed.). Upper Saddle River, NJ: Prentice-Hall.
Lloyd, J. W., Hallahan, D. P., Kauffman, J. M., & Keller, C. E. (1998). Academic problems. In R. J. Morris & T. R. Kratochwill (Eds.), *The practice of child therapy* (3rd ed.) (pp. 167–198). Boston: Allyn and Bacon.
Loeber, R., Farrington, D. P., Stouthamer-Loeber, M., & Van Kammen, W. B. (1998). *Antisocial behavior and mental health problems: Explanatory factors in childhood and adolescence.* Mahwah, NJ: Lawrence Erlbaum.

Patterson, G. R., Reid, J. B., & Dishion, T. J. (1992). *Antisocial boys*. Eugene, OR: Castalia.

Tankersley, M., & Landrum, T. J. (1997). Comorbidity of emotional and behavioral disorders. In J. W. Lloyd, E. J. Kameenui, & D. Chard (Eds.), *Issues in educating students with disabilities* (pp. 153–173). Mahwah, NJ: Lawrence Erlbaum.

E N D N O T E S

1. See Carnine, Silbert, and Kameenui (1997) and Lloyd, Forness, and Kavale (1998).
2. See Kauffman (2005).
3. See Kauffman (2005), Kerr and Nelson (2002), and Walker, Ramsey, and Gresham (2004) for a discussion of the relationship between academic failure and other characteristics of children and youth with emotional or behavioral disorders.
4. See Kazdin (1998), Loeber et al. (1998), Patterson, Reid, and Dishion (1992), and Walker, Ramsey, and Gresham (2004).
5. See Kauffman (2005) and Kaslow, Morris, and Rehm (1998).
6. See Kauffman (2005) and Loeber et al. (1998).
7. See Forness et al. (1999), Gresham et al. (1998), and Tankersley and Landrum (1997).
8. See Patterson, Reid, and Dishion (1992).

CHAPTER

3

Analyzing Behavior Problems

Skilled professionals in all fields analyze problems carefully before attempting to solve them. Physicians, engineers, lawyers, and merchants, as well as teachers and school administrators, are typically more successful when they are able to figure out why a problem exists and how bad it is before they start doing something to change it. People with little knowledge of a field of study or professional practice sometimes become impatient with a competent practitioner's approach to a problem because they believe the analysis should be simple and quick. The competent practitioner knows that apparently simple problems can be unexpectedly complex and understands that time spent in analysis can save time in the long run and prevent embarrassing, costly, or tragic errors. Two examples of teachers' reflections on their analysis of behavior problems can be found in the vignettes, Sally and Trisha.

If you approach a behavior management problem with the questions we posed in Chapter 2, you have already started the process of problem analysis. You will have begun eliminating wrong explanations for the behavior and be ready to analyze in more detail the extent of the problem, its possible causes, and where you might find a point of leverage in changing it. Understanding the possible and probable cause(s) of behav-

Tammy

When I first started working on the problems I had with Kevin, I wasn't aware of how often he failed to do what I told him. Actually, I had quite a few kids in my class who were noncompliant pretty frequently, but Kevin was really by far the worst. The thing that helped me most when it came to getting a handle on the problem was keeping track of my directions and Kevin's compliance for a while. I kept a daily record of how often I told Kevin to do something and the percentage of times he did what I told or asked him to do.

It was a little extra work to remember to keep track of my directions and his compliance, but it wasn't too bad. I was surprised by the numbers—by how often I was giving him a command of some sort and by the low percentage of the time he obeyed me. He seemed to give me the most trouble during reading, which he doesn't do very well, especially when I was working with another group. He also had lots of trouble during less structured activities, like lunch break and art. So I focused my record keeping on reading and lunch period, which included noon recess. I carried a little card in my pocket, and every time I told or asked him to do something I just made a tally mark. Then, if he complied within about a minute, I circled the tally. I divided the card into two sections, the top for reading and the bottom for lunch period.

By keeping track, I had a daily record of how often I was telling Kevin to do things and how often he complied in those two situations. I did this for about five days before I started the compliance training, so I had a pretty objective basis for judging whether the training was making a difference on compliance in reading and math. Of course, subjectively I felt things were getting a lot better too, but the data on the cards helped me confirm that he really was improving.

Trisha

It took me a while, but I finally figured out something that was a really effective reward for Sammy, this kid who was such a whiner and a crier. He was so spoiled by his mother and grandmother that there just seemed to be nothing I could offer him that he was interested in working for. Then one day I was talking to him about other things and he said something about not liking the name Sammy. He said his name was Sam, like his daddy's name, and that's what he wanted to be called. He thought Sammy was a "baby name," as he put it, and he didn't want to be called that anymore. So then I thought, aha! There's something he maybe cares enough about that I can use it as leverage to get him to stop crying. This is a kid who would have 10 or 15 crying fits just about every day, most of them lasting for just a couple of minutes but some going on for an hour. I think we really turned the corner with him when I had a little talk with him about his crying and his name and I told him I'd have to call him Sam, and so would all the other kids, as long as he wasn't crying. If he cried, we could call him Sammy, but otherwise we'd use his grown-up name.

Source: "Trisha" is based on S. Kaufhold and J. M. Kauffman, "Sammy: Frequent crying spells," in J. Worell and C. M. Nelson (Eds.), *Managing Instructional Problems: A Case Study Workbook* (New York: McGraw-Hill, 1974), pp. 188–193.

---

ior is often critical to choosing means for trying to change it. Measuring the level of the problem and having a way of judging progress are essential for making good decisions about whether to try a different strategy and when to consider a problem resolved. Setting clear and reasonable goals helps teachers avoid getting discouraged or becoming overly optimistic. In brief, as you analyze problems, you need to ask yourself important questions about your assumptions and intentions.

- What are my assumptions about why students behave the way they do?
- Can I identify causal factors that I can change?
- What is sufficient evidence that I am making progress in changing behavior?
- Exactly what am I trying to accomplish?
- What is the student trying to get?
- Could I help this student get what he or she is after in a better way?

These and other questions are part of a careful analysis of behavior management problems leading to well-planned strategies for change. They are also part of the functional behavioral assessment (FBA) that is required by federal special education law (IDEA, the Individuals with Disabilities Education Act).

Questions for Reflection

We suggest that after you have made an initial identification of a behavior management problem, you analyze the problem further before planning an intervention strategy to change it. Your analyses should include possible causal explanations for the misbehavior, measurement of its level and trend, and the goals you hope to accomplish. A careful analysis will greatly increase your chances of devising a management plan that is effective and efficient. The questions you need to ask yourself include the following:

- What are my assumptions about why students behave the way they do?
- What are the most important alternative explanations of the misbehavior?
- Are there causes of the misbehavior that I can control to a significant degree?
- How should I define the behavior I am concerned about and identify its antecedents and consequences?
- How might I identify the probable cognitive and affective aspects of the misbehavior?
- How should I measure the behavior problem and behavior change?
- What is a reasonable goal?
- How do I accomplish a functional assessment of behavior and write a positive behavior intervention plan?

What are my assumptions about why students behave the way they do?

Everyone makes certain assumptions about why people behave as they do. These assumptions are important because they are often the basis for one's attempts to change behavior. Examining your assumptions about the causes of behavior is important because beliefs are related to actions; what you do may change as a result of a change in your beliefs. But what you do also affects what you believe. Beliefs and actions influence each other, along with other factors in one's environment.

Historically, philosophers, religious leaders, and scientists have offered a variety of explanations for human behavior. Their explanations might be grouped into four basic categories:

1. *Biological:*   Physiological or biochemical factors, such as brain damage, disease, or malnutrition
2. *Environmental:*   Events in the objective external world, such as the consequences of behavior, the settings in which it occurs (e.g., signs or signals that certain behavior is expected or prohibited), and the examples provided by others
3. *Psychological:*   Internal mental characteristics or phenomena, such as thoughts, feelings, or emotional states
4. *Spiritual:*   Supernatural or mystical forces, such as god(s), devil(s), or other spirits

Present-day explanations also include all four of these categories of variables. None of these categories is entirely discounted by most people, although most people give more credence to some than to others, particularly in cases of highly unusual behavior. In analyzing a behavior problem it is important first to clarify the basic assumptions with which you approach human behavior.

- How do I typically explain people's behavior?
- What is the basis for my beliefs about behavior?
- To what extent are my beliefs based on scientific evidence about the causes of behavior?

The general notions you have about the causes of human behavior will likely influence significantly how you attempt to explain the misbehavior about which you are concerned.

What are the most important alternative explanations of the misbehavior?

Most people believe that there are multiple causes of human behavior, some of which are more important than others for explaining particular acts or patterns of conduct. For example, a person might believe that biological, psychological, and environmental factors are all involved to some degree in causing human behavior. However, in explaining why a given student behaves in a particular way in the classroom, this person might also believe that the most important causes are psychological (e.g., feelings of self-efficacy, predictions of the consequences of behavior) and environmental (e.g., the consequences of behavior and signals that certain behavior is expected). A task of the teacher is to identify the most likely and most relevant explanations of classroom behavior for individual students and specific circumstances.

We suggest that teachers pay particular attention to explanations of behavior that are supported by ample empirical research and that offer teachers the possibility of a reasonable measure of control. Concentrating on relevant and reliable explanations means, in our opinion, that the teacher will pay particular attention to environmental and psychological causes. These are the causes most directly related to teaching and the ones supported by the most scientific evidence. We are not suggesting that other explanations have no relevance or validity, but simply that in most cases the greatest research support and opportunity for a teacher's control are likely to be found in explanations having to do with environmental and psychological variables.[1]

Some of the potential causes of behavior problems are things that teachers cannot control, at least not directly. In nearly all cases of misbehavior caused by biological factors, the teacher can only make a referral or ask for assistance from a health care professional or social worker. Sometimes misbehavior is a result of brain dysfunction, disease, or problems of diet or health. The teacher must be aware of these possibilities and refer the student for evaluation by qualified health care providers. Sometimes misbehavior is a result of abuse or neglect at home or is related to other home or family conditions over which the teacher has no direct control. Again, it is extremely important for the teacher to be aware of these potential sources of problems and request evaluation or assistance when needed.

Being unaware of or ignoring potential causes of problem behavior can result in unfortunate outcomes. For example, missing or ignoring signs of malnutrition, seizures, abuse, and so on, will result in failure to address critical aspects of the problem and could frustrate the teacher's attempts to ameliorate it. Teachers must be keenly aware of possible causes of behavior problems other than those that are most obvious. This requires extensive knowledge of child development and a high level of sensitivity to children's life circumstances.

When analyzing a behavior problem, you should consider the range of possible causes and try to make sure that no plausible explanation for the behavior is ignored.

- What possible reasons for the behavior can I identify?
- Have I asked for evaluation by other professionals to eliminate certain explanations for the behavior that might be important?

We offer two cautions: First, possible or plausible causal factors often remain matters for speculation. In many cases, the precise cause(s) of misbehavior cannot be identified with certainty. Furthermore, there are typically several plausible causes, not just one. Second, finding the cause(s) does not necessarily lead directly to an effective intervention. That is, the cause does not necessarily tell us the "cure." Some causes cannot be reversed (e.g., brain damage, a history of abuse), whereas some interventions are effective even though the cause is not known. For example, stimulant medication may benefit a hyperactive child even though the cause of the hyperactivity cannot be found. Consistent consequences may result in improvement of an aggressive student's behavior even though one can only speculate about the causes of aggression.

Where does this leave you, as a teacher, who is trying to analyze a behavior problem? We reiterate two points made earlier. First, it is important to recognize the possible range of causes of students' behavior and to request the services of other professionals who may be able to rule out certain causal factors or obtain help that you may not be able to provide. Second, you should give your greatest attention to the causal factors that you can alter.

Are there causes of the misbehavior that I can control to a significant degree?

Teachers often can make a difference in the lives of their pupils by getting involved in matters that extend beyond the classroom or school. For example, some teachers make repeated home visits for the purposes of understanding and improving the home lives of their students by working with parents. Others are able to make a significant contribution to improving students' lives by counseling students or obtaining health and social services for them outside the school environment. We caution that teachers can become overinvolved in their students' lives and neglect their own needs (and those of their own families). We also recognize that there are limits to parental involvement in behavior management (see Chapter 8). Furthermore, circumstances such as living in a community far from the school in which you teach may preclude your extensive involvement with your pupils outside the classroom or school. Yet, you might ask yourself whether there are circumstances or conditions outside your classroom or school that may be contributing to a pupil's misbehavior and that you might be able to change.

Clearly, conditions and events in the classroom and school can contribute to behavior management problems. As we mentioned in Chapter 2, the curricula and teaching strategies teachers use, the demands and prohibitions of teachers and administrators, and the influence of peers are critical factors that can set the stage for appropriate or inappropriate student behavior. Of all the possible factors that can contribute to behavior problems, events and conditions in the classroom are the factors over which the teacher has the greatest control. Furthermore, a substantial body of empirical research suggests that teachers often can improve their students' behavior substantially if they change certain classroom conditions. In fact, teachers can most productively view behavior management problems as instructional problems. The most important consideration of the teacher is how to arrange the classroom environment to teach appropriate behavior. We elaborate on this concept in Chapter 4.

Of all the questions you could ask yourself about the causes of behavior, we believe the single most important one is this: What is happening in my classroom that might contribute to misbehavior? That is, how could I be teaching my student(s) to misbehave, albeit inadvertently? Or, how am I failing to teach my student(s) to behave as I would like?[2] Teachers can examine events and conditions in the classroom and their possible effects on behavior in a variety of ways. In our opinion, the most useful way of analyzing what happens in the classroom—what students are being taught—is to define the behavior of concern as an observable event and then examine what happens immediately before it occurs (antecedent events) and after (consequences).[3]

How should I define the behavior I am concerned about and identify its antecedents and consequences?

Defining a behavior problem is not always as simple as it first appears. Many times, students exhibit a wide array of "trashy" behaviors that are irritating and divert attention from the central issue (recall, for example, Sally's description in Chapter 2). Sometimes it is difficult to focus on the problem and describe it as a particular behavior the student does or does not do. Nevertheless, a precise description of what the student does or does not do is extremely important in identifying antecedents and consequences and devising an intervention plan. Moreover, precise description is important for measurement of the problem—asessing its severity and evaluating progress or success.[4]

Defining Behavior.   Defining a problem as something a student does or does not do requires that you observe carefully just how the student behaves and describe it clearly as an action. You must describe the behavior objectively and precisely enough that nearly anyone else observing the student independently could state whether or not the behavior occurred. You must take care not to describe the problem as your reaction or interpretation (e.g., "He irritates me") or the student's internal state (e.g., "She goes off into her dream world"), as these are too subjective and measurement of them will be too unreliable. "She cries," "She looks off into space with a blank expression," "He rummages in his desk," "She talks without permission," or "He does not complete his homework" are behavioral definitions that are probably objective enough that, with some clarifications, two or more independent observers could agree about whether or not they occurred in most instances.

If you have defined a behavior precisely and objectively, you will be able to observe when it begins and when it stops. That is, the behavior will not be described as a state of being ("unmotivated," "hostile," or "reticent," for example) but as a measurable event or episode (e.g., "slept," "cursed or hit someone," "did not respond to direct question"). A good test of whether you have defined a problem appropriately for our discussion here is to ask yourself these questions:

- Could I count occurrences of this behavior so that I could state how many times it occurred today?
- Could I measure the duration of these episodes so that I could state how many minutes of the period the student was engaging in this behavior?
- Could I glance at the student and tell whether or not the student was engaged in the behavior at that instant?

Once you have defined the behavior so that you can observe its occurrence accurately, you will be able to observe what happens just before and just after it occurs. As we discuss further in Chapter 4, the events that occur just before and just after a behavior can have a powerful influence. In fact, one explanation of behavior is that it is almost entirely a function of its antecedents and consequences. We urge you to take careful note of the events surrounding the behavior you are concerned about, because you may be able to alter these surrounding events and thereby modify it.

Identifying Antecedents.   You might begin by noting the antecedents. What are the events or conditions that immediately precede instances of the problem behavior? You may need to keep anecdotal records or other written notes in order to describe a pattern of when, where, and under what conditions the behavior most often occurs. Your objective in examining the antecedents of the behavior should be to anticipate it—to predict it accurately. If you find that the behavior occurs only under certain conditions or immediately after certain events, then you might be able to resolve the problem completely or in part by changing the antecedents. For example, if you find that the student nearly always exhibits the problem behavior when you give an instruction or make a request, you might try varying the way you present the task to avoid the problem. Sometimes giving a student a choice rather than a direct instruction (e.g., "Which of these pages would you like to do first?" rather than "I want you to complete these two pages") will make a significant difference in his or her compliance.

A particularly useful way of conceptualizing behavior problems is called *precorrection*, a type of lesson plan that we discuss further in Chapter 4.[5] Teachers who use precorrection see misbehavior as an error or mistake that they can teach the student to avoid. Precorrection requires taking *proactive* measures to keep misbehavior from occurring in the first place, not *reactive* measures taken after it has occurred. The teacher tries to anticipate the misbehavior and replace it with a desired behavior.

The critical step in using precorrection, after defining the problem objectively and defining the behavior the teacher would like to see instead, is describing the context in which the problem usually happens. Skilled teachers often can identify the antecedent—that is, the situation, circumstance, condition, or context in which a troublesome behavior is utterly predictable. If they can, then they may be able to modify that context to avert the trouble, saving them and everyone else the hassle of dealing with the problem. Good teachers find ways of helping students avoid making mistakes over and over, whether the skill being taught is academic or social. Helping students avoid the repetition of errors requires identifying a predictable pattern of behavior, beginning with the context in which the error is likely (e.g., in basketball, a particular play, perhaps a fast break; in music, a particular passage, perhaps a rest; in school conduct, a particular social demand, perhaps responding to a transition from one activity to another).

We are not suggesting that the antecedents of troublesome behavior can always be identified or that you can always alter them. Some behavior patterns are extremely hard to figure out. Sometimes the antecedents may be internal events or states. For example, a student experiencing high levels of anxiety or having a psychotic condition may be responding to perceptions or thoughts that you cannot observe directly. Sometimes the antecedents are things you cannot change. For example, you may find that the student exhibits the problem behavior whenever there is an announcement on the school intercom, a condition that you are not able to alter. At the least, however, identifying the antecedents should help you anticipate problems and know where and when to focus your intervention.

Identifying Consequences.   Equally as important as noting the antecedents is identifying the consequences—events that occur after the behavior about which you are concerned. What does the student "get" out of the behavior? You must remember that appearances can be deceiving; the student may appear to get nothing or to receive only negative consequences for the behavior, yet he or she persists in doing it. A rewarding consequence, or a punishing one, for one person is not necessarily the same for another. You must also look for multiple consequences.

Sometimes the "payoff" for behavior has several components, and the nature and sequence of these components can be highly significant. In the classroom, for example, a student may frequently misbehave in ways that result in criticism or punishment from adults (perhaps including restrictions or extra work) and the scorn of peers. A consequence of this kind of behavior is the attention—often the undivided attention—of one or more adults, several peers, or perhaps the entire class. Although the misbehaving student seems to earn only punishment, the attention that goes with the punishing consequences may be a sufficient reward to outweigh the intended effect of the punishment. For some students, seeing adults get upset is a very powerful rewarding consequence. Enticing the teacher into an emotional outburst may, for these students, be well worth enduring any punishment adults are likely to devise.

Identifying Chains of Events. Antecedents, behaviors, and consequences occur in continuous strings or chains of events. To analyze relationships among them, you may need to keep a running record of the sequence of events. Here is an example, drawn from a case written by John Shearer, "Foul Language: Classroom Trouble" included in *The Intern Teacher Casebook* (edited by Judith H. Shulman and Joel A. Colbert, ERIC Clearing House on Teacher Education). It recounts a sequence of events in a junior high school classroom. The incident involves a student's (Richard's) use of language that the teacher (John) considers foul:

1. John asks for volunteers to name sources of pollution
2. Richard raises hand, says, "I know, teacher! Farts!"
3. Boisterous laughter and noises from class
4. John calls class to order, cautions Richard
5. Richard flails arms in air, says, "Teacher, teacher! Malcolm just told me to [sexually graphic phrase]!"
6. Howling, whistling from class

We could label the first three events in this sequence in what is called an *ABC analysis.* For example, we might label these events as follows:

Antecedent ➤	*Behavior* ➤	*Consequence*
J asks for volunteers	R raises hand, says, ". . . Farts!"	Laughter, noises from class

We might go on to label the next three in a similar fashion:

Antecedent ➤	*Behavior* ➤	*Consequence*
J calls for order, cautions R	R flails arms, makes sexual comment	Class howls, whistles

Notice that in such analyses a given behavior can be both a consequence for the behavior it follows and an antecedent for the next behavior in sequence. Thus the teacher's behavior can be a consequence for the student; likewise, the student's behavior can be a consequence for the teacher. We might have chosen to diagram the sequence of ABCs as follows:

| *Antecedent* ⟶ | *Behavior* ⟶ | *Consequence* |
| R raises hand, says, "…Farts" | Laughter, noises from class | J calls for order, cautions class |

In interactions, individuals provide consequences and antecedents for each other in an ongoing chain of events. Where you start the analysis—which event you choose to label antecedent and whose behavior you choose as the focus—depends on your purpose. The purpose of an ABC analysis is to clarify the sequence of classroom events from a particular perspective, either the student's or the teacher's. It helps one understand what each party is responding to and what each is getting out of the interaction. ABC analyses are usually done for the events surrounding a specific behavior problem episode.

Doing an ABC analysis requires that the sequence of events be recorded accurately. Few teachers will have the help of someone who can observe classroom interactions and record them accurately, although sometimes a classroom aide or support staff (e.g., school psychologist, consulting teacher) can do so. If you must do the analysis yourself, you should attempt to jot notes to yourself whenever possible and reconstruct the sequence of events as soon after the episode as possible. Recalling the exact behaviors and their sequence is critically important. We suggest that if you plan to do an ABC analysis, you use a form similar to the one shown in Figure 3.1. We have added some possible written items to Figure 3.1 to illustrate how it might be used. Note that in our example, Chris is successful in avoiding his teacher's (Ms. P.'s) expectations and his involvement in academic work with the class. You may want to recall the example shown in Figure 3.1 when we discuss turn-taking interactions. The example shows how "turns" operate, with teacher and student each setting up the other for the next "turn" in an interaction.

FIGURE 3.1   Form for Recording ABC Analysis

Antecedents	Behaviors	Consequences
Ms. P. asks class to open books to p. 43	Chris does not open his book and pounds his book with his fist	Ms. P. says "Chris open your book."
Chris opens his book but closes it again	Ms. P. walks to Chris's desk	Chris puts book inside desk
Ms. P. puts her hand on Chris's shoulder	Chris brushes away Ms. P.'s hand and says, "Leave me alone."	Ms. P. moves away from Chris and talks to rest of class

Whenever you are perplexed by classroom behavior, you may need to answer these questions:

- What is the precise sequence of events surrounding this problem?
- Can I clearly identify the ABCs of the interactions that are troublesome?
- Most important, can I identify a predictable pattern of behavior, including the situation, circumstance, or context in which it usually occurs?

Answering these questions is particularly important for resolving the negative interactions that are called *coercion*. Answering them is also important to functional behavioral assessment (FBA), which means finding out what consequences a student obtains by specific misbehavior in a given setting.

Identifying Coercive Interactions. Antecedents, behaviors, and consequences sometimes are characterized by an escalating pattern of *aversiveness*. That is, starting with an antecedent that is aversive (unpleasant or painful, something the person would like to escape from or avoid), two parties attempt to control each other by increasingly powerful negative consequences. Positive consequences are not an outcome of these interactions. For example, abused and aggressive children often behave in ways that are extremely irritating to adults; they seem to "ask for" punishment, and adults typically oblige by providing it. Their irritating behavior typically is followed by harsh reprimands, if not physical abuse, from parents, which sets the stage for even more highly irritating acts. They and their parents become embroiled in a battle that someone "wins" (usually the parent when the child is younger) by being more obnoxious, threatening, or brutal and forcing the other party to stop. This type of interaction is known as *coercion*.

Coercion is sometimes a feature of classroom interactions between teachers and pupils and of interactions among classroom peers. The pupil may find the teacher's expectations and demands aversive and attempt to avoid them by misbehaving. The teacher finds this aversive and restates the demands or increases them, perhaps threatening or punishing the student. The student feels challenged to become more obnoxious, tempting the teacher to respond with more severe punishment or threats. This kind of coercive interaction continues until either the teacher or the student "wins" or an uneasy and temporary truce is made. Following is an example of a coercive classroom interaction.

Teacher asks student to complete page of math problems

Student says, "I don't know how to do this crap!"

Teacher says, "Yes you do, we just did some problems like these yesterday. Get started now."

Student slams book closed, saying, "Ain't doin' it!"

Teacher goes to student's desk, opens book, hands student pencil, says in angry tone, "Get started now!"

Student shoves book off desk.

Teacher squeezes student's shoulder, growls, "Pick that book up, young man!"

Student jumps to feet, says, "Get your hands off me, bitch! You pick it up! You can't make me do nothin'!"

Teacher yells, "That's it! I've had enough of this! Pick that book up and get to work now or you're outa here to the office!"

Many students are masters at drawing teachers into these power struggles; they know how to start wars of will, and often how to win them. Students sometimes lay coercive "traps" for teachers by engaging in irritating conduct, knowing that many teachers will respond to them by engaging in a power struggle, often over minor misbehavior. The more skillful the teacher is at behavior management, the more tactics she or he has for ending the struggle early, typically by finding a way to disengage and avoid stepping into the trap. Clearly, coercive interactions are not desirable, although they are common in many classrooms. Understanding the process of coercion is important in finding ways to deal effectively with it. We discuss the underlying process—negative reinforcement—in Chapter 4.

Becoming keenly aware of coercive interactions is critically important to the successful use of more positive behavior management strategies. In analyzing the ABCs of your classroom interactions, you should be especially concerned about those that involve a coercive process. Ask yourself questions about the early stages of the interactions.

- How do these interactions start?
- At what point could I avoid the process by disengaging from it?
- How could I start a different interaction that does not end in a power struggle?
- How could I try to replace coercive interactions with ones ending in positive consequences?

Sometimes you might discover that in trying to find answers to these questions you need to consider both your own thoughts and feelings and those of your students. Equally important, however, is being able to find the typical pattern of misbehavior and then observing how it begins and the stages through which it may go so that you can find effective ways of short-circuiting it.

Identifying the Patterns and Stages of Misbehavior.   Geoffrey Colvin and his colleagues at the University of Oregon have studied the classroom conduct of acting-out, aggressive students in great detail. Colvin has identified a typical cycle or sequence of phases that can help teachers see the early signs of misbehavior and take action to avoid an escalation of the problem.[6] In fact, most teachers, in reflecting on their experiences as children or youths or even their lives as adults, can probably recognize examples of these phases in their own conduct. Recalling or imagining how it feels to be in one of these phases or how these phases look to others, teachers are likely to be able to spot them in their students.

It is essential to recognize that all students are at least occasionally in the first and *desirable* phase: *calm*. When students are calm, they are on task and goal-oriented, follow classroom rules and expectations, respond well to praise and other forms of recognition, comply with suggestions and correction, and take the initiative in classroom routines and academic work. The reason it is essential to recognize this phase in the behavior of students, as we discuss further in Chapter 4, is that taking action to sustain this phase is the single most important behavior management strategy. This is the phase you want to draw out as much as possible, as it is the phase in which students are most teachable.

The calm behavior that teachers rightfully desire is often disturbed by incidents that they can identify. Teachers should be as aware as possible of events in or out of school that may launch students into the second, problematic stage: *trigger*. In the trigger phase, something happens that is anxiety provoking or discomforting to the student. Triggers may include, for example, conflicts with other students or adults, such as provocations or teasing, denial of a need, or the infliction of anything unpleasant on the student; changes in routine; pressure to perform or lack of the skills needed to respond appropriately to demands; making errors or being corrected; problems at home or in the community, including threats, abuse, or gang-related events; substance abuse; or health, nutritional, or sleep problems. Teachers sensitive to these triggers may be able to respond to students who have experienced them in such a way as to avoid the explosions that they may set off. The main purpose of looking for the phases is to keep the student's behavior from moving up the scale of seriousness.

If a student has experienced a trigger in school or out of school, he or she may show signs of the third phase: *agitation*. An increase or decrease in behavior may indicate agitation. Increases may demonstrate lapses in ability to stay on task and concentrate, such as frequent episodes of off-task behavior; moving in and out of groups, not able to maintain contact; constant motion, especially of hands; darting eyes or an apparent inability to maintain focus; or making vocal noises or using nonconversational language, such as repetition of words or phrases. Decreases in behavior may include staring into space; mumbling or other language indicating uncertainty; hands thrust into pockets or held in check under folded arms; or withdrawal from social interaction with others, especially groups. The perceptive teacher who spots these increases or decreases in behavior quickly and recognizes that something needs to be done to keep the student from becoming more agitated may move him or her toward the calm phase.

Agitation is often a prelude to the fourth phase: *acceleration*. In the acceleration phase, the student is looking for ways to draw other people, peers or adults, into a struggle. The student finds ways of inviting others to engage him or her in coercive interactions. Difficult students offer invitations that most peers and adults find difficult to turn down, and teachers often find that they have been drawn into the struggle before they know what has happened. Some students seem to have earned a Master of Engagement (M.E.) degree; they are exceedingly skilled at making themselves the center of attention by displaying behavior that others cannot ignore. Sometimes their engaging behavior cannot be ignored, as it is clearly intolerable in the classroom or is dangerous. The most difficult students have a special talent for engaging others in counteraggression or emotional upsets that put the student in full control of the situation. The engaging behavior—the invitations to coercive interactions—include such things as questioning and arguing, an especially useful ploy for adults who feel they must have the last word; noncompliance and defiance, directly challenging the teacher's authority; compliance accompanied by inappropriate behavior, so that the teacher is unlikely to be happy with the compliance; sustained off-task behavior, which a teacher tends not to ignore; provoking others by teasing, nasty comments, gestures, and so forth; whining and crying; running away from the teacher, leaving the room, or in some other way avoiding or escaping the task or situation; threatening or intimidating others through verbal abuse or physical acts; or destroying property. A teacher's response to a student's engaging behavior in this acceleration phase must be quick but insightful. Without skillful management of this phase, a blowup is highly likely. However, in most cases, there is still a chance to divert the student from a full-blown tantrum or assault.

If the student is not diverted, he or she goes "out of control" or enters phase five: *peak*. In this phase, one may see serious property destruction, physical assault, self-injury, hyperventilation, or a tantrum of considerable severity.

The peak phase cannot last forever; it is exhausting. The sixth phase, *de-escalation*, is sure to follow. After going out of control, students typically show signs of confusion. They may withdraw, deny that anything happened, or blame others. They may seek reconciliation or be responsive to clear directions. They don't want to discuss what happened at this point, but they may be willing to engage in some simple task.

Eventually, after a period of de-escalation, comes the final phase: *recovery*. The student may still be defensive and try to avoid discussing what happened, but he or she is likely to be relatively subdued in interactions with others and may show an eagerness for some sort of independent work. Recovery is a period of regaining equilibrium, or getting back on track.

Figure 3.2 depicts the seven phases of acting-out behavior. It is important to understand that a given individual may move very quickly from one phase to the next, seem to skip a phase, or remain in one phase for a protracted period of time. The key concept here is that there are various levels of intensity of behavior ranging from calm, task-oriented, compliant behavior to peak, out-of-control behavior. The most problematic types of behavior are repeated; they do not occur once but recur in a predictable pattern that skillful observers can recognize. The phases we have described and that are depicted in Figure 3.2 are a way of organizing observations and communication about these predictable patterns.

How might I identify the probable cognitive and affective aspects of the misbehavior?

Teachers who are expert in behavior management pay attention to more than what students do. They recognize that thoughts and feelings are intimately connected to the way people behave. They would like students to think rationally and feel good about themselves, and they know that helping students develop cognitive skills and appropriate affective responses is part of their responsibility. Furthermore, finding out what students think and how they feel, and reflecting on one's own cognitive and affective reactions, can provide useful insights into resolutions to behavior problems. We are not referring here to analyzing unconscious motivations or hidden meanings. Rather, we are referring to paying attention to what students say and their reactions to situations, which reveal their thought processes, preferences, and emotional responses.

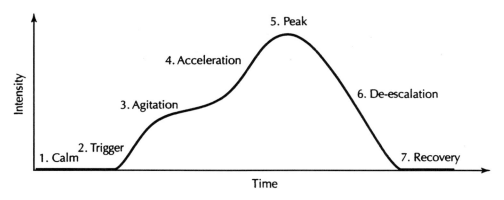

FIGURE 3.2 Phases of the Acting-Out Cycle

Source: From *Managing Acting-Out Behavior* by Geoffrey Colvin. Copyright © 1992 by Behavior Associates. Reprinted by permission.

Teachers often suspect that students' thoughts and feelings cause them to misbehave, and often they would like to change the way students think or feel about things. Someone else's thoughts and feelings cannot be manipulated directly, however. Furthermore, changing the way students think or feel will not necessarily change the way they behave. Teachers can directly manipulate many of the antecedents and consequences of students' classroom behavior, however, and in this way they may be able to alter thoughts and feelings. But how does one identify the thoughts and feelings that might be involved in behavior? The simplicity of the answer belies the complexity of the task: by watching and listening.

Observing and interpreting the affective components of students' behavior requires sensitivity to subtle individual differences and changes in posture, facial expression, behavior, and voice—the types of things we described in our discussion of the phases of acting-out behavior. Students who are the easiest to manage are likely also to be the easiest to "read." Those who are difficult to manage and interpret often express themselves in atypical ways or send mixed signals—verbal and nonverbal messages that contradict each other. In fact, they often put teachers in a quandary by saying one thing and doing another.

Teachers often learn much about students' thoughts and feelings indirectly through casual conversation. Perhaps most teachers could learn more by asking students directly what they think or how they feel about their own behavior and important aspects of the classroom and school. Some students are reticent in expressing their feelings, others tell teachers what they think they want to hear, and a few may make deliberately misleading statements. Teachers must be aware of these possibilities. Nevertheless, asking students is often better than relying solely on indirect interpretations. In Chapter 5, we discuss ways in which teachers might do this.

One important benefit of finding out what students think and feel about themselves and aspects of their school experience is that it often gives the teacher a clue about rewarding consequences for behavior. Trisha's reflection on Sam (at the beginning of this chapter) provides an example of a teacher identifying a student's feelings about something that could be used as a highly effective consequence. In Chapter 5, we discuss other benefits of talking with students about their behavior. For purposes of analyzing a behavior problem, however, we suggest you ask these questions:

- Are students giving me clues to their feelings about themselves and the classroom?
- Have I listened and observed carefully to detect the emotions that accompany their behavior?
- Have I asked the students directly what they think and feel about specific events or conditions?
- Can I connect what I observe and hear to a pattern or cycle of acting-out behavior?

How should I measure the behavior problem and behavior change?

Measurement is a fundamental requirement of many professional activities. Physicians, engineers, and economists, for example, typically rely heavily on measurements related to their analyses of problems and base their professional recommendations and judgments of success on measured outcomes. In education, measurement of students' academic skills is an accepted part of professional practice. Measurement of problem behavior is expected as an integral part of an intervention plan. A teacher cannot assess the effects of teaching without a reliable, accurate means of monitoring behavior.

We recognize that there are many different types of measurement ranging from subjective impressions to extremely precise quantitative assessments. Choosing the most helpful and efficient type of measurement and choosing to measure the right things are keys to competent professional practice. Your choice of measurement may depend on how you answer several questions related to the problem behavior.

- How serious do I believe the problem is?
- How am I going to judge the success or failure of my interventions?
- With whom do I need to communicate about the problem and my success or failure in dealing with it?

Ordinarily, the more serious you believe the problem is, the more concerned you should be about devising a precise way of measuring it. For minor problems, subjective impressions may suffice; for major problems, objective data are critical. More precise and objective measurement is needed for more serious problems for three reasons: (1) the consequences of the problem and its resolution are greater for both the student and the teacher; (2) the more serious the problem, the more imperative it will be for the teacher to communicate objective, reliable information about it to others; and (3) with more serious problems, subjective impressions can be very misleading.

Subjective impressions about behavior and behavior change are often included in summary reports of student progress. Some teachers keep diaries in which they record their impressions or reactions to students' behavior. These subjective, nonquantitative statements may be useful, but they have severe limitations in cases of serious behavior problems. Teachers seldom define problem behavior as precisely as they should when they record only their subjective impressions.

A systematic anecdotal record is a more precise level of measurement. Such a record requires that the teacher jot down observations about the student's behavior whenever it occurs or at regular times (e.g., daily). Anecdotal records can be quite helpful, but they do not allow one to make a careful assessment of the problem unless they include sufficient detail to allow an ABC analysis. An ABC analysis is actually a very careful anecdotal record in which specific events are recorded in time sequence to describe a behavior and its antecedents and consequences. A still more precise and quantitative level of measurement is often needed, however.

Direct daily measurement is extremely helpful in assessing serious problems and evaluating the effects of interventions. Measurement of this type requires that the teacher define the behavior as an objectively observable act, as we have suggested, and record occurrences of the behavior to establish its quantitative level. We cannot detail the methods of direct daily measurement here (you may want to consult one or more of the references at the end of the chapter). However, an example may show some of the advantages of such methods. We use the case of Trisha's work with Sammy, described in the vignette earlier in this chapter. We do not provide all the details of Sammy's case but focus on those aspects related to direct daily measurement.

Sammy was a third-grader who, Trisha realized, had a serious problem because he frequently disrupted the class with loud crying and whining. His peers teased him when he cried, contributing further to the problem. Trisha knew Sammy cried a lot, but she didn't know how to describe how much he cried or how to measure changes in this problem behavior. She knew that his crying episodes sometimes lasted only a couple of minutes and that others lasted for as long as an hour.

We considered how Trisha could measure Sammy's crying in such a way that she would have a more objective basis than her subjective impressions or general description ("He cries a lot!") for describing the seriousness of the problem and changes in the behavior. Trisha could have measured the duration of each crying episode by jotting down the time each crying episode started and when it stopped (or using a stopwatch). This would have had certain advantages, as she could then have described total crying time in minutes per day, percentage of the day spent crying, and number of episodes per day. Because she was responsible for the entire class and had no aide or other person who could keep such a record, however, we needed to find a measurement system that she could manage, but one that would still give her an objective description. Trisha agreed that she could keep an index card handy and make a tally mark for each crying episode. This gave her the number of episodes per day, but not their duration. She kept a daily log sheet on which she wrote down the number of tallies for the day.

By the time we began working with Trisha to resolve Sammy's crying, she had already tried several approaches: comforting, ignoring, and reprimanding him. None of these seemed to bring about improvement, although Trisha had no objective basis for judging the effects of her attempts to get Sammy to stop. She had given up on the problem until she could think of something new to try. We suggested, therefore, that she first record Sammy's crying episodes under "baseline" conditions before she tried anything else. After recording his crying episodes for 10 days, she reported that Sammy cried an average of about 17 or 18 times per day (see Figure 3.3). She felt that reducing the number to 6 or 8 times per day would be a reasonable goal. Next, Trisha tried totally and consistently ignoring Sammy when he cried. After 5 days of ignoring, the average was still about 15 (14, 15, 17, 15, 16 times per day), a little lower but not very close to her goal. Then she discovered that Sammy wanted to be called Sam. She designed an intervention in which she and his peers called him Sam—except when he was crying, when they tried to ignore him but could call him Sammy. Trisha also asked Sam to record his own behavior on her graph each day. The number of crying episodes then dropped to nearly zero (0, 0, 1, 4, 1, 0, 0, 0 for the next 8 days). Trisha continued counting for a while longer (during follow-up) but eventually was satisfied that the problem had been resolved.

Trisha's direct daily measurement helped her plot Sammy's progress more objectively and quantitatively than she could have using her subjective impressions. Her subjective impressions were useful, but her objective measurement gave her subjective perceptions a firmer base. Another method Trisha used was plotting her data daily on a graph, which is commonly done as a part of direct daily measurement. Her graph, shown in Figure 3.3, gave her a quick, easily interpretable picture of what was happening with Sammy's behavior.

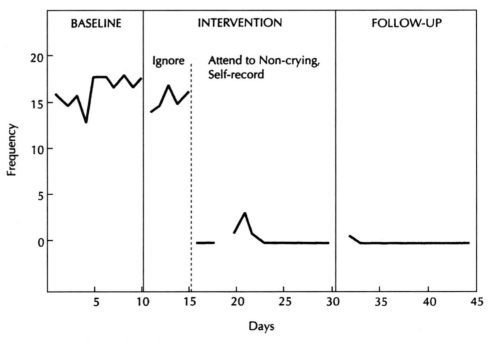

FIGURE 3.3   Sammy's Crying

What is a reasonable goal?

The ideal behavior management strategy resolves the problem immediately, completely, and permanently without creating any new ones. However, one nearly always has to settle for something less than the ideal. Teachers try to help their students learn patience and persistence and how to obtain gratification from partial successes. Teachers should be models of these characteristics by setting goals for themselves and their students that challenge but do not overwhelm. What does this mean for how you should approach setting a goal for the outcome of your intervention in a behavior management problem? We cannot answer this question directly because it is a matter for careful reflection in the individual case.

We can, however, suggest that goals are more likely to be reasonable when teachers define the problem behavior precisely and devise a way of measuring it objectively and accurately. Precise definition and quantitative measurement often help teachers notice progress that they might not have perceived if they had relied on more global, subjective impressions.

How do I accomplish a functional assessment of behavior and write a positive behavior intervention plan?

When a student is having extraordinary difficulty in school due to behavior problems, special education law may require a functional behavioral assessment, or FBA.[7] Actually, neither the federal special education law (the Individuals with Disabilities Education Act, most recently reauthorized in 2004) nor professionals in special education agree on just what a FBA is or how to do it.[8]

The basic idea of FBA is to ascertain by looking at the pattern of the student's behavior in its school context—using strategies like the ABC analysis we have already discussed—just why a student is exhibiting a particular behavior. Presumably, if you can learn *why* the student is behaving in a particular way, then you can help him or her learn to achieve the same goal in a more socially acceptable manner. This is more easily said than done, but FBA is at least intended to promote the analysis of why students misbehave and connect that information to a reasonable plan to do something about it.

There is much speculation about just what lawmakers and rulemakers intended or envisioned FBA to be. However, we think it is safe to assume that they intended to make the assessment of behavior *functional*—practical, useful, helpful in designing intervention plans, not simply an exercise in classification. This goal is entirely consistent with the purpose of this book. For details of current legal requirements related to FBA, you should contact your local special education administrator, who will know your state's requirements as well as the federal law.

Besides FBA, federal law may require a positive behavior intervention plan (BIP) for certain students. Again, consult your local special education administrator for details of the legal requirements, which are likely to change with each new reauthorization of the federal law and may vary from state to state. The procedures we suggest in this book are consistent with constructing a positive behavior intervention plan. There is nothing mysterious or peculiar about the essential features of a BIP that is outside the scope of our suggestions. If you implement our suggestions for analyzing behavior problems and changing behavior, then you will have a good basis for completing a functional behavior assessment and writing a positive behavior intervention plan.[9]

Summary

Careful analysis of a problem prior to designing a plan for attacking it is an accepted part of professional practice. Analyses of behavior management problems should include examination of one's assumptions about the causes of behavior, as beliefs may significantly affect the choice of intervention strategies. Some explanations of behavior are more important than others for teachers. We suggest that teachers focus on the causal factors that have the greatest support in empirical research and offer teachers the greatest opportunity for control. For teachers, classroom events are usually the most important causal factors. Analysis of classroom events should begin with a precise definition of the problem behavior. Particularly important in analyzing the problem is identifying antecedents (events immediately preceding the behavior) and consequences (events immediately following). Sequences or chains of antecedents, behaviors, and consequences (ABCs) may be described to clarify interactions from a particular individual's perspective. Coercive interactions, in which each party struggles for control by presenting increasingly aversive consequences for the other, are especially important to analyze carefully. Acting-out behavior typically occurs in a pattern of phases: calm, trigger, agitation, acceleration, peak, de-escalation, and recovery. The cognitive and affective aspects of behavior should be identified through careful listening and observation, as they may provide clues for resolving behavior problems. Analyzing behavior problems requires that the teacher select an appropriate approach to measurement. Direct daily measurement allows the most precise level of assessment and is particularly useful in evaluating the effects of interventions. Precise definition of behavior and accurate measurement of it help teachers set appropriate goals for behavioral change.

REFERENCES AND RESOURCES FOR FURTHER STUDY

The following references provided the basis for many of our statements in this chapter. You may wish to consult selected references for additional information on specific topics. Our reference notes for this chapter refer to sources in this list.

Causes of Behavior

Cullinan, D. (2002). *Students with emotional and behavior disorders: An introduction for teachers and other helping professionals.* Upper Saddle River, NJ: Merrill/Prentice-Hall.

Kauffman, J. M. (2005). *Characteristics of emotional and behavioral disorders of children and youth* (8th ed.). Upper Saddle River, NJ: Prentice-Hall.

Stoff, D. M., Breiling, J., & Maser, J. D. (Eds.) (1997). *Handbook of antisocial behavior.* New York: Wiley.

Definition and Measurement of Behavior and ABC Analysis

Alberto, P. A., & Troutman, A. C. (2003). *Applied behavior analysis for teachers* (6th ed.). Upper Saddle River, NJ: Prentice-Hall.

Colvin, G. (1992). *Managing acting-out behavior* [video lecture and workbook]. Eugene, OR: Behavior Associates.

Colvin, G. (2004). *Managing the cycle of acting-out behavior in the classroom.* Eugene, OR: Behavior Associates.

Colvin, G., Sugai, G., & Patching, B. (1993). Pre-correction: An instructional approach for managing predictable problem behaviors. *Intervention in School and Clinic, 28,* 143–150.

Kameenui, E. J., & Darch, C. B. (1995). *Instructional classroom management: A proactive approach to behavior management.* White Plains, NY: Longman.

Kerr, M. M., & Nelson, C. M. (2002). *Strategies for managing behavior problem in the classroom* (4th ed). Upper Saddle River, NJ: Prentice-Hall.

Kerr, M. M., Nelson, C. M., & Lambert, D. L. (1987). *Helping adolescents with learning and behavior problems.* Columbus, OH: Charles E. Merrill.

Walker, H. M. (1995). *The acting out child: Coping with classroom disruption* (2nd ed.). Longmont, CO: Sopris West.

Walker, H. M., Colvin, G., & Ramsey, E. (1995). *Antisocial behavior in school: Strategies and best practices.* Pacific Grove, CA: Brooks/Cole.

Walker, H. M., Ramsey, E., & Gresham, F. M. (2004). *Antisocial behavior in school: Strategies and best practices* (2nd ed.). Pacific Grove, CA: Brooks/Cole.

Functional Behavioral Assessment and Positive Behavior Intervention Plan

Fox, J., & Gable, R. A. (2004). Functional behavioral assessment. In R. B. Rutherford, M. M. Quinn, & S. R. Mathur (Eds.), *Handbook of research in emotional and behavioral disorders* (pp. 143–162). New York: Guilford.

Mulick, J. A., & Butter, E. M. (2005). Positive behavior support: A paternalistic utopian delusion. In J. W. Jacobson, R. M. Foxx, & J. A. Mulick (Eds.), *Controversial therapies for developmental disabilities: Fad, fashion, and science in professional practice* (pp. 385–404). Mahwah, NJ: Lawrence Erlbaum

Sasso, G. M., Conroy, M. A., Stichter, J. P., & Fox, J. J. (2001). Slowing down the bandwagon: The misapplication of functional behavior assessment for students with emotional and behavioral disorders. *Behavioral Disorders, 26,* 282–296.

Scott, T. M., DeSimone, C., Fowler, W., & Webb, E. (2000). Using functional assessment to develop interventions for challenging behaviors in the classroom: Three case studies. *Preventing School Failure, 44*(2), 51–56.

Yell, M. L. (1998). *The law and special education.* Upper Saddle River, NJ: Prentice-Hall.

Yell, M. L., Bradley, R., & Shriner, J. G. (1999). The IDEA amendments of 1997: A school-wide model for conducting functional behavioral assessments and developing behavior intervention plans. *Education and Treatment of Children, 22,* 244–266.

E N D N O T E S

1. See Kauffman (2005) for an extended discussion of causal factors, including how schools can contribute to students' misbehavior.
2. See Walker (1995), Walker, Ramsey, and Gresham (2004), and Kameenui and Darch (1995) for further discussion.

3. See Alberto and Troutman (2003), Cullinan (2002), Kerr and Nelson (2002), Walker (1995), and Walker, Ramsey, and Gresham (2004) for a further description of the role of antecedents and consequences.
4. See Alberto and Troutman (2003), Cullinan (2002), and Kerr and Nelson (2002) for more on the definition and measurement of behavior.
5. See Colvin (2004), Colvin, Sugai and Patching (1993), and Walker, Colvin, and Ramsey (1995) for a detailed description of precorrection.
6. See Colvin (2004) for a detailed description of the acting-out cycle.
7. See Yell (1998).
8. See Fox and Gable (2004), Sasso et al. (2001), Scott et al. (2000) and Yell, Bradley, and Shriner (1999) for a discussion of controversy about FBA.
9. See Mulik and Butter (2005)

4

Changing Behavior

Attempts to change behavior, whether by parents, teachers, politicians, or employers, have traditionally been impromptu. As reliable scientific evidence regarding behavioral change is accumulated and professional practices are more widely shared and evaluated, behavior management is becoming less improvised and more planned. Today, it is possible for teachers to select from a wide variety of strategies for managing classroom behavior. Some are "packaged" as programs, books, or workshops under special titles or trademarks. Others are presented in textbooks or resource manuals that focus more on underlying principles and their application to unique circumstances. Our approach is to present principles and suggest some initial questions teachers might ask themselves in selecting a management strategy. We also offer some specific suggestions and cautions for using specific strategies. This implies that teachers will not thoughtlessly follow a standard plan or passively accept whatever is offered but, rather, use their knowledge of behavior principles and best professional practices to select strategies with a high probability of success. Our intention is to foster reflective professional practice rather than provide a "formula" or "recipe" for teachers to follow. The vignettes of Mary and Tom provide examples of the kind of thinking we hope to encourage.

Mary

Two years ago, I went through a truly horrible time. I had one of the most difficult groups of kids I've ever taught. I was in terrible shape physically, psychologically, and financially. My whole world seemed to be a mess. I had back problems. My two grown kids both lost their jobs and came back to live with me. My husband had run away. I was deeply in debt. Maybe it was understandable, but I was not positive with the kids in my class. I was cranky. I yelled at them a lot. They got on my nerves. I was unhappy, and so were they. One day my supervisor was in my class and gave me one of those looks—you know, like, What's the matter with you? That was enough to make me stop and think about what was happening in my class and how I'd gotten into a lot of negativism, criticism, nagging, and other depressing kinds of interactions. My life outside school was bad enough, but my experiences in my classroom were just adding to my exhaustion. I knew I had to pull myself together and not let my personal life outside the classroom determine the way I behaved in school. It was really, really hard to do that! For a while, I kept an informal tally (on an index card) of my positive and negative statements to kids. Then I worked hard on being more positive when kids were doing what I wanted them to. I talked about this with my aide, too, and she helped me by watching for kids who were doing what they were supposed to and signaling me to let them know I noticed and approved. Fortunately, I got things turned around to the way I usually teach, with lots more positive than negative interactions with my students.

Tom

My sixth-grade group ate lunch in my room. They brought their lunch trays into the room from the cafeteria. After they ate, they were supposed to go out into the hall to scrape their trays into a waste can and stack their trays on a trolley. Even though I thought I had stated the rule clearly—no more than four students at a time in the hall—I had a lot of difficulty with too many kids going out together. Once five or six of them got out into the hall together, they started horsing around, shoving, pushing, doing gross things with the leftovers, and so on. Naturally, this made a lot of noise and led to problems with teasing, threatening behavior, spilled food, and soiled clothing. Finally, it occurred to me that what might work was some sort of "pass" or object to make the rule easier to monitor, something tangible that would regulate traffic for me. So I got four pieces of bamboo to use as "batons" or passes. The rule was that you could go out to scrape your tray only when you had a baton. The kids actually thought it was kind of fun because they made a game of passing the baton to the next person of their choosing. It worked for this group, but I was aware that it could have created problems, too. Kids could have started doing bad things with the batons. We could have had fights and teasing and hard feelings over who got the baton next. But we didn't. Other things could have gone wrong. But they didn't. If it had backfired—and I was ready for it to do just that—I wouldn't have lost much, if anything, by trying. What I learned was that sometimes little gimmicks work, especially in regulating kids' turns or movement. After all, why do you suppose some stores have customers take a number so they know when it's their turn to be waited on?

The wide range of methods and materials for behavior management available today requires a self-questioning strategy on the part of teachers. What have I tried, and how well have I implemented what I've done? Have I overlooked the simplest potential solution? What reasons do I have to believe that this approach might be successful? Given what I know about child development and this particular problem, what would be an appropriate strategy? Have I fallen into a pattern of negative or coercive interactions in trying to manage this problem? Am I employing best professional practices in dealing with this situation? Could I figure out how to precorrect the problem—to change the context somehow so that the problem doesn't occur in the first place, saving myself and my students a lot of needless hassle? These are only a few of the questions teachers must pose for themselves in tackling a behavior management problem after they have made an initial identification and analysis.

Questions for Reflection

When you have reached the point of planning a strategy for changing behavior, it is important to make a wise choice from the options you might try first. Sometimes the simplest and most obvious yet effective strategies are overlooked. We recommend that you consider how you might approach the problem from both behavioral and cognitive perspectives. Whatever the theoretical basis for the strategies you choose, it is critically important that you focus on what you want the student to do and that you provide a positive, supportive environment for appropriate behavior. You should ask yourself at least the following questions:

- Have I tried the simplest and most obvious strategies?
- What approaches to helping students change their behavior are most likely to be successful?
- How might I use the five operations of a behavioral approach?
- How can I capitalize on the cognitive and affective aspects of behavior change?
- Is my approach positive and supportive of appropriate behavior?
- Can I use an instructional approach to prevent this behavior problem?

Have I tried the simplest and most obvious strategies?

Amid the demands of teaching and the availability of relatively sophisticated or technical information regarding behavioral change, it is easy to forget that simple, direct approaches can be effective. When simple strategies work, they have the advantage of saving time and energy. They also tend to be more "natural" and may avoid the problems associated with highly technical or "artificial" approaches, including difficulties in implementation and failure to obtain long-term improvement in behavior. They are also easier to explain and defend to parents, administrators, and other teachers.

We are *not* suggesting that you take a simplistic approach to behavior management—an oversimplified view that justifies the use of discredited or unethical strategies (e.g., lecturing, sarcasm, corporal punishment). Many classroom behavior problems are complex and have no simple solution. Experience and research show, however, that such simple things as clear and consistent instructions and other uncomplicated strategies sometimes quickly and effectively resolve seemingly intransigent problems.

Simple things may seem obvious to someone else who is taking a fresh look at a situation, but they are easy to overlook when you are the teacher responsible for managing a difficult child or class. We suggest that before attempting a more complicated or elaborate approach you try to get a fresh look at the problem yourself, through self-questioning and reflection, to see whether a simple strategy might work: What is the simplest, most direct approach I could take to this problem? Have I overlooked an obvious tactic that might work? If I have tried a simple, direct strategy, have I implemented it well and consistently?

If a simple approach resolves the problem, you will have saved a lot of time and energy; if it doesn't, you will have lost little or nothing. We cannot catalog all the simple, direct, and effective strategies teachers might use. Teachers constantly amaze us with their creative but simple, direct solutions to common problems. We can, however, suggest several categories of interventions that are often overlooked. These include instructions, examples, and choices.

When faced with the problem of a student who either does things he or she should not or fails to do what is desired, we believe the simplest, most direct approach a teacher can take is using *instructions*—telling the student what is expected. You may at first think that this approach is unrealistic because the student obviously has been told how to behave. After all, most students who present behavior problems have been talked to quite a lot. Nevertheless, you might reflect on your communication with this student and consider whether you have used instructions in the most effective way:

- *Have I made the instruction as simple and clear as possible?* Adults often clutter and complicate their instructions with too much verbiage. Consider the differences between the following: (1) "It's time to get ready to go out to recess, so pick up everything and put it away and get ready to go, because, like I've told you, we're not going to go out to recess until everything's cleaned up and put away where it belongs and you're in your seats." (2) "It's time for recess. Put your things away so we can go."

- *Have I given the instruction in a clear, firm, nontentative, but polite and nonangry way?* Adults are more likely to get compliance when they speak as if they expect compliance and treat the student with respect. Questions are not instructions. For example, "Could you do this problem now?" indicates that you would like the student to do the problem but leaves you vulnerable to the response "No!" An alternative way of expressing your expectation might be "Please try this problem now."

- *Have I made certain I have the student's full attention before giving the instruction?* Students sometimes don't follow instructions because they never really "hear" them. Do not make the mistake of assuming that instructions are being received and processed when the student is doing something else or not looking at you when you give them.

Sometimes it is helpful to have the student repeat the instruction to make sure it was heard.

■ *Have I given one instruction at a time?*   Sometimes adults are unaware that they are piling instruction upon instruction without waiting for compliance with the first before giving a second. When repeated instructions are given in a short period of time, the student will likely perceive the adult as nagging.

■ *Have I been careful not to give too many different instructions?*   Students often feel they are ordered about constantly. Instructions will be more effective when they are carefully considered and only essential ones are given.

■ *Have I waited a reasonable time for compliance before assuming that the instruction will not be followed?*   It is easy to make the mistake of demanding instantaneous obedience. Giving the student the "room" of a few minutes often avoids noncompliance.

■ *Have I monitored compliances?*   Students with behavior problems often "tune out" adults because they are convinced no one will notice whether they obey. They are accustomed to adults assuming that instructions will be ignored.

■ *Have I provided appropriate consequences for compliance?*   Positive consequences for compliance, perhaps in the form of attention, recognition, or praise, will probably increase the likelihood that your instructions will be followed in the future. Adults often forget that reasonable compliance with instructions is learned—it needs to be rewarded consistently when it is a new behavior for the student, one we hope the student will acquire.

Depending on your responses to these questions, you might want to consider modifying your use of instructions. We have not exhausted the questions you might ask yourself. You might consider using models (drawing attention to other students who are following instructions), self-instruction (giving yourself audible instructions, then following them; asking the student to give himself or herself instructions and follow them), and making compliance with your instructions a kind of "game" (e.g., by interspersing "silly" or humorous instructions with serious ones).

We do not suggest that you train students to obey instructions without thinking. Unless students comply with most of the teacher's instructions, however, little learning will take place. Pupils who are highly noncompliant are at a severe disadvantage in school. They frustrate their teachers, but more important, they cut themselves off from many opportunities to learn. Helping students become reasonably compliant with classroom instructions is therefore a critical task of teachers.

Instructions depend on understanding the language used to describe an action or series of actions. People often take for granted that an individual will understand their instructions because they seem simple enough to them. "Oh, just write a little batch file and put it in the root directory" or "Now make sure you reduce the sauce before adding the mushrooms" may seem perfectly clear to some of people, but to others these instructions are as dense as Mississippi mud. The person being instructed has a much better chance of doing what is expected if the action is modeled for him or her—that is, if the person is shown how to do it with step-by-step instructions and feedback. The individual might need to be shown repeatedly or might do better if given a chance to practice under supervision before being expected to know what to do the next time he or she hears the instructions.

Examples are simple but indispensable tools in teaching. For some reason, teachers often forget that this is the case even when teaching children social and interpersonal behavior. It's easy to forget that the social skills that teachers assume to be second nature are unfamiliar, even mysterious, to some youngsters. "You need to pay attention" may mean little or nothing to many students with serious attention problems. Many of these children must be shown examples of what they typically do when they are not paying attention and how they might behave if they were paying attention. We and others have found that in teaching students to pay attention to their work it is typically necessary to (1) demonstrate for them the way they behave when they are not paying attention (e.g., looking around the room, playing with an object), (2) model for them the kind of behavior involved in paying attention (e.g., reading, writing answers, looking at the teacher when the teacher is talking), and (3) have them practice the behavior involved in paying attention and give them feedback on their performance. Being polite, sharing, waiting your turn, and so on, are examples of other types of behavior that some students may not understand without being shown examples.

When instructions are not working, we suggest that you ask yourself this question: Could I provide an example, model, or demonstration that would make my expectation clearer to this student? Can I show this student step-by-step just how I want him or her to behave? You might reflect further as follows:

■ *Have I provided both correct and incorrect examples and labeled them?*   Examples of desirable or correct behavior are essential. Typically, students will understand better what they are to do if you show them what is *not* correct as well as what *is* correct performance. Correct and incorrect examples must be labeled; that is, you must tell the observing student what is correct and what is incorrect (or appropriate and inappropriate).

■ *Have I demonstrated each step clearly and in sequence?*   Remember that unfamiliar tasks are difficult for most people to learn. The student will likely not acquire the skill you are trying to teach if you fail to give examples that are both clear and complete.

■ *Have I made sure the student is "with" me all the way?*   Watch for lapses in attention or points of confusion. Examples, like instructions, are useless if the student isn't paying close attention or doesn't comprehend what is happening.

■ *Have I given corrective feedback when the student makes an error?*   Students will learn slowly, or not at all, when they do not receive feedback about how they are doing.

■ *Have I maintained a positive instructional atmosphere?*   No one likes to be taught by someone who is impatient, uses sarcasm or ridicule, or otherwise causes embarrassment. Be careful to choose a time and place for giving examples that will avoid making the student feel inadequate or humiliated in the peer group. Maintain a supportive, positive attitude and recognize progress, even if it is slight.

Examples or models provided by the teacher can be extremely effective teaching tools. In addition, the models of behavior provided by peers can be extremely influential. We discuss peer models further in Chapter 6. Suffice it to say here that showing students how you want them to behave is a simple but often effective means of teaching. It is a strategy that has been used by master teachers in all fields for thousands of years.

One of the simplest but frequently overlooked techniques of managing problem behavior is giving people *choices*. Not only children in classrooms but also individuals in all kinds of social situations are likely to behave more constructively when they perceive that they have the power to make choices that are important to them. Conversely, people often behave badly when they feel "boxed in," perceiving that they have no choices. Students are likely to be less resistant to their teachers' instructions and control when they can choose certain features of their instruction or classroom environment. The savvy teacher is careful about the choices students are allowed to make for themselves.

Many teachers have found that students show less resistance to classroom demands and exhibit more appropriate classroom behavior when students are allowed to choose among several academic tasks, all of which are acceptable. For example, a student might be allowed to choose one of the following spelling tasks rather than being told which one he or she must complete:

1. Write each of 20 spelling words three times.
2. Write all 20 words one time in alphabetical order.
3. Look up and write the definitions for 15 words, and give the dictionary page number for 5 words.
4. Create 20 sentences, each using one of the spelling words.

Inventive teachers can find numerous alternatives to nearly any assignment, all of which have instructional value, and allow a difficult student to choose the one he or she prefers.[1]

Too few choices breed resentment and resistance to authority. Too many choices induce a kind of paralysis, leaving a person frustrated and unable to make a decision. For obvious reasons, some individuals should not be allowed to make certain choices. We know that if some individuals are given certain choices they are highly likely to make very bad ones. The teacher, then, is faced with this question: For a given individual, how many choices—and which ones—are appropriate?

Master teachers understand that choices must be structured for students to prevent catastrophic consequences and to foster interest and personal responsibility. That is, teachers must not allow students to make choices that will close off future options (e.g., deciding not to attend school or not to complete assigned work). On the other hand, teachers must try to encourage students to make wise choices and to present options that will heighten students' interest, satisfaction, and judgment. This requires helping students understand and be able to predict the consequences of their choices and constructing appropriate options in situations in which students have not ordinarily had them.

Students sometimes make choices in situations that you cannot control or structure. Under such circumstances, you can only try to help students make good choices.

Our point is that *constructing* options is a simple strategy that can be used very creatively and often successfully to manage behavior. The kinds of options we are referring to may appear to some teachers to be trivial, but to students they may be significant. They may involve such simple choices as which assignment or problem to do first, what color paper or pen to use, or where to sit for a particular activity. Students might be allowed to choose one of two or more tangible rewards or special activities when they have earned it or choose a friend with whom to work. When teaching, and especially when teaching a "difficult" student, you would be wise to ask yourself the following questions.

■ *What appropriate new options can I give this student?*   There are nearly always new choices that a student might be allowed, thereby increasing the student's stake in the classroom activity.

■ *Do I know that I can live with the choice the student makes?*   Be careful not to construct an option that is intolerable or unacceptable.

■ *Have I constructed an array of options that is consistent with the student's developmental level?*   The student's age, preferences, and decision-making abilities are important to take into consideration. The number and nature of options must be matched to the student's interests and ability to make choices.

What approaches to helping students change their behavior are most likely to be successful?

Teachers have many choices for approaching behavior management problems. More skillful behavior managers are aware of more options and able to make better choices among them. Regardless of the number of alternative approaches you may know about, it is important to be able to articulate your reasons for choosing one approach rather than another. Following are the primary questions we suggest you ask yourself when considering a particular approach.

■ *Is this approach consistent with professional practices?*   Teachers' practices must always reflect sound professional judgment. The fact that a particular approach has been used or suggested by other teachers does not necessarily mean that it is appropriate. Teachers must studiously avoid practices that are prohibited by law or school policy and those that are questionable on ethical grounds.

■ *Does my own experience or that of colleagues suggest that this approach might be effective?* Teachers themselves are often good judges of what is likely to work and what is likely not to work with a given class or student. We caution that some teachers find it easy to reject useful suggestions out-of-hand based on their personal biases; some cling to approaches that are familiar to them but are not very successful. Nevertheless, the judgment of experienced and highly skilled teachers must be viewed as an important test of the value of any suggested approach.

■ *What technical assistance can I find for helping me implement this approach?*   Guidance from colleagues, consultants, technical manuals, or professional publications is often a critical factor in determining whether an approach is successful. Trying to implement procedures on a seat-of-the-pants basis often leads to disappointment, and sometimes to mistaken judgment about the value or workability of the approach. Some approaches are failures, even when skillfully implemented; some are failures because their implementation was flawed. When you select an approach to a problem, make sure you use it skillfully.

■ *What empirical research supports this approach?*   In our view, support from empirical research should be a critical factor in selecting an approach to behavior management. Testimonial evidence alone ("I tried this, and it works!" or "I don't believe it's ever effective, because I've never been able to make it work!") does not seem to us as reliable as teachers' opinions that are supported by evidence obtained in carefully controlled research studies. Because we take the position that accumulated evidence from empirical research is the single best criterion for selecting strategies, we describe approaches based on the research literatures of behavioral psychology and social learning, particularly as they apply to the classroom.

How might I use the five operations of a behavioral approach?

Research in behavioral psychology has produced a wide range of techniques for changing human behavior. Here, we briefly describe only five basic operations that provide the core strategies for building all others.[2] With an understanding of these basic operations, teachers are able to create sound techniques for intervening to increase or decrease specific behaviors. We refer to "operations" because we are discussing "operant" behavior—actions that "operate" in the environment to produce certain outcomes. The operations we describe are ways of modifying the social environment so that specific behaviors will produce predictable consequences.

The five operations we describe here are all based on the principle that the events immediately following a behavior—its consequences—determine to a large extent how likely it is to occur again. Positive and negative reinforcement involve using consequences to increase the probability or rate of a behavior; extinction and punishment, whether by response cost or presenting aversives, involve using consequences to decrease the probability or rate of a behavior. Each of these operations has advantages and disadvantages, and some should be used more frequently than others. In most classroom situations, teachers' interventions will involve combinations of operations.

Positive Reinforcement.   Positive reinforcement is the staple of good behavior management, and it is a concept with which most teachers are familiar. It means that when the student behaves in a specific desirable way, the consequence(s) will be positive—something the individual student is willing to work to obtain. Positive reinforcement has the effect of increasing the behavior that produces such consequences. Providing rewards for appropriate behavior is extremely simple in principle, but putting positive reinforcement into practice in ways that are effective and self-enhancing for the student sometimes requires great creativity and finesse on the part of the teacher. Teachers are sometimes unsuccessful in using positive reinforcement because they neglect the fine points that are critical in using the operation effectively. Following are questions you need to ask yourself if you wish to use positive reinforcement to increase the behavior you would like to see a student exhibit more frequently.

■ *Am I sure the consequences I am using are positive reinforcers (rewards) for this student?* Not everyone finds the same consequences reinforcing; what is rewarding for one person may not be for another. To use positive reinforcement successfully, you must provide a consequence that is attractive to the particular student whose behavior you are trying to improve. Finding the right consequence is sometimes difficult. It must not only be something attractive to the student, but you must be able to control access to it. You might consider several categories of potential reinforcers:

1. Social reinforcers such as attention, praise, touching (these are among the most natural reinforcers)
2. Activity reinforcers such as talking with friends, reading, playing a game or sport, caring for pets, tutoring a peer, playing a musical instrument, working at the computer, watching a video (this category is nearly inexhaustible for the creative teacher and might be seen as only slightly more artificial than social reinforcers)
3. Tangible reinforcers such as edibles, toys, clothing, money, or any type of token that has no inherent value but can be exchanged for other desired reinforcers (tangibles are often considered highly artificial reinforcers)

You might identify reinforcers by asking a student what he or she is willing to work for, by observing the student's preferences, or simply by trying out things you think might work. The ultimate test of whether a consequence is a positive reinforcer for a given individual is whether he or she will work to get it. Bear in mind, however, that you can offer a potential reinforcer in ways that will make it useless, (i.e., that destroy its appeal). If you require too much for earning a reward, if you offer the reward in too small or too large an amount, or if you are inconsistent in providing the reinforcer, for example, you may be unsuccessful. Finally, sometimes students receive consequences that appear to be punishing, not reinforcing, yet they continue to behave inappropriately. In many cases, some aspect of the apparent punishment, perhaps the attention or the emotional behavior of adults who are upset, is actually a rewarding consequence of misbehavior that outweighs the intended punishment.

■ *Does getting the reinforcer depend on the student's exhibiting the appropriate behavior?* Reinforcers are typically useless unless they are made contingent on the behavior you want to increase. "Contingent" means that the reward is available when, and only when, the behavior is exhibited. If the reinforcer is available freely without performance, then the individual is unlikely to be motivated to earn it; "earning it" means that it is not available until after the appropriate behavior is exhibited. Teachers often experience failure in attempts to reward students' appropriate behavior with attention because they fail to respond differently to desirable conduct and misbehavior. When students get attention—either positive or negative—regardless of how they behave, they are unlikely to learn to behave as you would like them to. If you cannot control when the student has access to the reinforcer, then you probably cannot use it to improve behavior. You must attempt to use reinforcers that are under your control—things you can regulate.

■ *Is the reinforcer available soon after the student performs the appropriate behavior?* Much of behavior is controlled by immediate consequences. Smoking and overeating are common examples in which, even for many successful and well-adjusted adults, immediate positive consequences take precedence over long-term negative consequences. As people develop psychologically, they are able to tolerate greater delays in gratification and are controlled to a greater extent by long-term consequences in most areas of their lives. Young children and those whose psychological development is lagging, however, typically will not respond to rewards that are delayed for more than a very short time. Many teachers underestimate the importance of immediacy in using positive reinforcement effectively. Often, finding a way to decrease the interval between appropriate behavior and reward will be key to making positive reinforcement effective. Remember, too, that for many students the behavior that is rewarded is the one that occurs immediately prior to their receiving a reward. Regardless of what you intend to reward, the reinforcer will likely strengthen whatever behavior the student has just exhibited. We offer this caution: Be very mindful of the timing of your reinforcement.

■ *Am I providing an appropriate unit of reward for the expected unit of behavior?* Reinforcers are, in effect, like wages; they must be fair and effective compensation for performance. Fairness is not necessarily judged by what is typical. It is far more complicated than that. Perhaps the best way of determining what is fair is negotiating it with the student. Especially with young and developmentally delayed students, and especially when the student is learning a new skill, we recommend that you require only a little performance for reinforcement. Frequent small rewards are typically more effective than infrequent large rewards.

■ *Is the reinforcer a "natural" consequence or at least paired with one?* "Natural" reinforcers are ones that exist, or should exist, in a humane environment and effectively influence the behavior of most individuals. Most people agree that praise, recognition, and healthy recreational activities are natural reinforcers. "Artificial" reinforcers are those contrived for special purposes when natural consequences have failed (e.g., token systems in classrooms designed to remediate serious behavior problems). Natural reinforcers are preferred because they are likely to maintain behavior after artificial incentives are withdrawn. Artificial reinforcers are sometimes critical to initial success in changing behavior, and they should not be shunned when they are necessary. When they are used, however, they should be paired with (i.e., delivered concurrently with) more natural rewards. For example, social attention such as praise should nearly always be given along with tangible reinforcement. In this way, with time, natural consequences are likely to take on some of the power of artificial incentives.

■ *Am I careful to respect entitlements?* One of the more difficult ethical and legal issues involving positive reinforcement is the question of the conditions and privileges to which students are entitled regardless of how they behave. People may disagree about whether every student has a fundamental right or entitlement to certain activities (e.g., recess, all classroom privileges) or whether they may be made contingent on a standard of classroom conduct. Activities and privileges that are considered entitlements cannot be made contingent on desired behavior, and thus cannot be used as rewards. We cannot draw the boundaries of classroom entitlements for you; we can only urge you to be aware of the issues and take precautions against ethical and legal questions being raised. One precaution is making sure that your principal approves of any program that involves making any "standard" activity contingent on a student's behavior. Another precaution is using *additional* activities or privileges beyond those granted routinely to all students as reinforcers whenever feasible. A final precaution is reviewing the conditions of your students' lives from the perspective that every student has the right to be treated fairly and equitably and to receive recognition and rewards for appropriate behavior.

A problem that most teachers anticipate, and many experience, is the claim of entitlement to reinforcement by a student who has not behaved appropriately. That is, a student may deny that he or she has not met the criterion for reward or argue that he or she should receive the same reward as another student. In some cases, teachers become so weary of the carping of students who do not earn rewards that they eliminate special contingencies for students or groups with special needs. Some teachers become so frustrated by claims of entitlement that they conclude that positive reinforcement simply is not worth the hassle. When teachers abandon positive reinforcement contingencies because of this problem, the students are winning a contest of wills, but both they and their teacher are losing opportunities for more constructive interactions.

We have three suggestions for responding to inappropriate student claims of entitlement. First, you should be certain that every student in your class has a reasonable opportunity to earn frequent, meaningful rewards. Students' complaints sometimes mean that the opportunities for reward are simply too few, and you may need to alter your reward system accordingly. If rewards are scarce and given disproportionately, students may have a legitimate complaint. If the same contingencies do not apply to everyone, you may need to explain briefly and in simple language that different students need and earn different rewards.

Second, you should not become embroiled in arguments or long discussions about rewards. If you are confident that the reward system is fair to everyone in the class, then you have no need to offer repeated justifications or respond to nagging. Let one simple explanation of why the reward is given suffice; ignore further complaints.

Finally, teachers should commit to memory the suggestions of Ginger Rhode, Bill Jenson, and Ken Reavis about how to make positive reinforcement work, using the mnemonic IFEED-AV as a reminder.[3] If you want to be successful in using positive reinforcement, make sure that you give it as *Immediately* after desirable behavior as possible, give it *Frequently*, show *Enthusiasm* for the student's behavior and the reinforcement, make *Eye contact* with the student when you deliver the reinforcement, *Describe* simply and clearly what the student has done to earn the reinforcement, build the student's *Anticipation* of earning the reinforcement, and provide *Variety* in the reinforcements the student can earn.

Negative Reinforcement. The term *negative reinforcement* is frequently misunderstood to mean punishment. The term actually means reinforcing (strengthening) behavior by removing or preventing something unpleasant. That is, negative reinforcement strengthens whatever behavior allows the individual to escape or avoid a negative consequence. A few everyday examples may help to clarify how negative reinforcement works. Normally, people take analgesics to remove (escape from) pain; taking such pills is a behavior maintained by negative reinforcement. Also, people buckle their seat belts to avoid a negative consequence—injury or death; buckling up is a behavior that is negatively reinforced. Students may study for a test at least in part to avoid negative consequences such as embarrassment or a low grade; studying is a behavior that may be maintained in part by both negative reinforcement (avoidance of failure) and positive reinforcement (getting a good grade or learning privileges as well as—we always hope—the intrinsic satisfaction of learning).

Ordinarily, negative reinforcement should not be a prominent part of classroom behavior management for two reasons. First, negative reinforcement relies on the presence or threat of negative (aversive) consequences. Although some negative consequences or their threat are an unavoidable part of everyday existence, including a reasonably demanding learning environment, good teaching and management do not rely primarily on threats. Second, deliberate negative reinforcement sets the stage for coercion—the use of force or intimidation to achieve one's objectives. A coercive relationship is one in which both parties vie for control by increasing the level of pain or discomfort of the other, as we discussed in Chapter 3. Whoever wins the contest is negatively reinforced; the losing party withdraws his or her pressure, providing negative reinforcement for the winner. Coercion is, unfortunately, a part of the family life of many students with behavior problems. To make coercion a part of their school experience adds insult to injury.

When devising a behavior management program, ask yourself the following questions about negative reinforcement: What part does negative reinforcement play in my students' motivation to learn and behave appropriately? Can I rely more on positive reinforcement and less on negative reinforcement to motivate my students? Am I becoming engaged in coercive interactions—power struggles—with my students? Power struggles are sometimes difficult if not impossible to avoid. Nevertheless, they are a sign that your behavior management strategies need close scrutiny and possibly revision.

Extinction. One way of eliminating behavior, whether desirable or undesirable, is to eliminate its reinforcement—an operation called *extinction*. When a behavior no longer produces the desired effect (positive or negative reinforcement), it will eventually fade away (be extinguished). Using an extinction procedure assumes that you can identify the reinforcer for the behavior you are trying to eliminate and that you can terminate the reinforcer. The concept of extinction is indispensable in a behavioral approach to classroom management, but the procedure is never appropriate as a sole strategy.

Extinction has two major disadvantages as the primary focus of an approach to reducing problem behavior. First, it is a slow process, especially for a behavior pattern that has become well established. Second, when an extinction procedure is first implemented, the behavior is likely to become worse before it starts to improve. When people do not get what they have come to expect as a consequence of their behavior, they first try harder to produce the usual result. For example, if a child is used to getting what he or she wants by throwing temper tantrums, his or her tantrums will at first become more severe when adults place them on extinction (i.e., resolutely refuse to give in to them). Furthermore, extinction by itself is of little value. It does little or nothing, without reinforcement for desirable conduct, to improve behavior.

The central feature of a skillful behavioral approach is a combination of shifting reinforcement away from undesirable behavior (i.e., extinction) and toward desirable behavior (i.e., positive reinforcement). The critical concept in the approach is making sure that students receive ample positive reinforcement—but only, or at least overwhelmingly, for behavior that is appropriate. When using extinction, the following are important questions to ask yourself.

- *Have I identified and effectively terminated reinforcement of the undesirable behavior?* Occasional reinforcement during extinction is likely to make the behavior even worse. Try to make sure that you keep the behavior from resulting at any time in its former consequence.
- *Am I offering strong positive reinforcement for alternative appropriate behavior?* Remember, positive reinforcement for the behavior you want to encourage is a key to making extinction work.

Response Cost Punishment.   Like negative reinforcement, punishment is often misunderstood. Punishment does *not* necessarily mean causing pain, either physical pain or serious psychological distress. *Punishment* means providing a consequence that decreases the likelihood that a behavior will be repeated. True, punishment may involve causing physical or psychological distress, but the punishment procedures that are most effective for most individuals do not cause such trauma. The most effective punishment typically involves withholding or withdrawing a positive reinforcer contingent on a specific misbehavior. Punishment of this kind means that misbehavior "costs" something, hence the term *response cost*. It may mean the loss of money (i.e., a fine) or other possession or the withdrawal of a privilege (e.g., loss of a specific amount of time for TV viewing, recess, or another valued activity).

Punishment of any kind, including response cost, can be abusive if it is excessive or capricious. Nevertheless, it appears that rearing children who are reasonably socialized and maintaining a humane social structure require the judicious use of punishing as well as positively reinforcing consequences. When you are contemplating or evaluating the use of punishment, ask yourself the following questions.

- *Have I made every effort to use positive procedures to manage this student's behavior?* Punishment should never be your first resort. Consider it only after you have devised a behavior management scheme that emphasizes positive consequences for desirable conduct.

- *Am I generally positive toward my students, giving very frequent praise and other forms of positive attention to them when their behavior is appropriate?*   Punishment is most effective when it comes from people who are typically warm and loving toward the individual when his or her behavior is acceptable. If you are generally irritable or negative toward a student, your attempts to punish are likely to backfire. Punishment is most effective when it represents a stark contrast to the typical interactions between teacher and student.

■ *Am I able to administer punishment matter-of-factly, without a display of anger, and without nagging, threats, or moralizing (trying to induce guilt through sermonizing or shaming)?*　Displays of anger and lectures that accompany punishment will almost certainly have exactly the opposite effect you intend. Repeated warnings are actually nagging or threats, which are counterproductive. If you are going to give a warning before punishing, give only one. After the student has been punished, do not lecture him or her; pick up classroom activities as if nothing had happened and emphasize positive consequences for appropriate behavior.

■ *Is the punishment immediate, fair, and consistent?*　Delaying punishment, like delaying reinforcement, reduces its effectiveness. Effective punishment is reasonable—not trivial, but not out of proportion to the seriousness of the offense. And predictability is a critical feature of effective punishment. The student must know what behavior will result in punishment, and the punishment should be consistently applied for that behavior.

■ *Does the punishment quickly produce behavioral change?*　Effective punishment does not take a long time to work. If a change in behavior for the better is not quickly apparent (after it is administered a few times), you should revise or discontinue it. It is better not to punish at all than to persist in ineffective punishment (which is abuse). Punishing more severely is seldom the answer. Changing the nature of the consequence or making punishment more immediate or consistent is more likely to produce good results.

■ *Have I communicated my punishment procedures to all concerned parties?*　The student(s), parents, and your school administrators should know what punishment procedures you intend to use. Your best insurance against legal entanglements and unprofessional conduct is to keep concerned parties fully informed and your procedures open to inspection by others.

Punishment by Presenting Aversives.　Punishment may be accomplished in one of two ways, by either withdrawing valued commodities (as described in response cost) or by presenting aversive consequences such as reprimands, isolation, or noxious stimuli. Using noxious or painful consequences places the teacher in extremely dangerous territory, both legally and ethically, and our advice is to steer well clear of using them. However, reprimands and *brief* social isolation may be appropriate when used carefully and skillfully along with the positive procedures we have discussed. All the questions and caveats we offered in our discussion of response cost apply as well to presenting aversive consequences. In addition, consider the following regarding reprimands.

■ *Do I keep my reprimands brief and to-the-point?*　Lectures and general criticisms tend to be wasted words, if not inducements to further misbehavior. "Randy, stop talking to Rachel" is preferable to "Randy, I've told you I will not tolerate this kind of behavior, and I want you to stop it right now and pay attention to your work. Now shape up!"

■ *Do I keep my reprimands as private as possible?*   Private reprimands are ones given so that few if any of the student's peers can hear what is being said. Public reprimands are those that nearly everyone in the class can hear. Private reprimands, for which the teacher goes to the student and speaks quietly but firmly, are usually most effective. Public reprimands may sometimes be necessary, but more is lost than gained when the teacher uses primarily loud, public criticism or rebuke.

■ *Do I make sure I have the student's attention and attempt to get eye contact before reprimanding?*   Like instructions, reprimands will be ineffective if they are delivered to a student who is otherwise occupied. Use the student's name. Look directly at the student when speaking and use a direct, firm, but not angry tone of voice. There should be no misunderstanding about the fact that you are displeased with the student's behavior, but you should not be visibly upset.

Brief social isolation is sometimes referred to as *time out.* Nearly every teacher is familiar with the term, yet many teachers misuse the procedure in attempts to punish misbehavior. The technical meaning of time out is *time out from positive reinforcement.* That is, it means an interval during which positive reinforcement cannot be obtained. The implication is that positive reinforcement is readily available, except when the individual is in time out. As such, time out does not *necessarily* require physical isolation; it may not involve removal of the student from the group, only a period during which the student will be ignored or not allowed to earn the typical rewards for appropriate behavior. It may, however, involve placing the student for a brief period in a place where he or she is unable to interact freely with others and obtain attention and other positive reinforcers. When time out involves placing a student in a separate room, it becomes a highly controversial procedure and one that is easily abused. We recommend that you not use any such isolation procedure without the explicit approval of your school administrator and the student's parents and with consultation from a professional with extensive experience in appropriate use of the procedure. Brief social isolation of a less radical nature, such as having the student "sit out" of a game or move to another seat in the classroom, is less risky. Even with this kind of time-out procedure, however, you should be sure to keep our previous questions and cautions regarding punishment in mind.

In addition, remember that longer time outs are not typically more effective than shorter ones. The *maximum* effective time out period is usually not more than 5 minutes. To use time out appropriately, you will need a timer to signal when the time-out period has ended; you must *not* allow yourself to forget the student in time out. Finally, recall that time out means time out from positive reinforcement, not merely time out of the classroom or time out of your sight. Attempts to use time out often fail for one of two reasons: (1) the "time in" environment offers little positive reinforcement, so being excluded from it is not punishing, or (2) the "time out" environment is one in which the student obtains unintended reinforcement. The latter is often the case when the student is placed in a hallway or office, where interesting observations of and interactions with others are typically available.

How can I capitalize on the cognitive and affective aspects of behavior change?

A behavioral approach provides anchor points for devising specific management techniques. The five operations and combinations and variations of them are a core that enables teachers to plan explicit strategies. Nevertheless, the nuances of behavior management require that the teacher also approach students as thinking, feeling individuals. In fact, the teacher who ignores the way students think and feel about their behavior and about management techniques is doomed to be ineffective. Sensitivity to meanings and emotions is required for effective behavior management. Next, we briefly highlight the importance of cognitive and affective aspects of talking with students, choosing consequences for students, teaching self-control, and teaching social skills.

Talking with Students. In Chapter 5, we elaborate on the importance of teachers' verbalizations to students. Here, we merely wish to point out that the success of the strategies we have discussed may well depend on how the teacher presents them. Students' understanding of contingencies and their emotional responses to them will be determined in part simply by what the teacher says and how she or he says it. Words and tones that convey a positive attitude, respect for the student, self-confidence, and firm expectations that the student will behave appropriately will make a significant difference in the teacher's probability of success. What really matters to students? How do they feel about important aspects of school and the classroom? It should seldom be the case that a student can say, "No one ever asked me."

Choosing Consequences for Students' Behavior. "Different strokes for different folks" is a cliché that applies to selecting effective reinforcing and punishing consequences. Sensitivity to the student's preferences, which can be obtained only through careful observation and listening, is essential in choosing consequences of behavior that will have the desired effect. Talking with students about their behavior and its consequences is necessary. Nevertheless, talking is not enough. Watching and listening with understanding sometimes reveal that students' words do not reflect their true feelings. Many a student has fooled a teacher by saying, "I don't care." Sometimes verbal bravado masks real feelings; sometimes it does not. How can you tell what a student *really* feels about something? Perhaps another cliché will help: "Actions speak louder than words."

Teaching Self-Control Procedures. The ultimate goal of good behavior management is to help students learn to control their own behavior in self-enhancing ways. As we discuss in Chapter 5, teaching self-control is intimately connected to talking with students about their behavior. It is a way of getting them actively involved, cognitively and effectively, in their own self-growth.

Teaching Social Skills. Some students acquire social skills easily. They do not seem to require explicit instruction in order to learn the patterns of social interaction that teachers consider acceptable. As is the case with academic skills, however, some students do not learn the critical social skills as easily as other students. Students who need a more explicit instructional program for learning social skills must be helped to think through the demands of social situations and their own options for dealing with everyday interpersonal problems.[4] The teacher must help these students become cognitively aware of others' expectations, their choices in responding to those expectations, and the probable outcomes of making given choices.

Finally, it is important that you try to understand how your students feel about the conditions of their lives, both in school and out of school. Your knowing how a misbehaving student feels will not, in itself, change the student's behavior, nor will it necessarily enable you to resolve the behavior problem by other means. Understanding the student's feelings will, however, improve your chances of developing a helpful relationship with the student. A helpful relationship is one in which the student is open to positive influence through your listening, talking, and providing consequences. A student is more likely to be open to positive influence by a teacher whose behavior indicates awareness of the student's feelings.

Our belief is that students' cognitive and affective changes generally follow their behavioral changes, although thoughts and feelings sometimes determine how a student behaves. Attempts to change students' feelings and patterns of thinking in the hope that these changes alone will be followed by behavioral improvement are, in our judgment, not very likely to be successful. Thus our prediction is that your best bet for helping students understand and feel better about themselves will be to put your primary effort into helping them change their behavior for the better, with secondary emphasis on affective and cognitive changes related to their behavior. Of course, the goal of teaching is to accomplish improvements in both behavioral and cognitive-affective domains. The questions to ask yourself: Where do I begin? Where do I put my greatest emphasis? How do I view the relationship between what students do and how they think and feel about what they do?

Building helpful relationships with students requires both technical skills in using the operations of a behavioral approach and the ability to see events through the eyes and minds of pupils. Understanding the rage, loneliness, self-congratulation, suspicion, sadness, joy, or other emotions of the individual student is desirable in itself because it enables you to relate to that student as another human being. More important for you as a teacher, perhaps, such understanding might help you plan, and thus make better choices about, the way you talk to the student and the way you construct expectations and consequences in the classroom.

Is my approach positive and supportive of appropriate behavior?

In any attempt to modify behavior, you should reflect on the extent to which your approach emphasizes positive consequences for appropriate behavior. Negative reinforcement, extinction, and perhaps even punishment (within the guidelines we have suggested) may be justified as part of a management scheme. However, unless your approach is overwhelmingly positive and supportive of appropriate behavior, we feel it is professionally and ethically questionable. Teachers need to ask themselves questions about their own behavior in the classroom and take action accordingly.

■ *How frequently do I offer praise or other positive evaluations (e.g., smiles, pats, approval) of my students' appropriate behavior?*   Most teachers overestimate their positive interactions with students. You may want to keep a tally of your positive and negative responses to students during specified periods for several days to see just what your ratio of positive to negative is. Yes, it is possible to overdo praise statements, but few teachers are in any danger of doing so. No, it is not enough just to make many positive statements and show approval to students; your positive attention must be contingent on the type of behavior you want your students to exhibit. You must make sure that inappropriate behavior receives no rewarding consequences from you.

■ *Do I ignore most minor misbehavior?*   One of the most difficult behavior management strategies for most teachers to learn is putting minor misbehavior on extinction—simply ignoring it and focusing attention on desirable behavior. It is very easy to fall into the trap of giving negative attention to minor misbehavior, which results in inadvertent reinforcement of it. Attention—even negative attention in the form of reprimands—can be a positive reinforcer, particularly when a student seldom receives positive attention. Some misbehavior cannot be ignored because it is dangerous or too disruptive to allow it to continue. But most of the minor disruptions and irritating behavior we see in classrooms are best treated as if they didn't happen. No one can give you an exact formula for when and what to ignore and when and what *not* to ignore. Becoming a good judge of exactly what and when to ignore is an important aspect of becoming a master teacher.

■ *Do I emphasize positive outcomes of desirable behavior rather than avoidance of negative consequences for inadequate performance?*   The distinction between positive and negative reinforcement is subtle but important. Positive reinforcement induces a student to approach the teacher; negative reinforcement is based on avoidance. To the greatest extent possible, your behavior management strategies should be based on motivation to obtain rewarding consequences, not avoid unpleasantness.

■ *Am I able to avoid getting drawn into power struggles and other forms of negative interactions with students?*   Some students with behavior problems are masters at drawing adults into arguments and verbal power struggles that they typically win. Whatever you say, they will question. Before you know it, you are engaged in an argument and feeling emotionally upset, usually about something that in retrospect seems silly. Becoming aware immediately that you are being drawn in and terminating the interaction before it turns into a power struggle is an important skill for dealing with difficult students. In part, avoiding power struggles involves the recognition that you are responsible for your choices as a teacher and students are responsible for theirs.

■ *Do students like being in my classroom?*   One important test of whether your behavior management strategies are appropriate is whether students have generally positive feelings about your classroom. Certainly, you should not expect that students will never express unhappiness with you or the demands you make of them. Good teachers care about much more than their popularity with students. Nevertheless, if over a reasonable period of time students obviously do not like being in your classroom, you are probably not meeting their needs in a professionally defensible way.

■ *Are my students learning academic and social skills at a level commensurate with their abilities?*   For the competent teacher, students' good feelings are not enough. Students must make progress in acquiring the academic and social skills that are self-enhancing and give them increased options in important areas of their lives.

Can I use an instructional approach to prevent this behavior problem?

Too often teachers fail to see that social behavior can be taught and that an effective *instructional* program is crucial for classroom deportment, just as it is for the development of academic skills. Behavior management is often simply reactive (responding to misbehavior after it occurs) rather than proactive (preparing a program to teach desired behavior so that the misbehavior does not occur). During the past decade, researchers at the University of Oregon have been particularly adept at explaining how to *teach* appropriate behavior.[5] Here, we provide a brief explanation of the *precorrection* teaching strategy that we introduced in Chapter 3. Then we suggest strategies for managing the phases of the acting-out cycle depicted in Figure 3.2.

Precorrecting Problems.   Precorrection requires the teacher to specify the problem—to define precisely what the student does that is predictable but unacceptable. It also requires the teacher to describe the context in which this behavior is highly likely. The context is the set of circumstances under which the behavior is predictable. The rationale is that if one can predict the circumstances under which a student will make a mistake (be it academic or social), then one can teach the student how to avoid the mistake and do what is expected. This means that it is not enough merely to say what is unacceptable behavior; it means that it is essential to say, in addition, what is expected instead (a matter that is easy to forget in the heat of working with a difficult student). Then, the problem is this: How can the context be modified to help the student avert the mistake and do what is expected?

The precorrection strategy is both anticipatory and instructional. The teacher may think it through in this way: In this context (perhaps a transition from one activity to another, during which Fred must move from one place in the classroom to another), this behavior is highly predictable (perhaps Fred's teasing another student). Here's the behavior I expect (perhaps that Fred will mind his own business while going through the transition). And here is the way I can modify the context to make the behavior I expect more likely to occur (perhaps by specifying a particular route for Fred to take, clarifying my expectations for behavior during transitions, and giving Fred special recognition for doing what I expect).

Teaching generally involves not only instructions about what is expected but also rehearsals, prompts, and rewards for correct performance. Clearly stated expectations are essential, as we have discussed in previous chapters. But many students have to have more than that if they are to learn. They may have to practice the correct response under close supervision. This may involve the students actually doing the expected behavior or mentally rehearsing what they are to do, step by step. Most teachers easily get the hang of helping students go through academic problems in a step-by-step fashion; athletic coaches have long understood that this is critically important. Yet, when it comes to social behavior, teachers often seem to forget the principles of rehearsing, prompting, and rewarding.

For Fred, the precorrection plan might involve a mini-lesson in which the teacher explains the route from point A to point B that he is to take and the expected behavior: "Mind your own business on the way, which means don't get involved with anybody else along the way, hands to yourself, mouth closed." Rehearsal could involve either talking through the expected routine or actually showing Fred what you expect him to do and then having him practice it a time or two while you watch and give him feedback. Prompts could involve giving Fred a hand signal or perhaps handing him a brief written reminder just before the transition. Strong reinforcement could be given by allowing Fred to earn a special privilege after he has a string of several successive days of appropriate transition behavior. Monitoring could mean just keeping a simple log indicating whether Fred behaved as expected (perhaps just a plus or minus noted on the teacher's calendar).

The precorrection strategy may be used with an individual student or with a group of students. Figure 4.1 shows a completed precorrection checklist and plan for a student, Jimmy. Remember that each part of the plan is an essential element in teaching desired behavior. Key questions in using the strategy are the following:

- *Can I identify the context in which a predictable problem occurs?*   The context is the where and when. It is the situation or circumstance in which predictable behavior occurs.

- *Have I specified the expected behavior?*   Can you describe what you want the student to do instead of the predictable behavior? Both you and the student(s) must be very clear about just what you want.

- *How can I modify the context to make the expected behavior more likely to occur?*   Look for ways to change the situation, circumstances, or conditions to make the predictable behavior less likely and the expected behavior more likely to occur.

- *What is the best way I can help the student(s) rehearse the expected behavior?*   Think through and offer opportunities for the student(s) to practice. They will need a dry run, a tryout, a little drill to get the hang of it.

- *What reinforcement will be strong enough to serve as an effective reward for the expected behavior?*   You must find a consequence that is meaningful and arrange its occurrence when the expected behavior occurs.

- *How can I prompt the behavior I want?*   Prompts are gestures or other signals indicating, "Remember; do it now."

- *How can I monitor the behavior so that I have a reliable record of progress?*   A simple recording system will help you and others judge whether the student is behaving as you expect.

FIGURE 4.1   A Completed Precorrection Plan

Teacher: <u>Pat Puller</u>   Student: <u>Jimmy Ott (6th grade)</u>   Date: <u>Oct. 11</u>

---

1. Context [where and when; situation, circumstances, or conditions in which predictable behavior occurs]

   Upon entering the classroom in the morning, when at least one other student is in the room

---

   Predictable Behavior [the error or misbehavior that you can anticipate in the context]

   Jimmy describes his deviant behavior or deviant intentions (e.g., how he drank or did drugs or got into a fight or stole something or is going to "take someone out")

---

2. Expected Behavior [what you want the student to do instead of the predictable behavior]

   Jimmy will talk about appropriate topics when he enters the class

---

3. Context Modification [how you can change the situation, circumstances, or conditions to make the predictable behavior less likely and the expected behavior more likely to occur]

   Meet Jimmy at the door and immediately ask a question demanding appropriate talk as an answer

---

4. Behavior Rehearsal [practice; dry run; try out; drill]

   Practice with Jimmy coming into class and responding to my question, then talking about appropriate topics

---

5. Strong Reinforcement [special reward for doing the expected behavior]

   Praise for appropriate talk on coming into the classroom, plus 5 min. to talk with his choice of me, principal, cook, or custodian if no inappropriate talk before first period assignment is given (principal, cook, and custodian agreed and trained in how to handle conversation)

---

6. Prompts [gestures or other signals indicating "remember; do it now"]

   Hand signal to Jimmy when I first see him in the morning, worked out in advance to indicate "appropriate talk"

---

7. Monitoring Plan [record of performance; indicator of success that you can show someone]

   Jimmy and I to record daily successful school entry talk

Interrupting the Acting-Out Cycle.   As we suggested in Chapter 3 and in our earlier discussion of positive reinforcement in this chapter, the key to successful behavior management is focusing on what you want the student to do. The natural inclination is not to do this. In fact, most teachers are inclined to wait until a student is misbehaving in an obvious and intrusive manner before getting into the act and attempting to do something helpful. By that time, a teacher's efforts to correct are often unsuccessful and the problem gets worse—the student moves up to more intense acting-out behavior and may even reach the peak phase. (You may want to review Figure 3.2 and our accompanying discussion of the acting-out cycle.)

The most efficient and effective behavior management is achieved by concentrating on the earliest stages in the acting-out cycle. The principle is simple: If possible, keep the student in the calm phase; if not, then step in as early as possible to break the cycle and return the student to the calm phase. Following are a few questions and suggestions for responding to each phase.

■ *What can I do to keep a student in the calm phase?* A well-structured classroom in which expectations are clear and in which a high-quality instructional program exists will help. The most important thing you can do in addition is to initiate positive interactions with the student. Hill Walker and his colleagues emphasize *noncontingent attention* as a key concept and strategy here.[6] The idea is to catch the student when he or she comes through the classroom door and, before there is any chance for the student to become agitated or begin accelerating misbehavior, engage him or her in productive behavior. Engage the student in pleasant conversation; ask the student to help you do a job that's nonthreatening; give the student an assignment to do a favorite task; or in some other way recognize, approve, and engage the student. As the class or day progresses, take the opportunity *frequently* to show attention and approval for calm behavior. Do *not* assume that calm behavior is its own reward for the student or that it is a phase you can ignore. It is, in fact, the phase to which you need to direct as much attention as possible from the beginning of the student's time with you. Keeping the student engaged from the get-go in focused, productive activity is the best way to perpetuate the calm phase and avoid classroom triggers and the subsequent escalation of misbehavior.

■ *What should I do when I find that a trigger has occurred?* A trigger is an unresolved problem that upsets a person's calm. As we mentioned in Chapter 3, some triggers occur in the student's life before he or she enters your classroom. But regardless of where the trigger occurs, once you know it has happened your best strategy is to move quickly to resolve the problem. Begin by letting the student know that you are aware of what has happened and offering to help resolve the problem if you can. Just the reassurance that you know the student is experiencing discomfort, anxiety, frustration, or anger about the trigger may help. If you can resolve the problem right away, by all means do so. If you can't, then let the student know you will do what you can to help as soon as possible; meanwhile, help the student get focused on productive activity. If the trigger is something that is a recurrent problem, work out with the student how you will manage it together—identify the problem, possible solutions, the student's choices, and the outcomes of those choices. Time and energy spent helping students solve problems at this stage will save a world of effort and frustration.

■ *What should I do when I see signs of agitation?* Again, let the student know that you recognize the signs (see also our suggestions for talking to students in Chapter 5). Give the student time and space; at this point, don't crowd the student or demand instant performance. It may be helpful to move toward or to move away from the student, depending on his or her individual characteristic response to proximity. It may also be beneficial to let the student do independent work or to engage in some type of movement activity. Again, if possible, involve the student in a plan to manage agitation if you see a recurring pattern of behavior. Work out with the student what you will do and what you will expect of him or her when you see signs of agitation. Look for a solution to this problem: What can you and the student do to get him or her to return to a nonagitated state? What you should *not* do is ignore the agitation and provide a reason for the student to move into the acceleration phase.

■ *When a student is in the acceleration phase, what should I do?*   Remember that in this phase the student is inviting someone to engage in a "my turn–your turn" interaction, looking to draw someone into an argument or battle of wills. Your best bet by far is to decline the invitation. This means that you must avoid doing things that are likely to escalate conflict; avoid showing your own agitation, making challenging or demeaning remarks, touching or grabbing the student, or lecturing. Maintain calm behavior and an attitude of respectful detachment; refuse to be drawn in. Wise teachers plan ahead for a student's acceleration and establish a negative consequence beforehand (e.g., office referral, calling the parents, calling the police). Then, to avert a crisis, the teacher is able to do the following calmly: State the behavioral expectation (e.g., "Robert, you need to sit down now . . ."); state the consequence of not meeting the expectation (e.g., ". . . or I will call your parents"); allow the student some time to make a decision (e.g., "You have a few seconds to decide"); and follow through with the consequence (e.g., if Robert does not take his seat, then call his parents; if he does sit down, then proceed with the class). If you answer the student's invitation to argue, become upset, become belligerent, or otherwise "mix it up" with the student, you will almost certainly regret it. Be cool, be calm, be respectful, be certain that you have a choice to offer the student, and be sure to follow through with what you say will happen if the student does not choose to do what you expect. Later—after the student has returned to calm behavior and is accessible to productive conversation—talk to the student about the incident and how such conflicts can be avoided.

■ *What do I do with a peak phase?*   The main consideration is safety—yours and your students'. Get help. Restrain or isolate the student if that can be done safely. Besides safety, you should think about long-term interventions that might avoid future peaks: Making the school program more appropriate, getting additional evaluation of the student, obtaining counseling or other therapies to help the student manage problems more effectively, or changing your behavior management strategies. Once you hit the peak, it is too late to take preventive action except to keep anyone from getting hurt and to try to avoid a later peak.

■ *What are the best tactics for the de-escalation phase?*   Allow time for the student to cool down. Try to get him or her back on track with some routine, independent work. If possible, get the student to restore or clean up the physical environment if it was seriously affected.

■ *What should I consider during the recovery phase?*   Get back to normal routines, emphasizing attention on productive work and calm behavior. Talk to the student about the incident with emphasis on establishing plans to avoid future blowups. Express confidence that the student can learn to meet your expectations with help. Acknowledge any problem-solving behavior the student exhibits and focus on concrete plans for managing future issues.

Special Note on Digital Resources

Resources for behavior management are increasingly available on the World Wide Web. However, we caution that some sites offer misleading information or, frankly, misinformation. Our recommendation is that you avoid any site recommending against application of the principles we discuss in this book and that you view the information provided at that site with extreme caution. Many good sites are being developed on the Internet, and most provide links to other sites. Following are three that we recommend and that you might want to explore:

- The National Center on Education, Disability, and Juvenile Justice is found at www.edjj.org.
- The Oregon Social Learning Center is at www.OSLC.org.
- Sopris West has many helpful links at www.sopriswest.com.

Summary

Today's teachers have available to them a wide variety of behavior management suggestions, including "packaged" techniques. We urge teachers to use a reflective, self-questioning approach that makes creative use of basic principles. Before implementing elaborate or sophisticated management strategies, we suggest that teachers try the simplest, most obvious professionally defensible procedures. These include using instructions, showing and describing examples, and providing choices to students. When implemented very skillfully, these and other simple approaches are often sufficient to resolve behavior problems. In selecting other options for behavior management, teachers must weigh them in the light of best professional practices, personal experience and that of colleagues, available technical assistance, and reliable empirical research. Research in behavioral psychology and social learning applied to classroom problems provides, in our opinion, a sound basis for devising behavior management strategies.

The five operations of a behavioral approach—positive reinforcement, negative reinforcement, extinction, response cost punishment, and punishment by presenting aversives—are based on the principle that consequences (events immediately following a behavior) can be altered to change behavior. Positive and negative reinforcement are ways of increasing the strength or probability of behavior; extinction and punishment are ways of decreasing or weakening it. The key to good behavior management is emphasizing positive reinforcement of appropriate behavior; the other four operations should play a secondary role. Teachers who use behavioral operations successfully must capitalize on the cognitive and affective aspects of behavior change.

Students' thoughts and feelings must be considered when teachers talk with students, choose consequences for students' behavior, and teach self-management techniques and social skills. Understanding students' thoughts and feelings is important in building helpful relationships. Behavior management should be positive and supportive of appropriate behavior so that students receive frequent teacher approval, the focus is on motivation to obtain rewarding consequences, and students like being in the classroom and learn important academic and social skills. Instructional approaches to behavior management include the precorrection strategy and focusing interventions on the earliest stages in the acting-out cycle.

REFERENCES AND RESOURCES FOR FURTHER STUDY

The following references provided the basis for many of our statements in this chapter. You may wish to consult selected references for additional information. Our reference notes for this chapter refer to sources in this list.

Alberto, P. A., & Troutman, A. C. (2003). *Applied behavior analysis for teachers* (6th ed.). Upper Saddle River, NJ: Prentice-Hall.

Colvin, G. (2004). *Managing the cycle of acting-out behavior in the classroom*. Eugene, OR: Behavior Associates.

Cullinan, D. (2002). *Students with emotional and behavior disorders: An introduction for teachers and other helping professionals*. Upper Saddle River, NJ: Merrill/Prentice-Hall.

Kameenui, E. J., & Darch, C. B. (1995). *Instructional classroom management: A proactive approach to behavior management*. White Plains, NY: Longman.

Kauffman, J. M. (2005). *Characteristics of emotional and behavioral disorders of children and youth* (8th ed.). Upper Saddle River, NJ: Prentice-Hall.

Kerr, M. M., & Nelson, C. M. (2002). *Strategies for managing behavior problems in the classroom* (4th ed.). Upper Saddle River, NJ: Prentice-Hall.

Landrum, T. J., & Kauffman, J. M. (in press). Behavioral approaches to classroom management. In C. M. Evertson & C. S. Weinstein (Eds.), *Handbook of classroom management: Research, practice, and contemporary issues*. Mahwah, NJ: Lawrence Erlbaum.

Lane, K. L. (2004). Academic instruction and tutoring interventions for students with emotional/behavioral disorders: 1990 to the present. In R. B. Rutherford, M. M. Quinn, & S. R. Mathur (Eds.), *Handbook of research in emotional and behavioral disorders* (pp. 462–486). New York: Guilford.

Newsom, C., & Kroeger, K. A. (2005). Nonaversive treatment. In J. W. Jacobson, R. M. Foxx, & J. A. Mulick (Eds.), *Controversial therapies for developmental disabilities: Fad, fashion, and science in professional practice* (pp. 405–432). Mahwah, NJ: Lawrence Erlbaum

Powell, S., & Nelson, B. (1997). Effects of choosing academic assignments on a student with attention deficit hyperactivity disorder. *Journal of Applied Behavior Analysis, 30,* 181–183.

Rhode, G., Jenson, W. R., & Reavis, H. K. (1992). *The tough kid book: Practical classroom management strategies*. Longmont, CO: Sopris West.

Walker, H. M. (1995). *The acting out child. Coping with classroom disruption* (2nd ed.). Longmont, CO: Sopris West.

Walker, H. M., Colvin, G., & Ramsey, E. (1995). *Antisocial behavior in school. Strategies and best practices*. Pacific Grove, CA: Brooks/Cole.

Walker, H. M., Ramsey, E., & Gresham, F. M. (2004). *Antisocial behavior in school. Strategies and best practices* (2nd ed.). Pacific Grove, CA: Brooks/Cole.

Webber, J., & Scheuermann, B. (1991). Managing behavior problems: Accentuate the positive... eliminate the negative! *Teaching Exceptional Children, 24*(1), 13–19.

ENDNOTES

1. For further details of using choices to reduce behavior problems and increase desirable classroom behavior, see Kauffman (2005), Powell and Nelson (1997), and Rhode, Jenson, and Reavis (1992).
2. For a further explanation of basic behavior principles and their application, see Alberto and Troutman (2003), Cullinan (2002), Kerr and Nelson (2002), Landrum and Kauffman (in press), Rhode, Jenson, and Reavis (1992), Walker (1995), Walker, Colvin, and Ramsey (1995), and Walker, Ramsey, and Gresham (2004).
3. See Rhode, Jenson, and Reavis (1992) for a further discussion of IFEED-AV and other suggestions for using positive reinforcement.
4. See especially Walker, Colvin, and Ramsey (1995) and Rhode, Jenson, and Reavis (1992).
5. See Colvin (2004), Kauffman (2005), and Walker, Colvin, and Ramsey (1995) for a further explanation of precorrection, and Kameenui and Darch (1995) for a further explanation of an instructional approach to behavior management.
6. For a more complete discussion of managing the acting-out cycle, see Colvin (2004) and Walker, Colvin, and Ramsey (1995).

5

Talking with Students

Questions for Reflection

How does classroom talk differ from talking in other places?

How is talking with students about their behavior related to my teaching goals?

How can I avoid unproductive talking with students about their behavior?

What verbal and nonverbal communication skills must I model and teach?

Listening

Using Proximity

Speaking Body Language

Establishing Eye Contact and Varying Facial Expressions

Pausing, Reflecting, and Probing

Describing, Not Judging

Choosing the Best Words

Using the Best Voice

Setting the Right Pace

Summarizing

Questioning

Waiting

How can talking with students help teach them personal responsibility?

How should I talk with students about appropriate behavior?

How should I talk with students about unacceptable behavior?

How should I talk with angry or aggressive students?

How should I talk with students who are withdrawn?

Summary

References and Resources for Further Study

Endnotes

Talk is cheap—some of the time. It can also be very costly. Knowing when to hold your tongue can save you a world of trouble, especially when you are dealing with students who are masters in drawing adults into arguments or enticing others into a battle of insults. It is difficult to remember, when confronted by a direct verbal jab, that "a soft answer turneth away wrath" and that sometimes saying nothing is better than saying anything.

Knowing just what to say and how to say it are not only a very large part of knowing how to give effective academic instruction, but also of knowing how to manage behavior skillfully. Skill in talking with students is not just a matter of finding the right words but of being able to combine them with the right timing, intonation, eye contact, and nonverbal behavior to have maximum effect. The skilled teacher knows not only what to say and how to say it but also how to listen—what to listen for, how to interpret it, and how to judge whether a productive conversation is possible at the moment or whether it would be better to wait for a more opportune moment.

Some of the things teachers and students say to each other are not terribly important. Many, however, are critically important. They will make the difference between understanding and bewilderment, or between conflict and harmony. A few words carefully chosen—or a few spoken thoughtlessly—can have very dramatic results, as seen in the vignettes on Sarah and Natalie.

Sarah

I was prepared for a lot of things in my first year. I'd even paid attention to some professors who had reminded me to think through how I was going to set up my class routine, the rules I wanted to impose, and what to do if certain unacceptable student behaviors popped up.

Looking back, though, having my own class has taught me far more than I ever imagined about talking with my students. I assumed that I was prepared for communicating with them. After all, I had been able to talk to people all my life! Wow, was I wrong! David taught me the most. He was so unpredictable and very good at getting me hooked into verbal sparring matches. I remember one time when he really pushed all my buttons. We were doing math, and I had instructed David to begin the written work I had assigned. He turned his face to the wall, and that was that. I talked to him, but without eye contact I knew I wasn't getting anywhere. I tried everything from pleading and cajoling to shouting and yelling. Nothing. Not even a murmur. Then, as I walked away, he turned and said, quite deliberately: "You can't make me do anything I don't want to do!"

Well, that was all I needed. As I returned to his desk, I told him in no uncertain terms (I guess my voice was a little shaky though) that I was the boss, and that he'd toe the line or else. I still haven't figured out exactly why we ended up in the principal's office with David getting suspended, but in looking back I probably gave David exactly what he wanted.

Natalie

The cum folder from Anthony's former school described a child with mild mental retardation and hyperaggressive behavior, but my aide and I didn't need to read the folder. After four days in my classroom, several tantrums, and an aching jaw from a right to my chin, we knew he could accelerate from calm to explosion in a matter of seconds. Too often, we helped him along the way to a peak experience by what we said to him. Sometimes we were smarter and didn't get sucked into his verbal battles.

One morning, my aide was conducting an art lesson with Anthony's group when he began to brag about how frightened his mother was of him. My aide ignored him at first, then tried to defuse him with mollifying statements. "That's a terrible way to talk about your mother! I know how much you love your mother. You don't want to talk about her like that!"

It didn't work. Anthony continued to engage my aide, to draw her in, to rant about how intimidated his mother was and how if she ever crossed him again the rescue squad would have to pick up what was left of her. Then he got up and began to strut around the art table while expounding on his acts of prior and future terror. When he began to threaten the other children in the group with comments like, "And you're next! The ambulance can pick you up too," I intervened.

I had instituted a response cost system with Anthony—a laminated card with happy faces that I could mark off for misbehavior. When all the happy faces were crossed out, he lost his recess.

I picked up the card, approached Anthony, and said quietly, "Anthony, you only have one happy face left. You need to sit down and be quiet now, or you'll lose your last happy face."

Then I chatted with one of the other students in his group. He sat down. I placed the card and a crayon in front of the aide and returned to my instructional group. Anthony earned his recess that day.

Questions for Reflection

Talking with students is a complicated issue that permeates every level of behavioral assessment, the formulation of behavioral interventions, and the execution of behavior management plans. If you are constantly aware of effective communication skills and are able to put them into practice, you are more likely to accomplish your goals than if you forge ahead without careful reflection. As you approach the management of difficult students in your classroom, consider at least the following questions:

- How does classroom talk differ from talking in other places?
- How is talking with students about their behavior related to my teaching goals?
- How can I avoid unproductive talking with students about their behavior?
- What verbal and nonverbal communication skills must I model and teach?
- How can talking with students help teach them personal responsibility?
- How should I talk with students about appropriate behavior?
- How should I talk with students about unacceptable behavior?
- How should I talk with angry or aggressive students?
- How should I talk with students who are withdrawn?

How does classroom talk differ from talking in other places?

The language of the classroom is, for the most part and for most students, substantially different from the language of the home, the peer group, and the streets. It is typically more formal, more precise, and more directive than the conversational speech used by most students outside the classroom. Although this is true for most students regardless of their cultural identity, the cultural bases of classroom talk are not only very important but also highly controversial.[1] Two critical issues become apparent to any teacher who reflects on talking with students: the acceptability of language (both the students' and the teacher's) and the adequacy of communication (both the ability to decode others' messages and the ability to encode messages that are understandable to others).

- *What kind of language is acceptable in my classroom?*   In Chapter 2, we discussed teachers' expectations for their students' conduct. Deciding where and how to draw the line on acceptable language is one of teaching's great challenges. Language may be discouraged or proscribed in school because it is deemed to be foul, disrespectful, intimidating, impolite, or disruptive. The difficulty in knowing just where and how to draw the line on language stems from the fact that cultural and community definitions of "foul," "disrespectful," and so on, may differ markedly from the teacher's. Thus the teacher must be careful not to let cultural ignorance or bias be the basis for judging language as improper or unacceptable for the classroom. Moreover, it is important to recognize that language must not be considered unacceptable *simply because it is different from the teacher's.*

Nevertheless, just because a student uses certain language at home or on the street does not make it acceptable in the classroom. In fact, if the teacher does not draw clear limits on classroom language, he or she will undoubtedly encounter some very serious behavior management problems. Belligerent language is often a prelude to other aggressive behavior. Flagrantly disrespectful language, if not checked, encourages further disrespectful behavior. Yet, it is important not to let such clearly unacceptable language be the trigger for a teacher's inappropriate or unproductive use of words. Adults are tempted to respond to unacceptable language with outrage, lecturing, shaming, arguing, or even verbal counteraggression, responses that themselves are—or should be—considered unacceptable. Cool, calm, clear, and respectful responses to unacceptable language are difficult but necessary. They are necessary for two primary reasons: to avoid getting drawn into the student's escalation of misbehavior and to demonstrate the behavior expected of students.

■ *How can I make sure I understand and am understood by my students?*   Teachers often misunderstand the content of students' language or the intent of their verbal expressions because they do not understand their students' cultures and the language that is part of them. Teachers may not make themselves understood by their students for the same reason.[2] Becoming well acquainted with students' language, including slang expressions within any given culture, is critical to teachers' communicative competence. However, a full discussion of cultural diversity of language is beyond the scope of our task here. Beyond the matter of a teacher's competence in understanding language diversity, there are other issues about listening and talking to students that often make the difference between success and failure in managing behavior.

Listening effectively involves more than hearing the words; it demands attention to context, nonverbal behavior, and affect. The same verbal message may mean different things and require different responses depending on the social circumstances; in one context it is a joke, in another a serious matter. Sometimes a student's verbal and nonverbal behavior are contradictory, as when a student says, "No! I ain't gonna do it, and you can't make me!", followed almost immediately by the first step toward compliance. The teacher who focuses on the tough talk and applies sanctions may miss the real point of the communication and become embroiled in a needless struggle; the one who ignores the verbal challenge and focuses on the student's compliance may artfully sidestep an unnecessary confrontation. The teacher who does not understand the emotional meaning of what students say may respond in ways that are not constructive. Students may not understand the difference between street talk and classroom talk or may not have learned when certain expressions are inappropriate. It is important to set clear expectations for classroom talk but to decode students' communicative intentions regardless of the idioms they use.

Making sure that students understand what you say is no simple matter. Some teachers operate under the false assumption that loudness and reiteration will do the trick. While raising one's voice and repetition are sometimes necessary, more sophisticated communication strategies are required in most cases. The content, timing, posture, and other dimensions of teacher communication are typically the more important keys to being understood. For example, you may want to review our questions and suggestions in Chapter 4 for giving instructions. Sometimes it may be necessary for the teacher to use the idiomatic language of the student's home or the street rather than the typical language of classroom discourse. We discuss other aspects of making oneself clearly understood in subsequent sections of this chapter.

How is talking with students about their behavior related to my teaching goals?

A well-thought-out classroom structure will reduce the amount of time spent on unproductive dialogue about behavior, such as unnecessary repetitions of or arguments about rules, consequences, or classroom routines. A predictable daily routine and smooth transitions between activities allow a teacher to focus dialogue on instruction and expected behavior rather than on misbehavior. Moreover, talking with students about their behavior before their actions escalate to a major disruption is often effective, as we noted in Chapter 4 in our discussion of the acting-out cycle. (Review Figure 3.2 and accompanying descriptions.) If the overall approach to behavior management is proactive, then the teacher's talk will be primarily positive and instructive. This means that the teacher will frequently engage students in conversation when students are in the calm phase, minimize verbal engagement with students during the acceleration phase (avoid getting drawn into arguments), and use talking with students during the trigger and agitation phases to help students resolve their problems.

Many students act irresponsibly. A major reason for talking with students about their behavior is to teach them to assume responsibility for their actions and choices in social interactions and in their work. They may not accept responsibility for their own behavior but, instead, blame their actions on others (usually their parents, teachers, or peers), bad luck, a lack of ability, or the difficulty of the task. One way teachers can encourage students to assume responsibility for their own behavior is by questioning and commenting. For example, a teacher might say, "Anna, what will happen if you complete your work with 90 percent or more correct by 10:30?" [Pause for correct answer.] "Right, you'll be able to work at the computer until it's time to go to art class." It is usually wise to emphasize the description of the positive events that will follow expected performance rather than the unpleasant consequences of failure or misbehavior. Emphasizing the expected and the positive consequences helps keep the student focused on doing the responsible thing and is part of maintaining a positive, supportive classroom climate.

How can I avoid unproductive talking with students about their behavior?

One of the greatest challenges of working with difficult students is steering clear of nagging, wasted words, and verbal battles. Much of adults' talking with these students is ineffective or actually makes things worse. The students are masters at drawing adults into arguing, yelling, threatening, wheedling, berating, lecturing, and other forms of verbal struggle that they—the students—are very likely to win. They "win" by getting their way, getting the adult upset, diverting the adult from the real issue or problem, making the adult feel out of control or guilty, or in some other way making the issue the adult's problem. Here are some ways they do this:

- By not responding to adults' words, ignoring, pretending not to hear
- By doing precisely, deliberately, and obviously the opposite of what they have been asked or instructed to do
- By denying any knowledge or perception of something in which they have obviously been engaged
- By repeating a nonsense, inappropriate, or incorrect word or phrase in response to a question
- By repeating a question over and over, never seeming to hear or understand the answer
- By mimicking the adult or another person
- By interrupting, not allowing others to express themselves
- By insulting or verbally assaulting the teacher
- By changing the topic

Most teachers have difficulty not responding with corrections, arguments, or other forms of resistance to such verbal challenges. They want the last word. They want to insist on the student's admission of error and on his or her correct verbal representation of reality. And, in so doing, teachers nearly always set themselves up for defeat. It takes experience and a high degree of skill to recognize the bait and to resist taking it. Taking the bait and getting pulled into an unproductive verbal exchange usually involves making one or more of the following mistakes:

- Showing signs of agitation, such as raising one's voice, scowling, or making a threatening gesture
- Using verbal counteraggression, such as insults or threats of harm
- Repeating a statement over and over, answering each repetition of the student with another intended to counter or correct it
- Pleading with the student
- Stating a consequence for the student's behavior that is unrealistic or inappropriate, such as a penalty that the teacher cannot or will not levy.

Nearly always, teachers lose by these strategies. Usually, it is much more effective to do the following:

- Maintain calmness, showing as little sign of offense or upset as possible.
- Either ignore the student's verbal challenge or respond in a quiet but firm voice.
- Restate clearly and calmly—but only once—your expectation or answer.
- Move away from the student, giving him or her a few moments to calm down or respond appropriately.
- Look for opportunities to respond positively to the student's appropriate behavior, perhaps by changing the topic yourself.
- Give the student a choice of meeting the expectation or experiencing a negative consequence (one on which you know you can follow through).

After an episode of serious misbehavior has occurred and the student has calmed down and is able to engage in a productive conversation, debriefing is important. In debriefing, the teacher tries to structure a conversation that will help the student understand what happened, why it happened, how to choose a better alternative way of behaving, and how the student and teacher can plan to avoid further episodes of unacceptable behavior. The debriefing should be kept brief and focused. The teacher should initiate debriefing only after the student has gotten past the emotional arousal that typically goes with a serious acting-out incident and is able to talk about it realistically and without further emotional upset. That is, the debriefing should occur in the recovery phase of the acting-out cycle. Keep in mind that during debriefing, difficult students will not necessarily be completely rational (from your point of view) and may try to derail the conversation or engage you in argumentation. Your task is to stay focused, to avoid invitations to argue, and to move the student—if ever so slightly and grudgingly—toward more adaptive responses to the problems he or she encounters. For example, a useful debriefing might go something like this:

TEACHER: So, tell me what happened this morning that landed you in detention.

STUDENT: Hell, I dunno. It wasn't my fault, it was Henry who got it going.

TEACHER: Well, let's start with what happened first. What was the first thing that happened?

STUDENT: When I came in, Henry, he started on me. That's what happened first. It was his fault, and you know it, and I don't want to hear about it.

TEACHER: What did Henry do? How did he start on you?

STUDENT: He called me a dope. You heard him, and I'm gonna git that sucker, too. And then he called me other names, like "welfare queen" and other stuff.

TEACHER: So, Henry called you a dope and other names. I understand. That's pretty hard to take, and Henry needs to learn not to do stuff like that. But what happened after he called you names?

STUDENT: I punched him, you saw that! I punched him in his fat mouth, that's what I did.

TEACHER: Yeah, I saw you hit him. And then what?

STUDENT: Well, you know what happened, he hit me back.

TEACHER: Yes, it looked like you guys were gonna take each other down.

STUDENT: We woulda, too, if you hadn't come 'round.

TEACHER: So, what's the rule if you get into a fight in this school?

STUDENT: Detention.

TEACHER: Right, after-school detention, and we call your parents.

STUDENT: And it ain't fair when you didn't start it, and I didn't start it, it was Henry's fault, and you know it.

TEACHER: Well, the rule is, it doesn't make any difference who started it, if you get involved in hitting someone you get detention.

STUDENT: You may think so, but I don't. And somebody calls me those names, I'm gonna hit 'em, and they gonna know it.

TEACHER: I know you'd want to hit 'em, and I probably would too. But what could you do besides hit somebody who calls you names?

STUDENT: I dunno. I'm gonna hit 'em,' cause I can't stand it.

TEACHER: I know it's tough to do, but what are the things we've talked about that you can do besides hit somebody who gets on you?

STUDENT: Ignore them, I guess, but I can't do that.

TEACHER: Right, ignoring them and just going on about your business as if they weren't there—that's a good idea, that's a good alternative. It's hard, but you can learn to do it and not get sent to detention.

STUDENT: But they shouldn't be callin' me names.

TEACHER: You're right. If they're doin' that, then they've got a problem, and they need to learn not to do it. But if they get you to react by hitting them, then what happens?

STUDENT: I get detention. But I don't care. I ain't gonna have it.

TEACHER: Right, if you hit, you get detention and then it's your problem, too. So, how could we work on your not getting detention?

STUDENT: You stop them calling me names, that's how.

TEACHER: Well, yeah. I'll do what I can to stop that. They shouldn't do it. But if they do, then what can you and I do so that you don't get detention?

STUDENT: You stop them.

TEACHER: How will I know when they're doing it? I couldn't hear Henry this morning when he was calling you names. You guys were over on the other side of the room.

STUDENT: Well, I can tell you.

TEACHER: Right, you can tell me. But how would you do that? Would you yell out, "Hey, Henry's calling me names!" or how would you do it? How about you just walk away and come toward me and give me a signal?

STUDENT: Like what?

TEACHER: Like just walk toward me and pull your ear, like this. That'll mean you are just walking away from somebody who's calling you names.

STUDENT: I dunno, man, I'm gonna just hit' em.

TEACHER: Well, let's give it a try, OK? Just give it a try next time, and then if you can do it and not hit, you won't end up going to detention. OK? Will you try that?

STUDENT: OK, I can't make you no promises, but I'll try.

TEACHER: Great. We'll give it a shot. Let's just try it.

In this verbal interaction, how did the teacher avoid getting sidetracked into an argument about who was at fault? How did the teacher sidestep invitations to argue about the fairness of the consequence for fighting? How did the teacher avoid lecturing or other forms of unproductive verbalization?

What verbal and nonverbal communication skills must I model and teach?

Teachers must model and teach the self-control skills that are prerequisites for effective communication. Students may need to be taught to:

- Take turns talking, allowing one speaker to speak at a time.
- Not interrupt while someone else is talking.
- Maintain a focus on a topic (especially if it is their own behavior) without wandering.
- Understand how much to say about their behavior without being repetitive or evasive.
- Avoid ambiguity or vagueness while at the same time being polite and considerate.

No adult is likely to teach these critical communication skills unless he or she can demonstrate them in verbal exchanges with students.

The nonverbal prerequisites for effective communication are also important. Students may need to be taught how to:

- Use eye contact during conversation and show understanding that different cultures and individuals have different expectations about looking and talking.
- Listen to what others are saying and use appropriate facial expressions and body language to maintain social connection.

Again, if you want to teach students these skills, you must demonstrate them yourself.

Listening.   Through the use of *active listening*, teachers can learn to differentiate between the emotional and intellectual content of what students are saying. Active listening requires giving the student your full attention by blocking out other distractions. Pay close attention to the verbal and nonverbal actions of the student and try to decide which parts of what the student is saying are facts and which are emotional messages. It is important to gauge the student's feelings and reactions. Listen long enough to evaluate the student's behavioral status. In addition, because active listening is an intensely individual activity, remember that your personal feelings toward the student will influence the unspoken messages you hear.

Active listening provides the student with an opportunity to deal with inappropriate behavior and frustration. Utilizing good listening skills will also convey a sense of empathy to the student and support the possibility of behavioral improvement. Demonstrating these skills may encourage students to listen appropriately when you talk, but the demonstration alone may not be enough. You may need to describe how people behave when they are listening and ask the student to practice that behavior. However, you must be careful to look for the teachable moment when the student will not interpret your instruction as criticism or nagging.

Using Proximity.   Personal proximity is important in communication, especially if the speaker has poorly defined personal boundaries. Being too far from a student while talking may be misinterpreted as disinterest, whereas getting too close may be threatening. A comfortable distance for most students is about an arm's length, although you may find that some students appear to need more personal space than others. Angry and aggressive students probably need more space than calmer or compliant pupils. Proximity during verbal communication is partly a cultural phenomenon, and you should be aware of cultural expectations. However, even within cultures students may respond very differently to proximity. The key point is to watch for signs that an agitated student is best managed by closer proximity or by keeping more distance.

Speaking Body Language.   Body language and posture convey a sense of interest or lack thereof. Slouching or leaning back is more likely to communicate disinterest, while leaning slightly forward may indicate an attentive attitude. However, try not to be physically rigid or "posed" either. You want to appear confident, in control, and assured, but not arrogant. Body movement and gestures can be seen as either encouraging or disapproving during a conversation, so be aware of any personal gestures that may interfere with what you are trying to communicate.

Body language varies considerably from culture to culture. It is essential to take into account, when interpreting the meanings of body language or choosing a posture or gesture, the culture of the student and the meanings attached to movement, position, posture, and gesture in his or her culture. If you're not sure about these meanings, ask an adult who is competent in that culture to help you understand.

Establishing Eye Contact and Varying Facial Expressions.   Eye contact conveys a sense of interest and friendliness to most listeners, and adds to your credibility. However, staring is usually interpreted as intimidating and should be avoided. Facial expressions can be helpful in conveying what you are thinking during your conversation. It is important to listen carefully to what the student is saying so that you will not be caught unexpectedly, perhaps responding to a comment intended to shock with an inappropriate or exaggerated expression. In addition, prolonged disapproving expressions can be very distracting. It is more appropriate to match your expression carefully to the conversational content.

Again, you must be aware that eye contact is an aspect of communication that is highly grounded in cultural expectations. In some cultures, students are expected to avoid eye contact most of the time; in others, students are expected to look into the eyes of the adult who is talking to them. Expect and give eye contact that is consistent with the expectations in the student's culture.

Pausing, Reflecting, and Probing.   In talking with students, teachers should make careful use of language to convey very definite and clear messages about their demands. Think through what you intend to say before talking with a student about behavior. Taking a moment to consider how you will phrase a question or comment and being aware of your body language can save a great deal of energy and frustration. If possible, put yourself in the student's place and see what it would take to answer your question or respond to your comment appropriately.

Learn to use verbal cues that will enhance conversations about behavior. For example, silence can encourage a student to be reflective or to expand an explanation of his or her behavior. True, silences that are too long create "dead space" that is disconcerting. However, most adults tend to rush in, to fill all seconds with words, to be too hurried. This is understandable, as schools are busy, even frenetic, places, and many other students besides the one you are talking to at the moment need attention. Still, what you communicate by appropriate pauses is that this conversation is important, that you are thinking carefully about it, and that you want the student, too, to think carefully.

You may prompt students by using recognition statements, which simply acknowledge that you have heard what they have said to you (e.g., "I see . . . , yes . . . "). Another way to prompt students is to use reflective statements that mirror what the student has said (e.g., if the student says, "I hate Sally!" you might respond with something like, "So, you hate Sally . . . ").

Describing, Not Judging.   Language may be either descriptive or judgmental. *Judgmental language* automatically elevates a situation or behavior to a level at which conflict is more likely. Applying a judgmental label to behavior (e.g., "awful," "bad," "stupid," "wrong") often ruins the chance for further communication. Although it may be quite true that in the eyes of many, the student's behavior merits a highly negative judgmental label, but the objective is to establish and maintain communication with the student, not merely to render and communicate a judgment. *Descriptive language* is often preferable, as it describes what happened without attaching subjective judgment. Such language does not label behavior with an emotional overlay that may truncate communication. The more objective and factual the language, the more precise the feedback to the student about his or her behavior, and the easier it is for both teacher and student to remain calm. Furthermore, descriptive language is less likely to provoke an escalation of misbehavior. For example, a judgmental comment might be, "Sean, that was an awful way to treat Jean." A related descriptive comment might be, "Sean, you pushed Jean into the wall."

Choosing the Best Words.   The wise teacher selects vocabulary carefully to reflect what has happened or is happening as calmly and objectively as possible. Familiar words are usually better than words the student may not understand. Brief statements are typically better than long ones. Language should be appropriate for the occasion and apply specifically to the student, the behavior, and the social context. This requires careful judgment of the student's language abilities and responses to verbal expression. Sometimes, vivid language in the form of metaphors or similes works well. For example,

"Peter, don't take the bait" may communicate either nothing or a clear and effective warning, depending on the student's understanding of and response to figures of speech. Remember, too, that the line between an effective figure of speech and sarcasm is fine and that you want to stay clearly out of sarcasm territory.

Specific words may be appropriate and understood in one language but inappropriate or even incendiary in another. The key point is to know your audience. As you are teaching, you must listen carefully for words that are particularly loaded for particular groups or individuals. An expression that has meaning for your audience that you do not attach to it can lead to a serious social faux pas.

Using the Best Voice. Voice tells us a great deal about the speaker's expectations and emotional state. Students are extremely sensitive to changes in a teacher's voice, including loudness and pitch. In some circumstances, success in talking with students about their behavior may depend as much—or more—on how you sound as the words you say. Your voice should be loud enough so that students can hear you clearly, although talking in too loud a voice is just as detrimental to conversation as speaking too softly. A shouted command may sometimes be necessary, and a strong voice is often appropriate. However, a quieter voice than usual is sometimes highly effective in getting a student's attention. Speaking at one volume level, however, will mean that nothing you say will stand out from your other comments. Varying the volume of your voice will stimulate interest and help the student maintain focus on what you are saying. Varying your voice pitch will convey different messages to students. A shrillness or monotone will decrease your ability to hold a student's attention and is often a good indicator of your emotional state. Some teachers use a tentative and questioning voice when giving instructions or commands (e.g., "Could you please sit down?"). Typically, it is wiser to use a firmer voice that indicates the expectation that the student will do what you want (e.g., "Rodney, please sit down now"). Practice using a tone and inflections that communicate calmness, firmness, confidence, and assertiveness but not harshness.

Setting the Right Pace. The pace at which you converse is also important. There is a good chance that when you are talking with a student about his or her behavior you may be extremely excited, frustrated, or angry. These emotions may tend to make you speak more quickly. Speak slowly enough so that your words are not garbled or incompletely formed. On the other hand, do not speak too slowly or hesitantly, as this may communicate that you are unsure of yourself and not in control of the exchange.

Most people have a pace of speaking that is natural for them, and pace may vary considerably, depending on the culture or geographical home of the speaker. However, some teachers need to slow down and some need to speed up their pace to be most effective.

Summarizing. You may wish to interject brief, intermittent summaries of what the student has been saying. Summarizing student talk will reflect back to the student what has been said, and will also provide a point of reference that the student can use for further discussion. Rephrasing what a student is communicating by asking for confirmation may also help (e.g., "Let me see if I understand what you are trying to say. Did you mean that . . . ?"). That is, you may wish to repeat the views of the student without attempting to evaluate the student's feelings or nonverbal impressions. Keep in mind, too, that summarizing or rephrasing can be overdone.

Questioning.   Most teachers see questioning as part of teaching the academics. It is also a critical part of talking with students about their behavior. The way a teacher asks questions about students' behavior may mean the difference between effective communication and alienation or disruption. Questions may be used to motivate students, help them think about their behavior, or provide them with information about more appropriate behavior.

Questions come in two major varieties: open and closed. Both have advantages and disadvantages. Choosing the right kind is a key factor in a teacher's ability to engage students in productive interactions.

Closed questions are the more restrictive of the two types because they ask for either very specific information or a yes/no response. Their advantage is that they focus on a specific issue or event and typically yield explicit, if limited, information. However, it is wise to avoid excessive use of yes/no questions except as a warm-up for other questions (e.g., "Did you tear the page?" would be a warm-up question for discussing alternatives to tearing pages), as they have several disadvantages. One disadvantage of closed questions is that they allow only a simple choice between two alternatives. This means that the student is forced to choose one answer over another, effectively preventing discussion or reflection on more appropriate behavior. Another disadvantage is that closed questions do not give the teacher much information about what the student is thinking. Also, unless closed questions are used sparingly, teachers often end up asking one yes/no question after another—a practice that is ineffective and frustrating for both teacher and student.

Open questions are less restricting because they allow students to formulate their own answers from an unlimited array of possibilities. That is, students who have to think of their own answers must engage in internal self-talk to select from a variety of responses to your question. For example, instead of saying "Did you tear the book?" (closed question), you may make more progress by asking an open question, such as, "What can you tell me about the torn book?"

Bear in mind that questions should contain natural, everyday language, as opposed to "textbook" or highly formal language, and should be simply worded at a level appropriate to the age and language ability of the child. Many students are easily confused by questions containing unfamiliar words. Make questions brief and ask only one question at a time. Some students find it difficult to remember long or multiple-part questions. Questions should be purposeful and address exactly the behavior you wish to discuss. However, good questions demand that the student think carefully before answering.

Waiting.   Wait-time in conversation is especially important when questioning students about their behavior. It is also important when giving commands or choices. Expecting an instantaneous answer or response is a mistake, but so is waiting too long, which indicates either that you are not monitoring the student's behavior or that you are not following through with an appropriate next step. Waiting patiently communicates that an answer is expected and simultaneously allows the student sufficient time to think about a response. Most researchers believe that three to four seconds is appropriate when waiting for a student response. Many teachers do not allow enough time for students to formulate answers before prompting answers or asking another question. Not waiting for a student response may communicate to the student a feeling of being rushed or pressured to answer. However, waiting too long before applying a consequence, repeating the question or command, or taking other appropriate action indicates that you are unaware or unconcerned. There are times, certainly, when you need to disengage from an interaction or avoid a coercive struggle by not responding. Nevertheless, if you intend to continue to interact with the student, then judging just how long to wait for a response is critical.

How can talking with students help teach them personal responsibility?

The ultimate goal of behavior management is to help students become more self-controlled and self-directed. The debriefing session after a major acting-out incident should include a discussion about how to avoid future upsets. During debriefing, you will want to discuss what led up to the incident, what the student might have done instead of act out, and how future incidents can be avoided. In other words, the object of debriefing is to help the student understand what went wrong and what you and she or he might do to make things go right next time.[3] Furthermore, the idea of precorrection, as we discussed in Chapters 3 and 4, is to work with the student to make a plan and follow it—a plan that will lead to the student's learning strategies of self-management. Externally imposed controls are often necessary, but they are only a first step toward giving the student skills for adaptive independence.[4]

Teaching students to be responsible for their own behavior is a difficult task, so avoid using language that makes someone else responsible for their personal conduct (e.g., "I guess Sally made you very angry"). Instead, describe the situation in language that emphasizes personal decisions and responsibility for one's actions (e.g., "So, you got really angry when Sally..."). Try not to become sidetracked by the student's attempts to avoid being held accountable for his or her actions. Many students are provocative or hostile as a means of maintaining their control. For example, if a student can engage you in talking about how others are to blame for his or her behavior, then you will waste valuable time attempting to convince the student otherwise. By this time, the student will be in control of the conversation and an opportunity for teaching will have been lost.

In order to maintain control of the conversation for the purposes of teaching responsibility, you can respond to the student in one of two ways. First, you may use a directive response with students who have limited problem-solving skills. Offer the student one of two choices (e.g., "Either sit down now, or I'll call Mr. Harrison") and allow him or her a few seconds to decide which will occur. Make sure you monitor the student's behavior and follow through with the appropriate consequence after a few seconds.

Achieving a large measure of self-control and autonomous selection of appropriate behaviors is a prime goal in dealing with students with mild disabilities. Talking with students about their behavior is a first step toward getting them to assume control over their actions. Some students consistently show only small gains in transferring what they learn about their behavior in specific situations to more generalized social skills. A major aim of talking with students, therefore, must be to help them monitor, evaluate, and modify their behavior on their own. Your responsibility for student behavior will be lessened over time as the student gains greater self-control.

A student's assessment of his or her own behavior is the initial step toward self-control.[5] To encourage self-assessment, your first task as a teacher is to help the student decide whether his or her behavior is appropriate or inappropriate. In order to make this discrimination, the student must carefully compare personal actions to the standard set by the classroom rules of conduct, learning, and peer social interaction. If the behavior is inappropriate, encourage the student to modify the misbehavior by considering several possible solutions to the problem. Discuss each option with the student and be supportive of the process of selecting a more appropriate behavior. Reinforce the student for choosing an appropriate behavior to be used in the future.

Self-assessment depends largely on the willingness of the student to change his or her behavior to more acceptable alternatives and the ability to understand why the behavior change is necessary. Negotiation of the new behavior will be shaped by the expectations of both the teacher and the student. Negotiation is effective because there is little point in using teacher-imposed expectations that students are unable or unwilling to attain.

When the replacement behavior has been agreed on, devise a self-recording system so that the student can accurately note how often the new, appropriate behavior occurs and how well it was implemented. The recording system provides a measure of the student's awareness of behavior change. Self-recording of the replacement behavior encourages the student to use self-talk. Further, it helps the student keep a record of the degree of control he or she has over the change in behavior. Self-recording also helps the student internalize control of the new behavior. In turn, the more internal control the student can exercise over his or her new behavior, the greater the likelihood that what is learned in one specific behavioral situation will generalize to other behaviors and situations. Once self-recording has begun, you can talk with the student about his or her progress. Be sure to reinforce increases in appropriate behavior. As the new behavior emerges, the student can evaluate the success of the replacement of the old misbehavior. It is important that you keep a tally of the appearance of the new behavior. When you talk with the student about how well he or she is doing, you can compare your tallies to those of the student. Such a comparison will help refine the accuracy of the self-recording and will be a "reality check" for unrealistic expectations held by you or the student.

As progress is made in a self-assessment program, the student may begin to administer his or her own reinforcement for increased appearance of the new appropriate behavior. At this point, the student can be instructed to rehearse the steps necessary for maintaining an appropriate behavior either by internal dialogue or by whispering. Self-talk helps the student improve behavior by talking through the steps necessary to assess and, if necessary, modify behaviors.

How should I talk with students about appropriate behavior?

We hope that you recall our discussion in previous chapters of the crucial role of teacher attention to desirable behavior, especially our discussion of positive reinforcement in Chapter 4. Positive recognition of what you want from students is the keystone of behavior management; without it, your other behavior management skills will fail. Positive reinforcement may include special privileges or tangible rewards, but it should be accompanied by your positive comments—social praise in some form.

Experienced teachers know that effective praise is not merely the stereotyped, "I like the way you raised your hand and waited for me to call on you," although such statements clearly have their place in good teaching. The trick is, first, to be aware of the student's behavior that is desirable, to catch it in progress, and then to accompany it or follow it immediately with something that communicates approval and encouragement. This is not as simple as it might first appear. To most teachers, students' misbehavior is more conspicuous than their desirable behavior. If you are dealing with an especially difficult student, you may need to observe carefully to find brief periods of the student's calm, on-task behavior or evaluate the student's behavior carefully to see that it is more appropriate than is typical for him or her. The temptation is to expect too much before recognition is given. True, expectations for students' conduct can be too low and praise can be too generous. But that is not the failing of most teachers; many teachers are too ready with criticism, too stingy with recognition of the expected behavior. The teachers most students are drawn to, and from whom most students learn best, are those who recognize effort and achievement, even if it is small, who are encouraging and supportive, and who take obvious pleasure in a student's success. The important point to remember is that praise is due for whatever represents improved effort or a worthy achievement *for a particular individual*, not for the typical person or someone of great accomplishment. The beginning student of any age—whether learning the piano, math, writing, or basketball, turning in homework, or behaving appropriately in a group—thrives on recognition and encouragement for what, to the advanced student, look like small achievements.

The language of effective praise is at once simple and complex. Almost everyone knows the typical words and phrases that convey public approval or recognition, and in this sense the language of praise is simple. Certainly, most people also recognize that particular words, phrases, gestures, facial expressions, and other acts can convey a more significant level of approval than others, depending on the person from whom they come and the context in which they are given. Likewise, people understand the expression "to damn with faint praise"—to signify contempt by "praise" that is sarcastic or compares an accomplishment to something worse (e.g., "*That* sentence was not total nonsense"). It is important that effective praise be a sincere expression, verbal or nonverbal, that recognizes the value of what a student has done in a way that the student understands and appreciates.

Communicating approval and encouragement depends on your understanding the developmental level, individual characteristics, and cultural identification of the student. Some students may react negatively to praise to which others respond positively. Getting a positive reaction may depend on timing, the use of particular words or gestures, or the privacy of the communication. For some adolescents, for example, the typical public praise statement may discredit them with their peer group and be ineffective or worse. For some students, low-key indications of approval are best; for others, an animated display is most effective. The key is understanding how to communicate approval that is meaningful to the individual, and for that kind of praise, one can make this generalization: Nobody doesn't like it.

The purpose of approval of desirable behavior is twofold. First, it is an invitation to positive social interactions that are adaptive and mutually beneficial. It is the first step toward social bonding. Second, it is a model that is intended to induce imitative self-evaluation in the student. Our hope is that students will learn to evaluate their own behavior, to see their own accomplishments, to internalize teachers' valuing of them, and to respond with self-approval of desirable conduct. Teachers want students to notice their own improvement and learn to celebrate their own successes. This is not done by focusing on criticism or correction or by abstaining from any evaluative statements. Rather, teachers do so by showing their approval of students. True, there is a time to ask students for their self-evaluation (e.g., "How well do you think you did just now?" "Do you think you did the right thing?" "I wonder what you think of the fact that you brought your homework in for four days in a row"). However, many difficult students have received so little positive feedback and recognition that to begin with self-evaluation is to leave them adrift in a sea of uncertainty or starved for a kind and encouraging word. Having so seldom received praise, they do not know how to evaluate their performance or praise themselves.

We cannot overemphasize the importance of noncontingent attention as a preventive behavior management tool, a means of engaging students in positive social interaction before misbehavior has a chance to emerge.[6] Noncontingent attention means that you are *not* looking for a *particular* appropriate behavior and making your attention contingent. Rather, you are engaging the student in positive, productive activity *before* he or she has a chance to start misbehaving. Anticipate the student's entry into your classroom. Have a positive comment to make and engage the student immediately in an activity that he or she enjoys—a little chore or a favored activity, for example. Look for opportunities to talk to the student about something pleasant and nonthreatening, if not highly rewarding. Think of it as a preemptive positive strike. "Hi, Chas. Cool shirt! I like those colors. I've got all these books to straighten up on this shelf. Would you help me out by doing this job for me?" Know your student. Short-circuit the tendency to exhibit undesirable behavior by taking the initiative in a positive vein.

How should I talk with students about unacceptable behavior?

Negative teacher talk is often detrimental to appropriate student behavior and achievement. Constant negativity or belittling talk is unlikely to convince a student to improve behavior. It may easily, however, have the opposite effect. There is little point in embarrassing students when talking about their behavior, especially in front of the rest of the class. Resorting to language that causes shame is a personal attack on the student's self-esteem. Your objective should be to address the student's behavior and promote responsible actions. Avoid sarcasm, insults, and offensive language. Courteous language is not only professional, it also provides a model for students.

If possible, address misbehavior confidentially. When you talk to students about their behavior in the presence of their peers, confine conversation to the behavior itself. If it becomes necessary to confront or reprimand a student, give him or her an opportunity to save face. Keep it as private as possible; position yourself near the student and speak in a soft voice to reduce the chances of other students overhearing what you are saying. Doing this also teaches the rest of the class that they may expect the same dignified treatment.

An increase in positive messages and a reduction of negative messages will extend the chances of favorable behaviors recurring. For example, even critical feedback can be worded without being attacking or personally offensive. Using "I" messages that take responsibility for your feelings are helpful (e.g., "I feel that throwing the book on the floor was a poor choice of behavior"). In this way you express disapproval without attacking the character of the student. It does not follow, however, that the more positive the teacher talk, the better the student behavior and achievement. A neutral and businesslike approach in talking with students is at least as effective as an overly positive approach when the topic is misbehavior. Most successful teachers maintain a supportive but controlled attitude in their classrooms. Less successful teachers tend to engage in talk that is either excessively positive or excessively authoritarian and harsh. Also, teachers who are more internally controlled take responsibility for their talk and the progress of their classes and are more effective than teachers who blame the way they talk with students on circumstances or their students.

You should have three objectives in communication about misbehavior: (1) indicating clearly that the behavior is unacceptable, (2) indicating clearly what is expected, and (3) finding a way to help the student learn to do what is expected. Your communication should not give the student a reason to flare up. Keep it clear but brief, low key, and as private as possible. At the same time, make sure you tell or signal what you want, not just to desist. When you have an opportunity, talk to the student about the misbehavior and how you can help him or her learn acceptable alternatives to it. For example, you may have a brief discussion of specific things the student might do to avoid blowing up in response to not understanding an assignment. You may say something like, "What can we do so that, when you don't understand, you can stay calm and get the help you need?" Look for opportunities to develop precorrection plans, including rehearsal, prompts, and strong reinforcement for the expected behavior.

How should I talk with angry or aggressive students?

Sometimes students who are angry or upset become verbally abusive. They may seem intent on insulting or assaulting the teacher for no apparent reason except to establish their control and dominance in the classroom. For example, students may say to the teacher—or to someone else so that the teacher is certain to hear it—such things as these:

"Man, you a weird lookin' dude."

"Why do you wear such nerdy clothes?"

"She's got the ugliest nose I've ever seen!"

"Your breath stinks like shit."

"You don't know how to teach at all! Why didn't nobody teach you how to be a teacher?"

"Look, you just leave me alone or I'll punch your face in."

"You like your job, then you stay outa my face."

"You don't get off my case, my momma will come get you."

"You're stupid, and you lie!"

It is easy to take these remarks personally and respond in kind. Students know that teachers are vulnerable to personal attacks, and some seem to have an uncanny sense for knowing what will be especially hurtful and offensive. Refusing to take students' remarks to heart will help you avoid becoming angry or hurt and getting drawn into power struggles. Feeling personally affronted by every negative student comment will distract you from the real work of teaching and signal to students that they have found a victim.

Certainly, it is unrealistic to expect teachers, as anyone else, to be without emotions. Nevertheless, it is critically important for teachers to model restraint in the face of provocation and to show by word and deed that they will not be sidetracked from their professional responsibilities. This is not to suggest that effective teachers are unfeeling robots who simply grind away at getting through the curriculum. There are times when expressing frustration with a student in a controlled, appropriately responsible way can be extremely effective. Such a strategy, however, should be used sparingly and under extenuating circumstances.

Most prospective teachers have not carefully prepared and rehearsed responses to angry or aggressive students. Sometimes teachers fail to prepare for this eventuality because such incidents are usually few and far between. It is also difficult to prepare for every possible situation because the circumstances of each encounter are unique. You can, however, prepare yourself in a general way. First, define for yourself as carefully as you can the verbalizations that you will tolerate and the kinds that are unacceptable. Clearly unacceptable verbal behavior usually involves a situation in which a student says things that are likely to lead to serious classroom disruption or property damage. Such verbalizations may be a clear prelude to fighting, self-injury, or destruction of property. Second, once you have a clear set of limits, think through as many problem situations as possible, envisioning how you will act and what you will say. Work out a "prepackaged" strategy for dealing with the situation and rehearse the physical and verbal steps that will be necessary to regain control of the communication. Third, practice speaking in a calm tone and rehearse giving firm directions and commands. This kind of "imaging" and rehearsal will not prepare you for every eventuality, but it will provide enough preparation so that you will have time to think of other solutions or, if necessary, get assistance.

When you see a crisis brewing, you may initially try to buy time to allow you to regroup and move into your "prepackaged" verbal strategies or consequence. To buy time, you can direct students to go to different parts of the room, instruct them to engage in a new or different classroom activity, or insist on silence among arguing or fighting students until the situation is calmer. Sometimes an angry student can be deflected by your suggestion of an alternative behavior or activity. This also provides an interim time for the student to regroup and to regain some control. Another useful intervention involves asking the students to comply with a small request rather than insisting on a total move from anger to compliance.

As suggested by our discussion of the acting-out cycle, preventive talking is preferable to reactive talk. More can be gained by nipping a problem in the bud by a simple comment than by trying to deal with a full-blown crisis, where talking with a student tends to become less and less effective as the crisis escalates. Important as it is to try not to let a situation get out of control in the first place, you should not overreact to the buildup to a crisis or blowup in which the student gets out of control. Overreaction to minor infringements sometimes causes major problems that could have been avoided in the first place. Judging what to ignore and what to attend to will increase with experience, but your decisions will be helped by constant vigilance and a clear understanding of what you are prepared to tolerate in your classroom.

Besides mental or actual rehearsal, you must have an explicit plan for negative consequences that will follow intolerable behavior. Preplanning is absolutely essential, or you will find yourself in the position of having no effective consequence that you can be assured will occur and saying that something will happen when you cannot be assured that it will. The consequence may involve suspension, calling parents to come to take the student home, calling the police or a probation officer, and so on. Work with your principal and other staff who may be involved and with parents or guardians to make sure that everyone's clear about what will happen as a consequence of the intolerable behavior.

If you are forced to deal reactively with a suddenly out-of-control situation, your first concern should be to prevent harm to anyone in the room and to deescalate the emotionally charged situation as quickly as possible. In this situation, attempting a conversation with the student is rarely effective. For example, if two students are fighting, you are quite unlikely to be successful in asking questions about what started it or how the students feel about it. It's time for clear, short commands related to your preplanned consequence, time to get help, perhaps time for physical intervention.

Assuming that there is no immediate physical danger, talk in a firm yet calm, non-threatening manner. If an angry student perceives that you are afraid or feeling intimidated, there is a very good chance that he or she will respond with increased aggression. Speak calmly and in a natural voice. Simultaneously lower and relax your hands and arms to appear nonthreatening. Be alert, however, for any physical threat to yourself or other students. Avoid touching the student, as this may escalate her or his anger. Talk only about what is happening at that moment and avoid reciting past problems or transgressions. It is best, too, in spite of any personal feelings that you may have, to avoid having the last word. Do not, at all costs, taunt (e.g., "OK, just try it, go ahead and see where it gets you") or threaten (e.g., "You do that and you'll be sorry!"). Instead, give a clear and simple choice between the expected behavior and a consequence that you know you can deliver (e.g., "Bob, either return to your room now, or I'll call the police"). Don't get in the student's face. Give the student a few seconds to decide what to do. Then follow through, either by resuming the expected activity or applying the consequence.

Once you have given the student a choice, given the student a few seconds to decide, observed that the student is not complying with your expectation, and stated that the consequence will occur, do not let the student talk you out of it; you must follow through on what you have said will occur. The student may well try to draw you into an argument, protesting that he or she is now complying with your expectation (e.g., "I'm going, I'm going!") or pleading that you are not being fair (e.g., "I didn't know you really meant it," or "You didn't give me enough time"). Decline to be drawn in by ignoring the protestations or pleading. You made your decision; stick with it, or your subsequent statements will be taken as hollow threats.

How should I talk with students who are withdrawn?

Aggressive, acting-out students are an obvious challenge, as you must think on your feet and respond quickly to in-your-face behavior. Withdrawn students are not so obvious a problem in grabbing your attention, but they are no less daunting. The student who shuts you out and will not respond to your questions can be very frustrating indeed, leaving you feeling defeated in your attempts to build a meaningful teacher-pupil relationship.

The rules of engagement with withdrawn students are not so clearly developed as those with aggressive, acting-out students. However, we can suggest that you avoid several strategies because they are highly likely to fail. You would be unwise to bore in, to insist on a response, or to wheedle and cajole. Often, withdrawn students are highly reinforced by attention from adults who are obviously frustrated by their unresponsiveness and seem determined to hound them into talking. Punishing the student for not talking is foolish. Expecting a sudden or dramatic breakthrough is unrealistic. Other approaches may give you a considerably greater chance of success, although careful observation, sensitivity, patience, and satisfaction with small gains are required.

Spending time in proximity to the student, perhaps engaging in parallel activities and certainly watching carefully for signs of attention, may pay off. Your behavior and speech should indicate awareness of and interest in the student, not criticism. Look for what attracts the greatest interest of the student. Offer opportunities to engage in appropriate activities related to those interests and, if possible, arrange the activities to require some minimal verbal response from or interaction with someone else. Try communicating through written messages or use nonverbal communication (e.g., gestures, signals) if the student is persistently unresponsive to your speech. Be gently persistent, even relentless, in your attempts to communicate, but do so without conveying a sense of frustration or anger. That is, don't give up, but don't try to drag responses out of the student; the student will win this battle easily. Invite at every opportunity, entice if you can, but do so in a way that conveys calmness and confidence that you know what you're doing, not that you are at your wit's end.

A major factor in achieving success with withdrawn students is looking for successive approximations of normal social interaction. That is, you must be able to see and reinforce small steps in the direction of normal interaction. For example, if you have a student who simply will not respond in a large group of peers, then look for opportunities for that student to respond in a group with just one other. If you have a student who will respond to your questions with only one-word answers, then set your sight first on this student's responding with only a very few words. You may never make—and should not intend to make—a social butterfly of a student who is severely withdrawn. You should, however, attempt to draw the student into successively closer approximations of normal social interaction.

Some students are persistently, consistently withdrawn. Others withdraw periodically, often after an emotional blowup or acting-out incident. In either case, it is critically important to be sensitive to signals that a student wants to be left alone. Nothing is to be gained by invading a student's "space" when he or she is clearly indicating that you are not welcome to be close by and that he or she does not want to talk to you. However, it is also important to monitor the student's behavior carefully, looking for opportunities to draw the student into appropriate interaction.

Summary

Talking with students about their behavior is one of the most complex aspects of teaching. The teacher must understand how classroom language is different from the language students use at home or in the community. Particular care is required to develop communication skills that are sensitive to cultural differences.

Talking about behavior should be consistent with other instructional goals; the objective is to talk with students in ways that teach self-control. Teachers must learn how to avoid getting drawn into unproductive verbal interactions with students, such as arguments. They must also teach, through modeling and direct instruction, a variety of verbal and nonverbal communication skills such as listening, using proximity and body language, making eye contact, varying facial expressions, pausing, reflecting, probing, describing, choosing words and voice, pacing, summarizing, questioning, and waiting.

Talking with students about their appropriate behavior is critically important. The key is finding ways of expressing approval of the student's behavior that are meaningful to him or her. In talking with students about unacceptable behavior, it is important to keep the communication as private as possible and to highlight what is expected instead. Talking with angry and aggressive students requires preplanning, emotional detachment, and calmness in setting expectations and applying consequences. Students who are withdrawn present a different and daunting challenge, and the best approach involves persistent but gentle, calm, and careful attempts to establish communication and induce social interaction.

REFERENCES AND RESOURCES FOR FURTHER STUDY

The following references provided the basis for many of our statements in this chapter. You may wish to consult selected references for additional information.

Alber, S. R., Heward, W. L., & Hippler, B. J. (1999). Teaching middle school students with learning disabilities to recruit positive teacher attention. *Exceptional Children, 65,* 253–270.

Alberto, P. A., & Troutman, A. C. (2003). *Applied behavior analysis for teachers* (6th ed.). Upper Saddle River, NJ: Prentice-Hall.

Banks, J. A., & Banks, C. A. (Eds.). (1997). *Multicultural education: Issues and perspectives* (3rd ed.). Boston: Allyn and Bacon.

Carnes, J. (1994). An uncommon language: The multicultural making of American English. *Teaching Tolerance, 3*(1), 56–63.

Colvin, G. (1992). *Managing acting-out behavior* [video lecture and workbook]. Eugene, OR: Behavior Associates.

Colvin, G. (2004). *Managing the cycle of acting-out behavior in the classroom.* Eugene, OR: Behavior Associates.

Colvin, G., Sugai, G., Good, R. H., & Lee, Y. (1997). Using active supervision and precorrection to improve transition behaviors in an elementary school. *School Psychology Quarterly, 12,* 344–363.

Cushner, K., McClelland, A., & Safford, P. (2003). *Human diversity in education: An integrative approach* (4th ed.). New York: McGraw-Hill.

Deffenbacher, J. L., & Swaim, R. C. (1999). Anger expression in Mexican American and white non-Hispanic adolescents. *Journal of Counseling Psychology, 46,* 61–69.

Delpit, L. (1995). *Other people's children: Cultural conflict in the classroom.* New York: New Press.

Dilg, M. (2003). *Thriving in the multicultural classroom: Principles and practices for effective teaching.* New York: Teachers College Press.

Foster, H. L. (1986). *Ribbin', jivin', and playin' the dozens: The persistent dilemma in our schools.* Cambridge, MA: Ballinger.

Gersten, R., Brengelman, S., & Jimenez, R. (1994). Effective instruction for culturally and linguistically diverse students: A reconceptualization. *Focus on Exceptional Children, 27*(1), 1–16.

Gersten, R., & Woodward, J. (1994). The language-minority student and special education: Issues, trends, and paradoxes. *Exceptional Children, 60,* 310–322.

Gollnick, D. M., & Chinn, P. C. (2002). *Multicultural education in a pluralistic society* (6th ed.). Upper Saddle River, NJ: Merrill/Prentice-Hall.

Hallahan, D. P., & Kauffman, J. M. (2006). *Exceptional learners: Introduction to special education* (10th ed.). Boston: Allyn and Bacon.

Hallahan, D. P., Lloyd, J. W., Kauffman, J. M., Weiss, M. P., & Martinez, E. A. (2005). *Learning disabilities: Foundations, characteristics, and effective teaching* (3rd ed.). Boston: Allyn and Bacon.

Irvine, J. J. (2003). *Educating teachers for diversity: Seeing with a cultural eye.* New York: Teachers College Press.

Jacobson, T. (2003). *Confronting our discomfort: Clearing the way for anti-bias in early childhood.* New York: Heinemann.

Kameenui, E. J., & Darch, C. B. (1995). *Instructional classroom management: A proactive approach to behavior management.* White Plains, NY: Longman.

Kerr, M. M., & Nelson, C. M. (2002). *Strategies for managing behavior problems in the classroom* (4th ed.). Upper Saddle River, NJ: Prentice-Hall.

Lassman, K. A., Kristine, J., & Wehby, J. H. (1999). "My teacher said I did good work today!": Using collaborative behavioral contracting. *Teaching Exceptional Children, 31,* 12–18.

Pullen, P. L. (2004). *Brighter beginnings for teachers.* Lanham, MD: Scarecrow Education.

Rhode, G., Jenson, W. R., & Reavis, H. K. (1992). *The tough kid book: Practical classroom management strategies.* Longmont, CO: Sopris West.

Rogers-Adkinson, D., & Griffith, P. (Eds.). (1999). *Communication disorders and children with psychiatric and behavioral disorders.* San Diego: Singular.

Singh, S. D., Ellis, C. R., Winton, A. S. W., Singh, N. N., Leung, J. P., & Oswald, D. P. (1998). Recognition of facial expressions of emotion by children with attention-deficit hyperactivity disorder. *Behavior Modification, 22,* 128–142.

Walker, H. M. (1995). *The acting out child. Coping with classroom disruption* (2nd ed.). Longmont, CO: Sopris West.

Walker, H. M., Colvin, G., & Ramsey, E. (1995). *Antisocial behavior in school. Strategies and best practices.* Pacific Grove, CA: Brooks/Cole.

Walker, H. M., Ramsey, E., & Gresham, F. M. (2004). *Antisocial behavior in school. Strategies and best practices* (2nd ed.). Pacific Grove, CA: Brooks/Cole.

Wood, F. H. (Ed.). (1990). When we talk with children: The life-space interview. *Behavioral Disorders, 15,* 110–126.

Wood, M. M., & Long, N. J. (1991). *Life-space intervention: Talking to children and youth in crisis.* Austin, TX: Pro-Ed.

ENDNOTES

1. See Hallahan and Kauffman (2006) for further discussion.
2. See Banks and Banks (1997), Carnes (1994), Deffenbacher and Swaim (1999), Foster (1986), Gollnick and Chinn (2002), and Pullen (2004).
3. See Colvin (2004) and Walker, Colvin, and Ramsey (1995) for a further discussion of debriefing.
4. See Chapter 4 and Colvin (2004) and Walker, Colvin, and Ramsey (1995) for a further discussion of precorrection.
5. See Hallahan et al. (2005) and Kerr and Nelson (2002) for a further discussion of self-management procedures.
6. See Colvin (2004) and Walker, Colvin, and Ramsey (1995) for an extended discussion of noncontingent attention.

CHAPTER

6 Using Peer Influence

People usually assume that the most important things students learn in school are the things they learn from their teachers. This assumption may or may not be correct. It is well known that students learn a great deal from each other. Our hope is that what they learn from each other improves their conduct and achievement, but we know that this is often not the case. Students learn much by observing each other, and their observations sometimes lead to conflicts or withdrawal. Frequent serious conflicts with peers, minimal interactions with peers, and association with deviant peers are indications that a student is likely to have long-term personal problems, as we noted in Chapter 2.

Teaching requires the management of groups to foster positive and satisfying peer relations. Teachers must recognize the pervasive influence of peer groups in nearly every person's life. A peer group is a relentless influence on one's behavior, regardless of age or societal role. As adults—more specifically, as teachers—we are concerned about what our peers think of us. Moreover, behavior of one's colleagues influences one's perceptions of important events, many of one's decisions, and significant aspects of one's professional relationships.

Adults are aware of peer influences. They may consciously choose certain friends and control their relationships with peers to enhance their professional skills, ethical conduct, and personal satisfaction. Many students, however, are not so aware of peer influence nor so astute in choosing their associations. Teachers have an obligation to

Sally

Kevin, as I said, was a real problem because he didn't comply with my requests or commands. That's the reason I made up little compliance lessons in which I had him practice doing what I told him. My first thought was to teach him individually, but then two things occurred to me. First of all, he didn't interact much with any of the other kids in my class. He was a very, very strange little boy in many ways and didn't seem to pay much attention to his classmates. Most of the time he seemed "spaced out" and not in touch with what was going on around him. Second, I had another child in my class, Derrick, who was a lot more compliant than Kevin but still needed a little improvement. I thought it'd be a good idea to teach Kevin and Derrick together in my compliance lessons. Derrick could serve as a model for Kevin because he would usually do what I asked. My strategy early in the lessons was to get an appropriate response from Derrick to one of my instructions, reinforce him, then ask Kevin to do the same thing. I also alternated instructions so that Derrick wasn't always the first to respond. This approach worked really well because Derrick was, at first, a good model for Kevin. But I also found that Kevin started interacting with Derrick at other times during the day.

Chris

Ned was considered a "nerd" by his classmates. I even heard some of them say things like "Oh, God, it's Ned the nerd!" to his face or call him "Dopey" or "Sleepy." The teasing he took from some of the less thoughtful kids was awful. He was an easy target because he was so painfully shy and got terribly flustered if anybody asked him anything. He almost never talked to anyone in school, peers or adults. I found out that he spent most of his time at home in his room. The kids in the neighborhood that he had anything to do with were 8- and 10-year-olds, and he was 14. The school counselor and I noticed that Ned had just about zero social skills. He didn't look people in the eye when he talked to them, he didn't have any idea how to start up a conversation with his peers, and he didn't know how to respond when someone tried to start a conversation with him. We developed some lessons in conversational skills for Ned, including how to initiate conversations, how to respond to others' initial comments, how to show interest and emotional responses, and how to handle eye contact during conversations. The counselor taught these basic skills in one-to-one sessions with Ned at first. She would discuss the importance of the skill, model it, and then have Ned rehearse using it with her. Ned not only learned the social skills we taught him in these sessions but he also learned how to use them with his peers. In fact, he started asking classmates to visit him at home, began dating, and even tried out for a school team.

Source: "Chris" is based on D. P. Franco, K. A. Christoff, D. B. Crimmins, and J. A. Kelly (1983). Social skills training for an extremely shy young adolescent: An empirical case study. *Behavior Therapy, 14,* 568-575.

---

do what they can to make positive peer influence an important aspect of their students' lives in the classroom and to help students learn to make wise choices about peer relationships. The vignettes of Sally and Chris illustrate some of the issues teachers face in helping students get along with, and learn appropriate behavior from, their peers.

Peer pressure will be at work in the classroom whether the teacher harnesses it or not. Social pressure from peers is more obvious in some classrooms than in others. In some classrooms it obviously affects every student; in others it is seen most clearly in an "in-group." In some classrooms the pressure of the in-group is for academic achievement, but in many classrooms there is pressure to resist academic learning and to be disruptive. Some classrooms are characterized by feelings of belonging or togetherness of all the students, whereas others are characterized by tension, divisiveness, scapegoating, exclusive cliques, and destructive competition.

Experienced teachers know that every group, like every individual student, is different from every other. Some groups are easy and some are difficult to manage. The group's character seems to depend on the mix of individuals comprising it and the circumstances that bring it together. The dissimilarities in peer relations that we observe in various classrooms are not due only to differences in teachers' skills in managing groups. Still, there are enough common or predictable features of groups and peer interactions that we can offer suggestions about strategies that are likely to be useful in accomplishing specific goals. Important questions teachers need to ask themselves about managing peer influence include these:

- How can I harness peer pressure as an effective force for improving my students' behavior and achievement?
- How can I encourage cooperation and caring for each other among my students?
- How can I help students on the social fringes of the class become better accepted among their peers?

Questions for Reflection

As you contemplate what you might do to foster good peer relations among your students and how you might use group pressure effectively and humanely, you will need to keep in mind the basic psychological processes involved in social groups. For example, people in groups learn much by observing each other, especially by noticing the positive and negative consequences others experience. Watching what happens to others not only reveals how to obtain consequences but it also allows the observer to experience those consequences *vicariously*—as a substitute for one's own experience. Finally, individuals in groups are loosely or tightly bound together by structures that are imposed by group leaders or by an outside authority. The way individuals relate to each other as group members depends partly on the rules for sharing in each others' success and failure. We suggest that you ask yourself at least the following questions about specific strategies:

- How might I use observational learning and vicarious consequences to affect the behavior of my students' peers?
- What type of group contingency might I use to create desirable peer pressure?
- How might I engage classroom peers as confederates?
- How might I use peer tutors as a classroom resource?
- What options should I consider in teaching social skills?

How might I use observational learning and vicarious consequences to affect the behavior of my students' peers?

Teachers must always be aware that they are serving as models for their students. Youngsters learn a lot about teaching, parenting, relating to peers, and other aspects of socialization by watching adults. You need to be particularly concerned about practicing what you preach, as your students probably will learn at least as much from what they see as they do from what they hear. One question that should be in your mind is whether your students would be behaving appropriately if they imitated you. We recognize that adults have prerogatives that children and adolescents do not have. Yet, you do not want to lose sight of the importance of adults providing good models for younger generations.

Children and adolescents are also keen observers of each other. Perceptive teachers use students' tendency to watch and imitate their peers as a means of improving the conduct of those who exhibit inappropriate behavior. They do this by having students whose conduct is desirable serve as models for others who are misbehaving or having difficulty learning. The inappropriate conduct that may be improved through peer modeling includes a wide range of problems such as inattentive, aggressive, or socially withdrawn behavior; it may also include lack of study skills or specific academic difficulties.

Using observational learning successfully requires careful selection of the model (student) whom you hope will be imitated. You also must reward the model and the student(s) you want to imitate the model in ways that do not discourage the observers. When you use procedures that are intended to enhance observational learning, it is likely that most or all students in the classroom will experience vicarious effects. That is, when any student receives reinforcing or punishing consequences, those who are watching probably will be affected indirectly through their vicarious experience of the reward or punishment.[1]

Models Who Are Likely to Be Imitated. Some individuals are much more likely than others to be imitated by their peers. This means that when you use an observational learning strategy, you must attempt to choose a model whose behavior probably will be most influential with the target student. Research does not indicate precisely the type of model who is most likely to be imitated in every circumstance, but we can offer some general guidelines. Usually, you would be wise to choose a model whom the target student sees as attractive, competent, and similar to himself or herself in important ways (e.g., someone of the same sex and close to the same general ability level). If the behavior you hope the target student will imitate is one that he or she has had considerable difficulty learning, then a coping model is best—a model whom the target student can see overcoming difficulties on the way to mastery, not one who has already mastered the behavior and performs it effortlessly and flawlessly. For example, if you are looking for a model to help a target student overcome a serious fear of talking in class, the best classmate to serve as a model will not be one who enjoys public speaking. Rather, it will be one who has some hesitation about speaking up but manages to overcome his or her anxiety about it. Watching someone who shares your anxiety or difficulty overcome it and perform successfully tends to make you feel that you can do the same; observing someone who apparently never shared your struggle isn't nearly as encouraging.

There are two principles to keep in mind: First, the model must be personally attractive to the observer, or imitation is not likely to occur. People tend to imitate those they admire, as well as those they perceive as sharing similar characteristics but as somewhat "better" than themselves along certain dimensions. Second, the model must exhibit behavior that the observer believes he or she can imitate successfully. People often imitate those they admire, even if they are very different from themselves in most respects. In fact, what they imitate may have little or nothing to do with the primary reason they find others attractive. For example, an individual might imitate the dress or mannerisms of popular musicians but have no intention of imitating—and no ability to imitate—their musicianship. If someone is just learning to play a musical instrument, or learning another skill, the best model is someone who can demonstrate a level of skill just above his or hers. Virtuosic performances may provide inspiration to continue learning, but beginners who are expected to imitate a master are likely to get discouraged and give up. Teachers sometimes make the mistake of choosing models who are too "good" or too competent to be encouraging of imitation by the target student.

Rewarding the Model and Target Student.   Sometimes models are imitated even though the imitators are not directly rewarded. However, the target student is much more likely to imitate the model you have chosen if he or she sees the model receiving reinforcement for appropriate behavior. Thus it is important to provide the reinforcement for the model when the target student is watching. In some cases, if the target student is unaware that the model is to be imitated, you may need to prompt the target student by telling him or her to watch the way the model behaves (or solves a problem). Then you must be sure to reinforce the target student immediately when his or her behavior approximates that of the model. If the target student observes that others receive rewards for a given behavior, but that he or she is not rewarded for the same behavior, the result may be demoralization or inappropriate behavior. The model's behavior should demonstrate the kind of behavior or performance you expect; your response to the model should demonstrate that such behavior will be rewarded; and the target student's attempts to imitate the model should be rewarded.

In the typical classroom, a lot of things are going on simultaneously. Individual students' behavior is sometimes good, sometimes not so good. You will be more likely to encourage good behavior in the group if you call attention to the specific conduct of well-behaved students. Make your social reinforcement of desirable conduct as specific as possible, so that the behavior you want to encourage in observing students is not only demonstrated by the model but described. "John, I like the way you waited to be called on" is better than "Thank you, John, for being polite" because it is a more specific description of the behavior you want observers to imitate.

Limits of Vicarious Effects.   Teachers who are excellent behavior managers often make good use of vicarious effects to encourage good conduct. For example, when they observe minor misbehavior, they ignore it and show obvious approval for appropriate behavior of another student, usually someone in close proximity to the one who is misbehaving. In this way they offer a vicarious prompt to the misbehaving student; they are saying, in effect, "Behave in this way (like the appropriately behaved student), because then you will get my attention and approval." They focus on desirable conduct, knowing that the observing students may not only be prompted to behave appropriately but also experience vicarious gratification when they behave in the same way as those who are being rewarded.

Rewarding models in the hope that observers will imitate desirable behavior can backfire if you are not prepared for at least two possible complications. First, you must be careful not to rely on a single model or a small group. If only one student or a small group of students is constantly featured as fulfilling your expectations, then the rest of the class is likely to see you as playing favorites or having "pets." This will quickly destroy the effectiveness of the models and undermine your use of rewarding consequences. Make sure that you catch the good behavior of as many different students as possible and call attention to it. Second, in some groups—and this tends to be a particular problem among adolescents—"teacher-pleasing" behavior is an anathema, taboo, something that carries a stigma. You must be prepared for groups in which typical statements of praise or approval are not rewarding and may, in fact, be punishing. This does not mean that you cannot use vicarious consequences or that you must become punitive. It means that you must be very shrewd in rewarding the behavior you want to encourage. You may need to keep your praise and approval minimal and emphasize—matter-of-factly—rewarding consequences that are meaningful to the group. These consequences may be activities or privileges that members of the group see as desirable.

We caution further that few people, if any, can live by vicarious effects alone. A person may be able to share to some extent in the joy and pain others are experiencing directly, but others' lives cannot become a substitute for his or her own direct experience. Compared to direct experience of consequences, vicarious effects are weak. Furthermore, vicarious approaches typically work well with groups that are generally well behaved; they are not likely to work with groups that are highly disruptive or out of control. For very poorly behaved groups, frequent direct rewards for individuals who are behaving appropriately are typically necessary.

We offer an additional caution about the limitations of vicarious effects. If an individual observes others receiving consequences for certain behavior but receives no consequences for the same behavior, the effect is likely to be the opposite vicarious consequence. For example, if a student in your class sees others receiving rewarding consequences for certain behavior, yet he or she seldom or never is rewarded for behaving similarly, then the effect will in all likelihood be vicarious punishment—he or she will feel, by comparison to others who are being rewarded, punished. Alternatively, if a student sees others being punished for certain behavior, yet he or she is not punished for similar behavior, then the effect will be vicarious reinforcement—he or she will feel rewarded. This principle suggests that favoritism or bias in a teacher's consequences will compound behavior problems. Students who observe their classmates receiving rewarding or punishing consequences for a specific kind of behavior should receive the same treatment. If they do not receive at least similar treatment, then the effect on their behavior is likely to be the opposite of that for those who are receiving direct consequences.

What type of group contingency might I use to create desirable peer pressure?

The contingencies of reinforcement teachers use often apply to individuals without any reference to the peer group. However, contingencies can also be arranged for groups in a variety of ways, some of which produce considerable peer pressure on individuals to behave in ways that earn rewards or avoid punishment.

The phenomenon of group pressure is well known, and it is a pervasive feature of social groups. Consider the group pressure that is part of political parties, unions, professional organizations, fraternities and sororities, and religious groups. All of these rely on peer pressure as one means of controlling the behavior of members and furthering their collective aims. One cannot conclude that group pressure is undesirable, although there are examples in which groups have destructive aims or use excessive and cruel peer pressure. As a teacher, your task is to encourage peer pressure for appropriate behavior and keep it from becoming excessive or inhumane.

Any contingency that is oriented toward a group will create some level of peer pressure. Group-oriented contingencies include those in which the same rules apply to all individuals independently, those in which consequences for the entire group depend on the behavior of one member, and those in which the consequences for the entire group are interdependent (all members of the group obtain the same consequences based on the combined behavior of the members). Each type of contingency has certain advantages and disadvantages in the classroom. Combinations of group and individual contingencies are possible, and you may want to consider how you could combine contingencies to structure the most effective learning environment for specific individuals and groups.

Independent Group Contingencies.   Independent group contingencies are those that apply uniformly to each student, regardless of the performance of the group. For example, you might establish the following contingency for students in your classroom: "If you turn in acceptably completed homework, you are allowed to participate in a five-minute period of free time for talking with friends." This is a group contingency, in that it applies to the entire class; it is independent, in that one student's behavior does not affect any other student's consequences.

Independent group contingencies have the advantage of focusing on individual responsibility. Their disadvantage in managing a group is that they do not generate much peer pressure. About the only pressure from peers will be that which is already present in the form of friendship ties and the relatively weak and indirect influences of modeling and vicarious consequences.

Dependent Group Contingencies.   Dependent group contingencies are those under which rewards are available for all group members only when requirements are met by one member or a small subset of the group. An example of a dependent group contingency is the "hero procedure" used by Gerald Patterson and his colleagues.[2] They made class "heros" of hyperactive, disruptive students by setting a contingency under which these students earned rewards for the entire class by paying attention and behaving appropriately.

An advantage of dependent group contingencies can be positive peer pressure—peers may "root for" the target student and do whatever they can to encourage him or her to behave appropriately because they have something to gain by doing so. Another possible advantage is that the social status of the target student may be improved if his or her behavior becomes a source of rewards for peers. A disadvantage is that the misbehaving student can become a target for peer harassment and the other members of the class can feel that they are being denied an "entitlement" when they do not receive a reward. The way the dependent group contingency is presented, as well as the nature of the group to which it is applied, may determine whether the advantages outweigh the disadvantages or vice versa. The reward earned for the entire group by the target student must be an extra—an add-on to the rewarding consequences routinely available to the group—or there is too much risk of negative peer reactions when the reward is not earned.

Interdependent Group Contingencies. Interdependent group contingencies are those in which a specific requirement for a reward applies to all members of the group but the reward depends on the combined or total performance of the group, as well as the behavior of individuals. That is, the group's combined performance is the criterion for anyone to receive reinforcement, and all share equally in the reward. For example, a teacher might allow the class to participate in a special activity after each member of the class completes an assignment successfully. Basically, team sports are interdependent group contingencies—individuals contribute to the team's success, but it is the team, not an individual, that wins.

The "Good Behavior Game" is an interdependent group contingency that has been used in a variety of forms by teachers.[3] The essential features of the game are these: (1) the teacher states certain rules that apply to all members of the class; (2) all members of the class can earn points for the class (or their "team," a subgroup of the class) by behaving according to the rules; and (3) the class (or team) earns rewards, depending on the total number of points earned by the group's members. In some variations on the game, the class or team has earned a reward for accumulating less than a certain number of points given for specific misbehavior (i.e., the rules of the game were reversed, with low misbehavior points "winning").

Interdependent group contingencies typically create peer pressure; whether it is primarily positive or negative pressure depends a lot on the composition of the "teams." One member can sabotage the team, creating considerable hostility among other team members. Teams that are clearly unequal in ability quickly create problems. Overemphasis on competition can cause scapegoating and other negative peer interactions. Our suggestion is that you consider using interdependent group contingencies, as they are powerful devices for harnessing peer pressure, but that you use them with considerable caution.

Cooperative Learning.   Nearly every teacher has at least heard the term *cooperative learning*, if not read about or been instructed in cooperative learning procedures. Many variations on the theme of cooperative learning are possible, but they all have in common the combined use of independent and interdependent group contingencies. Pairs or larger teams of students work under contingencies in which their combined performance, as well as their individual improvement, is evaluated and rewarded. Some variants of cooperative learning deemphasize individual achievement and concentrate on group performance and reward. Cooperative learning procedures hold great promise as a means of fostering positive peer interactions. We encourage the use of cooperative learning strategies with the cautions we offer for all group contingencies.

Cautions about Group Contingencies.   Group contingencies of the types we have described can encourage positive peer pressure, but they can also backfire and result in negative pressure and coercion if they are not carefully managed. We offer five suggestions for avoiding the common problems of threats, criticism, and harassment from peers when a student does not perform as his or her peers would like. If, in spite of following our cautions, a group you are managing is putting negative pressure on certain of its members, we recommend that you revise or eliminate the contingency.

1. Be certain that the performance standard you set is not too high. You must begin with a criterion for reward that the target student or group can meet easily, then gradually increase the requirement for reward. If you set the standard too high in the beginning, everyone may be disappointed; if you expect gradual improvement over time, however, the target student or group is more likely to win approval from the rest of the class. Early success in achieving the reward should be virtually guaranteed in the beginning by setting a requirement that represents slight improvement over current behavior.

2. Emphasize reward for appropriate performance rather than punishment for undesirable behavior. Whenever possible, state the contingency positively and reward the group for good behavior (e.g., "We'll all take a 10-minute break when everyone has finished this math assignment" is preferable to "Nobody can take a break until everyone has finished this work"). The alternative—stating rules not to be broken and giving points for misbehavior—mean that one or a few students can easily sabotage their peers' efforts by deliberate misbehavior. These "spoilers" may encounter a lot of hostility and threats from their classmates, and this may set the stage for escalating coercive interactions.

3. Keep the competition fair. If you divide the class into teams, make certain that the teams have about equal chances to "win." Whenever possible, allow everyone to earn a reward for good performance and the "winners" to earn a little extra.

4. When using interdependent group contingencies, encourage everyone to participate, but do not require it. Forced participation will almost certainly set up the group for failure. Group contingencies will not work for all students in all circumstances. Use the group only for students who are willing "players." Let those who do not want to be team members "sit out."

5. Make allowances for those who do not work well as part of any group you can construct. In spite of your best efforts, some students may repeatedly or purposely torpedo their group's efforts. Do not merely exclude these students from participation in groups. Set up individual contingencies for them, and keep open the possibility of their rejoining a group when they are willing to work cooperatively with their peers. Removing one or a few individuals from the group contingency is often better than abandoning it for the majority. For those who are removed, however, you must have individual expectations and provide rewarding consequences for appropriate behavior.

How might I engage classroom peers as confederates?

Students are a potential classroom resource as teachers' confederates—accomplices, allies, or assistants of the teacher in specific interventions. Sometimes a peer confederate is able to extend the teacher's reach by carrying out specific intervention procedures that the teacher cannot implement because of a lack of time or because the object of the intervention is to enhance peer relations that only another student can initiate directly. When a peer is serving as the teacher's confederate, the confederate's role may be explained to the target student, but this is not always the case. Depending on the specific role of the confederate and the nature of the target student's behavior, you may need to obtain parental permission and administrative approval before implementing the intervention procedures. You must exercise careful professional judgment in deciding whether the interactions between confederate and target will be such that parents or school administrators might question their appropriateness. If in doubt, discuss the role you propose for the confederate with your supervisor or principal before proceeding.

Peers are particularly useful as models and tutors for specific skills, as we discuss elsewhere in this chapter. Students may also learn to deliver social reinforcers very effectively in naturally occurring peer interactions. In addition, peers may be very helpful as confederates in initiating social interactions with students who are socially isolated or withdrawn. Confederates must be carefully chosen and trained. The teacher must know precisely the role the student is to play in the intervention, model that role for the confederate, and provide feedback as the confederate rehearses precisely what to do. Moreover, the teacher must monitor the confederate's performance to make sure he or she is implementing the procedures as intended.

Not all students are capable of serving as confederates, and any student who does so will require careful training and supervision. Peer confederates must be reliable in several respects. They should have good school attendance so that you are able to depend on their availability. In addition, confederates should be generally positive in their interactions with peers, able to avoid negative interactions with peers under nearly any circumstance, and able to follow your instructions. You should not select as a peer confederate a student who is not liked by the target child; the confederate should be socially attractive to the target student, or at least socially neutral.

Some interventions may be appropriate if implemented by the teacher but not if they are implemented by a peer confederate. Using a peer confederate to assist in punishment is not, in our opinion, justifiable (with the possible exception of some peer-implemented conflict resolution procedures). Peer confederates are best used to provide good models, tutor or coach fellow students in specific skills, initiate positive social interactions with target classmates, and deliver positive reinforcement for specific desirable behavior as determined by the teacher.

Conflict resolution by trained peers is a strategy that has been implemented in some schools and classrooms. Students serve as counselors or mediators who try to help their peers resolve disputes in nonviolent ways. They are trained in specific negotiation procedures to resolve minor problems, the goal being to catch conflicts before they escalate into major struggles. Some conflicts clearly are too much for peers to manage, and proper training will help students recognize problems that need to be dealt with by an adult. However, many students at all grade levels can learn to help their peers step back from minor confrontations, to ask questions that clarify each party's goals and point of contention, and to negotiate a nonviolent solution that is satisfactory to both parties. In some schools, mediation or conflict resolution has been made a part of the social studies curriculum. We note that not every attempt to train and use peer mediators has been successful. Training takes time and special expertise on the part of teachers, and peer mediators need time and a private place in which to resolve disputes. The resources required for successful peer mediation are not always available.

How might I use peer tutors as a classroom resource?

Peer tutoring became an extremely popular idea in the 1990s.[4] No teacher should plunge into peer tutoring, however, without a clear idea of what the tutoring is to accomplish. The skills to be acquired by the tutees must be stated explicitly. Also important are the objectives for the tutors. Using a classroom peer as a tutor solely to save the teacher's time and effort is highly questionable. Tutors should be learning valuable skills themselves during the process of tutoring, and the teacher should be able to state exactly what those skills are. Some studies have shown that tutors' academic performance or social behavior improves, but such improvement cannot be taken for granted. Before launching a peer tutoring intervention, you should be able to answer these questions:

- What specific skills do I expect the tutee to acquire from this tutoring?
- What specific benefits do I expect for the tutor?
- Is peer tutoring the most effective and efficient way I can attain my goals for the tutee and tutor?

Choosing and Training Tutors.   Ordinarily, teachers assume that when they enlist peers as tutors they are making better use of their time and operating a more efficient and effective instructional program. Before assuming that peer tutoring makes better use of your resources, however, you must consider how much time and effort will be required to train and supervise the tutor(s). Some teachers have implemented relatively unstructured and unsupervised tutoring. The teacher has merely told students to work in small groups and help each other learn academic tasks, such as spelling words. Other teachers have given tutors very explicit and relatively extensive training in how to teach specific skills. This kind of training has sometimes involved modeling by the teacher, rehearsal by the tutor under the guidance of the teacher, and frequent feedback on performance. Obviously, the specific objectives for the tutor and the tutee as well as their abilities will determine how much training and supervision are required and therefore how much of the teacher's time, if any, is saved.

Classwide peer tutoring has been implemented by some teachers, whereas others have involved only a few of their students. Sometimes same-age peers have been used; sometimes tutors have been substantially different from their tutees in age. In spite of the popularity of peer tutoring as an academic intervention, research does not yet indicate clearly the characteristics of the optimum tutor-tutee match. In any case, you should consider how a variety of characteristics of the students involved as tutors or tutees might contribute to the success or failure of peer tutoring: relative ages, gender, social class, ethnicity, and skill development, for example. Also critically important are behavioral characteristics, especially the tendency to be punitive toward others, the ability to give contingent praise and other rewards, and susceptibility to peer influence. The specific tutoring arrangements you choose must be based on your knowledge of the individual students involved and your estimate of how they will interact, given the specific tasks you have set for them.

Limitations of Peer Tutoring. Effective teachers and aides are not easily recruited, trained, and evaluated. We doubt that untrained and unmonitored peer tutors will provide instruction equal in effectiveness to that of most classroom teachers and aides. Although we recognize its potential benefits, the simplicity and cost effectiveness of peer tutoring are exaggerated in some reports of its use. Peers can and often do help each other, but they do not always do so, and they are not likely to do so without careful planning, monitoring, and training.

Peer tutoring might create more behavior problems than it resolves if it is not carefully implemented. Depending on the match of tutor and tutee, the specific skills being tutored, and the training, supervision, and reinforcement for the students involved, peer tutoring can have remarkably positive or negative outcomes. Some disruptive, unmotivated students will learn a great deal and become more tractable when they serve as a tutor for a peer or when they are tutored by another student. Students who are socially withdrawn and unresponsive in a larger group may develop close relationships and learn critical social skills when involved in a peer tutoring arrangement. Others, however, will carry their behavioral difficulties into the tutoring interactions. Some students may engage their tutees or tutors in coercive interactions or fail to use their assigned time together in the manner intended by their teachers. You must be aware that peer tutoring has the potential for negative outcomes and be ready to modify or terminate tutoring arrangements in which coercion or inappropriate use of time allocated for tutoring is a problem.

What options should I consider in teaching social skills?

Within the past decade, teachers and researchers have begun to recognize the fact that social skills are perhaps as important as academic skills in determining students' futures. Without good social skills, students' academic progress is likely to be less than optimal, their future educational opportunities are likely to be restricted, and they are less likely to make a successful transition to adulthood and employment. Consequently, most educators now place more emphasis on the social learning that occurs in the classroom.[5]

Social skills are taught by parents, families, peer groups, and teachers. To a large extent, the social skills training children receive is informal and incidental—we might even say haphazard. Educators are now beginning to realize that many students fail to learn social skills under these conditions, just as they fail to learn academic skills when instruction is haphazard. As is true in the case of academic instruction, most teachers have neither the time nor the expertise to develop their own curriculum and instructional materials for teaching social skills. Fortunately, social skills training programs, including specific materials and lessons, have been developed for students at both the elementary and secondary levels. We urge you to consider using one of the social skills training programs listed in our references and resources at the end of this chapter if you teach students with apparent social skill deficits. Regardless of what program you adopt or what social skills training activities you plan for your students, you will need to ask yourself the following questions:

- *What are the particular social skills that my students need to learn?* Careful observation and reflection may help you understand exactly what it is about the social behavior of particular students that is problematic (e.g., inappropriate eye contact during interactions, lack of response to social initiations from others, maladaptive responses to instructions from authority, giving or responding to criticism inappropriately, impulsive or aggressive responses that provoke social conflict, inability to demonstrate appropriate affect, etc.). Understanding the demands of positive social interactions and relationships is critically important in describing the social skills one needs. Try to describe precisely what your students need to learn to do, as well as what they need to learn not to do, if they are to become more successful in their relationships with others.

- *Do my teaching strategies promote social competence?* Some teachers employ instructional approaches that minimize social interaction, providing almost no opportunity to learn social skills. These teaching strategies, which focus almost exclusively on independent work and individual responses, demand so little interpersonal competence that social skills become relatively trivial.

- *Do I teach social skills explicitly?* Most teaching activities should encourage social interaction. However, providing opportunities for social interaction is not enough for many students. Explicit instruction is often necessary. A social skills curriculum must focus on helping students acquire and use an acceptable level of specific social skills. Talking about social skills is not enough. Rehearsing and practicing them with feedback on performance are necessary.

■ *Am I able to generalize training in social skills from simulated to actual social situations?* It is one thing to be able to exhibit social skills in a familiar and friendly environment; it is quite another to exhibit the same skills in the presence of unfamiliar and unresponsive or antagonistic individuals. Your curriculum and instructional strategies for social skills must take into account the importance of helping students extend their skills beyond the training sessions in which you teach them.

■ *Is my approach to social skills training consistent with the needs of students with mild disabilities and students at risk?* Students with disabilities—especially mild mental retardation, learning disabilities, and emotional or behavioral disorders—may need social skills training that most students do not. Likewise, students at risk (i.e., seemingly headed for academic or social failure but not yet identified as having a disability) may not respond like most students to particular social situations. Students with disabilities and students who are at risk may need more explicit and directive instruction in social skills than the more typical student.

Summary

Teaching requires managing the behavior of groups. Peer pressure is always present in groups, whether harnessed by the teacher or not. The teacher must attempt to foster positive and humane peer pressure that encourages a sense of togetherness or belonging among members of the class, cooperation and caring of students for each other, and better acceptance of those who are at the social fringes of the group. Students are keen observers of each other, as well as of adults. Teachers often use observational learning and the tendency to imitate certain peers and adults as a means of improving behavior. Effective observational learning procedures highlight the appropriate behavior of attractive models, and that includes rewarding consequences for both the model and those who imitate the model. The vicarious experience of consequences by those who witness models being reinforced for desirable conduct may influence the observers' behavior. Vicarious effects are relatively weak, however, and direct consequences are necessary for managing serious behavior problems.

Group contingencies create peer pressure and can be used in a variety of forms, including independent, dependent, and interdependent contingencies. Cooperative learning procedures involve a combination of individual and group contingencies. Care is needed to avoid possible negative peer pressure when group contingencies are used. With proper selection and training, many students can serve as effective confederates of the teacher in implementing positive behavior management procedures. Also with proper selection and training, most students can also serve as effective tutors for their peers. Teaching social skills necessarily involves group learning and a curriculum designed to teach appropriate interpersonal responses.

REFERENCES AND RESOURCES FOR FURTHER STUDY

The following references provided the basis for many of our statements in this chapter. You may wish to consult selected references for additional information on specific topics. Our reference notes for this chapter refer to sources in this list.

Antil, L. R., Jenkins, J. R., Wayne, S. K., & Vadasy, P. F. (1998). Cooperative learning: Prevalence, conceptualizations, and the relation between research and practice. *American Educational Research Journal, 35*, 419–454.

Babyak, A. E., Luze, G. J., & Kamps, D. M. (2000). The good student game: Behavior management for diverse classrooms. *Intervention in School and Clinic, 35*, 216–223.

Bandura, A. (1986). *Social foundations of thought and action*. Upper Saddle River, NJ: Prentice-Hall.

Bowers, F. E., McGinnis, J. C., Friman, P. C., & Ervin, R. A. (1999). Merging research and practice: The example of positive peer reporting applied to social rejection. *Education and Treatment of Children, 22*, 218–226.

DuPaul, G. J., Ervin, R. A., Hook, C. L., & McGoey, K. E. (1998). Peer tutoring for children with attention deficit hyperactivity disorder: Effects on classroom behavior and academic performance. *Journal of Applied Behavior Analysis, 31*, 579–592.

Gumpel, T. P., & Frank, R. (1999). An expansion of the peer-tutoring paradigm: Cross-age peer tutoring of social skills among socially rejected boys. *Journal of Applied Behavior Analysis, 32*, 115–118.

Gumpel, T. P., & Golan, H. (2000). Teaching game-playing social skills using a self-monitoring treatment package. *Psychology in the Schools, 37*, 253–261.

Hallenbeck, B. A., & Kauffman, J. M. (1995). How does observational learning affect the behavior of students with emotional or behavioral disorders? A review of research. *The Journal of Special Education, 29*, 45–71.

Kerr, M. M., & Nelson, C. M. (2002). *Strategies for managing behavior problems in the classroom* (4th ed.). Upper Saddle River, NJ: Prentice-Hall.

Lane, K. L. (2004). Academic instruction and tutoring interventions for students with emotional/behavioral disorders: 1990 to the present. In R. B. Rutherford, M. M. Quinn, & S. R. Mathur (Eds.), *Handbook of research in emotional and behavioral disorders* (pp. 462–486). New York: Guilford.

McConaughy, S. H., Kay, P. J., & Fitzgerald, J. (1998). Preventing SED through parent-teacher action research and social skills instruction: First-year outcomes. *Journal of Emotional and Behavioral Disorders, 6*, 81–93.

Presley, J. A., & Hughes, C. (2000). Peers as teachers of anger management to high school students with behavioral disorders. *Behavioral Disorders, 25*, 114–130.

Skinner, C. H., Cashwell, T. H., & Skinner, A. L. (2000). Increasing tootling: The effects of a peer-monitored group contingency program on students' reports of peers' prosocial behaviors. *Psychology in the Schools, 37*, 263–270.

Strayhorn, J., Strain, P. S., & Walker, H. M. (1993). The case for interaction skills training in the context of tutoring as a preventative mental health intervention in the schools. *Behavioral Disorders, 19*, 11–26.

Tobin, T., & Sprague, J. (2000). Alternative education strategies: Reducing violence in school and the community. *Journal of Emotional and Behavioral Disorders, 8*, 177–186.

Utley, C. A., Mortweet, S. L., & Greenwood, C. R. (1997). Peer-mediated instruction and interventions. *Focus on Exceptional Children, 29*(5), 1–23.

Walker, H. M., Ramsey, E., & Gresham, F. M. (2004). *Antisocial behavior in school. Strategies and best practices* (2nd ed.). Pacific Grove, CA: Brooks/Cole.

ENDNOTES

1. See Bandura (1986) and Hallenbeck and Kauffman (1995) for further information on modeling and vicarious effects.
2. See Utley, Mortweet, and Greenwood (1997) for additional description of group contingencies.
3. See Babyak, Luze, and Kamps (2000) for a description of the "Good Behavior Game."
4. See Kerr and Nelson (2002), and Utley, Mortweet, and Greenwood (1997) for details on peer tutoring.
5. See Walker, Ramsey, and Gresham (2004) and Kerr and Nelson (2002) for specific suggestions for teaching social skills.

7 Working with Other Educators

The map is not the territory.
—Alfred Korsbybski

Collaborative arrangements between and among special and general educators is now considered to be an intervention that can be used to create more successful and inclusive classrooms, schools, and school districts. But is this goal justifiable? If so, how do we go about accomplishing it?

Perhaps Korsbybski's quote can help explain the need to examine this issue in a comprehensive manner. This quote is a reminder that a map depicting the physicality of any place provides only a superficial understanding of that place. Even though people are made privy to directions from one location to another within the territory, they are unable to fully appreciate and understand this unfamiliar terrain until they have experienced it socially, culturally, and historically. As time passes, people develop a more substantive awareness of the area and revisit assumptions formulated earlier in their interactions with it. For example, through observation and discourse with more knowledgeable others, individuals learn how the roads, streets, and highways are connected. As a result, the individuals learn more shortcuts, become more efficient, and discover that the quickest route between points A and B may vary depending on the time of day or the day of the week. Perhaps most important, people learn that the shortest route might not always be the best route.

Landmarks further assist people in their attempts to negotiate new surroundings. Maps only reveal the geographic location of a locality, but continued interaction with the locality and its inhabitants who exist within it provides the newcomer with richer descriptions of past occurrences that have shaped the present and will influence the future (e.g., consensus, conflict, boundary shifts, and redistribution of power). In turn, this knowledge influences how the newcomer will function in the new environment (e.g., how he or she will react to "Based on what I've been told, it's dangerous to frequent this section after dark, especially if you're alone"). And then, just when the newcomer thinks he or she knows everything there is to know, when there appear to be no more unanswered questions or contradictions, he or she views the territory from a different stance and the cyclical, developmental learning process begins anew. Deeper understandings ensue, we hope. However, failure to move beyond the superficiality of the map will thwart the emergence of a deeper, more contextual understanding of the territory. Growth is stifled, and much is lost.

Interestingly, we can use Korsbybski's idea to think about the collaborative process in schools, especially collaboration designed to achieve more inclusive environments for students with disabilities. In many instances, school personnel who undertake such endeavors believe that, in short order, a common vision will lead to mutually satisfying relationships and desired outcomes for their students and themselves. All that's needed is two or more "like-minded" individuals who plan, teach, and evaluate together. Soon after the initiation of collaborative yet linear activities, students' behaviors will improve immensely; their levels of achievement will soar; parents, administrators, and policymakers will be pleased; and teachers will honor and value the importance of collaboration. Mass replication will follow, and all will be right with the world!

Unfortunately, this belief could not be farther from the truth. Collaboration entails much more than presumed common visions and sustained efforts. Moreover, addressing academic and behavioral problems at the classroom level *only* may not result in efficacious and sustained school and districtwide reforms. Effective collaboration entails a more complex process that is developmental, interactive, evaluative, and cyclical. Furthermore, the degree to which participants achieve mutual goals will depend largely on their ability to engage in honest, interactive, and constructive problem solving that is both process and outcome driven.[1]

Of course, there is no right or wrong way to create and sustain collaborative communities. The way groups go about problem solving is based largely on individual perspectives (including individual histories) and the interaction of these individual perspectives within the collaborative community. However, there are models and processes that can be adapted, refined, and transformed within different contexts that may result in sustained and effective problem-solving practices. As evidenced in the Du Bois Elementary School vignette, help from outside sources may lead to a deeper and richer understanding of the map and the territory, and provide more opportunities for all community members to grow. So, we ask: Why go it alone?

Based on the vignette, it appears that these educators have adopted a problem-solving approach that views the collaborative process in a broad context, views problems as a means for growth, and uses past decisions and actions to inform present and

Du Bois Elementary School has been recognized for its exemplary cooperative teaching model. The teachers and the principal, Jim Davidson, believe this recognition is due to the excellent teaching that takes place between Latisha (the special education collaborative teacher) and her colleagues, and the ongoing communication and support that exists among the teachers, the principal, and the two lower-level central office staff who support general and special education collaboration at the district level. In a joint interview, Latisha, Bill (a third-grade collaborative teacher), and Jim stated that they have been able to solve problems that thwarted their efforts to sustain an effective cooperative teaching model. Interestingly enough, though, mutually constructed solutions have often led to the emergence of new contradictions, tensions, and disruptions. According to Jim, "The process is cyclical. No relationship develops without problems—it's just a part of life. Despite your best efforts, new problems always show up and the only way to solve them is to see them as opportunities for growth and face them head on. We spend a lot of time planning and talking, sometimes arguing, around here. It's healthy, though, because we know that this is the only way we can resolve problems and keep things moving the way we want them to."

"That's so true," responded Latisha. "One of the problems in the beginning was that my LD students were spread out among all teachers on a certain grade level. For example, the seven LD students who are now all in Bill's class this year were disbursed between all four second-grade teachers. This made it virtually impossible for me to work collaboratively with all four teachers, teach my resource program in the afternoon, and serve as a member of the prereferral and child study teams. We talked to Bill about this and he set up meetings with me, the general educators I work with, and Stacy and Kim, our central office facilitators. After a few meetings of establishing clear goals and outcomes and some healthy arguing and debating, we agreed to try placing all my kids in one classroom per grade level."

"Yeah," chimed in Bill, "and remember how we thought this solution would work like a charm? Actually, things did work great when you were in the room with me."

"Uh-huh, it's good that we can look back and laugh about it now, even as we try to solve this new problem," said Latisha. "We have learned so much from working with each other. I know I really got comfortable teaching a larger group of students and really got a handle on using the whole language approach. Most of my methods' classes focused on direct instruction."

At this point Bill sat up in his chair and shared excitedly what he had learned from his colleague. "And I learned so much about b-mod, strategy instruction, social skills instruction, and instructional modifications. I'd never heard of this wonderful stuff. Before we started teaching together, your kids came in from resource and I was totally clueless about how to help them continue using these skills in my classroom. Actually, I didn't even know you were teaching them these skills and that was such a shame because, as you now know, many of my unlabeled kids needed them big time. Now, I use them with the whole class—and it's funny, I don't feel like just a third-grade teacher any more. I'm also beginning to feel like a special education teacher."

Jim chimed in at this point. "Umm, interesting you should say that, Bill, 'cause I've been thinking the same thing lately. Sometimes when I observe you guys, I have to stop and think about who is the LD teacher and who is the gen-ed teacher. The lines are getting blurry and I think this is good. Still, I remember when you came into my office and plopped down in that chair right over there as if you'd been working at a sawmill cutting lumber all day."

"Hey man, don't remind me," said Bill. "Like I said before, things were great when Latisha was in the room with me because we planned, divided responsibilities, taught, and evaluated together. BUT, when she left to team with another teacher or to do the gazillion other things she does...man...things started getting a bit out of hand. Honest to goodness, sometimes I felt like I wasn't doing a good job for *any* of the kids. There were just too many kids functioning at too many different levels. Because of this, there were lots more behavior problems that also influenced academic performance."

"So now we're trying to solve *this* problem by looking at what we've done in the past and figuring out how to refine and modify things to make it better," Latisha added.

future decisions and actions. However, despite this problem-solving process, dilemmas emerged that could not be resolved by anyone at the school level without the support of higher-level central office administrators. For example, Jim believed that higher-level central office administrators didn't know enough about the effectiveness of the model and would therefore not be able to help with administrative problems that went beyond his jurisdiction. This belief proved to be prophetic. The program was so effective that the LD rolls and special education referrals dropped significantly until the school no longer qualified for a full-time LD teacher. Central office administrators would not bend the rules, even in light of the positive outcomes for teachers and students, and Latisha was transferred to another school. Less than a year later, the referral rate increased significantly and a half-time LD teacher was hired who found it difficult to run the program. Consequently, this program, like so many other successful school initiatives, was discontinued. It became merely a speck on the map, abandoned territory that was easily overlooked and bypassed despite its immense value and potential.

Questions for Reflection

So, what contributed to the demise of this program? Reflect on this question as you read about collaboration and the three collaborative models presented in this chapter. In addition, think about other questions you need to ask when engaged in collaborative work at the classroom, school, or district level. These questions may include but are not limited to:

- When do I need to seek assistance from colleagues?
- How might I work with others to solve problems?
- What are some of the principles that can guide collaborative work?
- What specific processes can be used to implement and evaluate collaborative work?

When do I need to seek assistance from colleagues?

You may follow the steps we have presented in the first six chapters of this book and still find that you are unable to handle behavior problems to your satisfaction. For example, as a teacher, administrator, or school psychologist, you may have analyzed the problem, and used behavior modification strategies such as positive reinforcement and extinction, contracts, or modified instruction to address circumstances that might lead to inappropriate behaviors. One can see from the vignette that the collaborative community has engaged in effective problem-solving practices. They addressed the problem created by placing students with learning disabilities across different grade-level classrooms. However, this organizational change resulted in the emergence of another problem: Bill found himself overwhelmed with such a heterogeneous group of students when Latisha was not in the room. Even though Bill is extremely frustrated by this situation, he is very empathic toward his students and desires to help them optimally. Latisha (special educator), Jim (principal), and Stacy and Kim (lower-level central office personnel) also support him. These factors indicate that the time is ripe for this community to continue its collaborative work.

Currently, several different models of collegial support are being implemented in schools. These include (1) consultation, (2) collaborative teaching (CT), and (3) intervention assistance teams (IATs). We present definitions, a brief description of the models, existing research, and more specific information about the general collaborative process in the next two sections.

How might I work with others to solve problems?

In this section, we define and describe the three collaborative models identified above. We present these models from a developmental perspective, starting with the classroom level and moving to the schoolwide or district level. However, we strongly recommend that educators attempt to move toward more expansive models that extend beyond the classroom, placing collaborative efforts within the context of school- and districtwide reforms. From this standpoint, all participants—including school personnel from the district to the classroom level, parents, communities, and outside agencies—should be engaged in the collaborative process. If building level and central office administrators are not interested, a more individualized, classroom-by-classroom model is much better than no plan at all. However, use of these models within the broader context of the districtwide collaborative work may result in more sustained, widespread, and effective practices.[2]

Expert and Collaborative Consultation.   In an expert consultative relationship, a consultant with expertise in a given area is assigned to work with teachers who are experiencing problems with students in these areas. A collaborative consultative relationship is similar to an expert consultative relationship; the major difference is that both the consultant and the consultee may take on expert roles.[3] Both approaches may be used to address commonly identified problems within schools and across school districts. Beginning with an iterative process (restating the problem until it is clear), the consultant helps plan interventions to the extent desired by other educators who are seeking assistance. The consultant and the consultee meet to monitor and modify the interventions that are implemented. The result should be resolution of the problem or the realization that other steps need to be taken to handle the problem adequately (e.g., direct administrative and/or parent involvement). Also, the process is designed to improve the skills and the problem-solving repertoire of the consultees so that they may use the strategies in the future when similar problems arise with other students. In an expert consultative relationship, a consultant with expertise in testing might teach consultees how to modify tests for students with reading or writing problems. On the other hand, there is more parity and reciprocity in a collaborative consultative relationship. The consultant facilitates the sharing of expertise among consultees to address the issue of test modifications and adaptations.[4]

Collaborative Teaching.   In collaborative teaching, also referred to as *cooperative teaching*, teams divide responsibilities according to the strengths and weaknesses of individual teachers. In many cases, pairs are created so that regular classroom teachers can work cooperatively with special education teachers. In this way, the teachers plan and teach the academic curriculum to all students within the general education classroom. Collaborative teaching can be implemented based on at least three different arrangements—team teaching, complementary teaching, and supportive learning activities.[5] *Team teaching* occurs when the general and special educators alternate their presentation of segments of a lesson, with the nonteaching educator monitoring student performance or behavior. *Complementary instruction* allows the regular educator to maintain the primary responsibility for teaching the academic curriculum, while the special educator teaches the organizational and study skills necessary for students to master the material. *Supportive learning activities* are devised by the special educator to provide students with practice activities based on the skills presented by the regular educator. As illustrated in the vignette, sometimes these different types of collaborative teaching arrangements might all be used in one classroom.

Research on collaborative teaching has revealed inconclusive results. However, findings reveal characteristics and actions that promote or hinder the development of collaborative teaching models that improve academic and behavioral outcomes for students with disabilities significantly. For example, teachers report that administrative support, voluntary involvement, ownership, common planning times, attention to process, and training in problem solving and conflict resolution contribute to growth for students and teachers.[6]

Intervention Assistance Teams.   Intervention assistance teams (IATs)—sometimes called *prereferral teams (PRTs)*, *child study teams (CSTs)*, *teacher assistance teams (TATS)*, or *school-based teams (SBTs)*—are comprised of educators who function as problem-solving units that provide ongoing assistance to referring teachers. In some instances, these teams do not fulfill any requirements set forth by federal and state mandates to provide special education services to students who qualify. However, in other instances, they are used to address the requirement of IDEA that prior to special education referral, adequate interventions have been tried to meet students' behavioral and academic problems without special education intervention.

One review of the literature on intervention assistance programs found that two approaches predominated: TATs and PRTs.[7] However, the results of studies on both approaches have been inconclusive. Teacher assistance teams are designed to provide immediate support to teachers whose students are not performing at expected levels prior to, during, or after assessment for special education.[8] Participants responding to questionnaires and surveys have reported critical factors that influenced the effectiveness of TATs, such as administrative support and characteristics of team members. Barriers to TATs include inadequate planning time, insufficient intervention strategies, and insufficient problem-solving skills.[9]

Prereferral teams were developed to satisfy the requirement of IDEA that implementation of interventions such as modifications and adaptations must be documented prior to an assessment for special education placement. This model is supposedly more systematic and structured and focuses more on expert consultation delivered by ancillary personnel and administrators. In cases where implementation of PRTs has been considered effective, participants reported that there was a significant decrease in testing for special education assessment, and significant increases in the number of PRT cases and in student achievement. School psychologists and teachers of children with learning disabilities trained in consultation for prereferral interventions were a part of the PRT in these studies. Barriers to the implementation of PRTs include lack of administrative support, lack of fiscal and human resources, insufficient time for meeting and planning, and resistance to the use of nontraditional assessment processes and expert consultative practices.[10] In addition—and consistent with research on TATs—the efficacy of PRTs has mostly been determined through self-report data with little documentation of student outcomes.

What are some of the principles that can guide collaborative work?

As already noted, research on collaboration has yielded mixed results. Moreover, much of this work has not examined the processes used to implement and sustain collaborative initiatives and how these processes affect student outcomes. In addition, most researchers have focused on collaborative relationships between teachers. Few studies have explored how collaborative teaching is influenced by forces outside the classroom (e.g., federal, state, and local guidelines; school agendas; school district policies; parental influence; support from central office; the ability to engage in critical problem-solving across all levels within a school system). For these reasons, in this section, we do not provide lists of separate processes for each of the models presented here. Instead, we provide a general framework that can guide educators who are interested in creating effective collaborative communities from the classroom level to the central office level.[11]

Context, History, and Problem Solving. Two of the most important things to remember about collaborative work are that it does not occur in a vacuum, nor does it have a beginning, middle, or end. Rather, it is an ongoing, cyclical process that should always be changing and evolving over time. There are many, many complex factors that predict whether a collaborative initiation will thrive or constrict.[12] Three such factors can be viewed as principles that can guide collaborative work. These include context, history, and problem solving. We return to the vignette to illustrate how these factors influence collaborative processes and outcomes.

Context.   Understanding of context is critical to the growth and sustainment of a collaborative community. When considering how best to serve students with disabilities in inclusive classrooms, personnel must not focus attention solely on the children. Instead, analysis of the situation should view the child within the context of the entire community. If not, it is quite possible to develop a "blame the victim" mentality where school failure is mainly the result of deficits within the child with little or no analysis of the environment *surrounding* the child. Now, think about Latisha, Bill, and Jim. In order to meet the needs of all their students more effectively, they had to consider many aspects of the environment. For instance, Jim had to change the master schedule of the entire school and place students with disabilities in one class per grade level so that Latisha would have the time to collaborate with all general/inconclusive education teachers. Even though these changes created another problem, the sustained focus on the environment as well as the students' well-being kept the teachers, their principal, and the central office support staff engaged and committed. They did not give up on themselves or their students. Unfortunately, however, for whatever reason they were unable to include the higher-level central office administrators in their collaborative community.

History.   There is an inscription in a Washington, DC, museum that reads, "Past is prologue." The past influences both the present and the future. Although it is not beneficial to dwell on the past in ways that paralyze individuals or communities, it is important to study the past to identify patterns that may lead to the growth of a community. In other words, how can you know where you are going if you don't understand from where you have come? From this standpoint, when engaged in collaborative work it is extremely important to reflect on personal histories of individual members, and the collective, longitudinal history of the community. Once again, we use the vignette to illustrate this point. When Latisha and Bill began their work together, they did not begin collaborative teaching immediately. The first thing they did was to have talks about their beliefs about teaching and learning, their similarities, and their differences. Also, they observed each other for about a week prior to teaching together in the same room. As they worked together, confidentiality became one of their rules. As Latisha stated, "I needed to know that if I made a mistake, I would not hear about it from another teacher in the teachers' lounge." This process, they said, helped them build a trust that also allowed them to be more critical with each other in respectful ways.

As they continued to work together, Bill and Latisha began sharing stories about prior experiences, even their school experiences as children. They believed that this sharing of history helped them understand the rationale behind actions, especially those that didn't appear to be compatible. Before responding in a negative way, they began to think about how their respective histories might have influenced thoughts and actions. Bill stated, "I still might disagree with the way Latisha does things, but understanding the *why* behind her actions helps us to first identify *common ground* that might lead to more effective interventions based on what we both bring to the situation." As they continued this process, they could begin to identify patterns in behavior that contributed to growth for them and their students. For example, sharing of histories revealed that Latisha was more skilled in teacher-directed instruction, strategy instruction, and social skills. Bill, on the other hand, was more informed about process-oriented approaches, such as whole language. Gradually, as they shared perspectives and skills through discussion, modeling, and evaluation, they found themselves borrowing from each other. As Jim said, the distinction between who was the special educator and the general educator began to fade.

Problems and Disagreements Just Might Lead to Growth.   Do you find it difficult to confront family members and friends? Do you hate to hurt others' feelings even when you disagree with them? If this is the case, then you may find it quite difficult to work with colleagues collaboratively when problems arise. Three questions to ask in this vein include:

- How do you and I view problems and conflicts that threaten the sustainment of effective collaborative relationships?
- Are problems viewed as sources for growth or signals of impending deterioration of a collaborative community?
- Do you and I expect problems to be solved immediately without consideration of the complexities involved in schooling?

Answers to these questions will, to some degree, predict the degree to which a collaborative community will be sustained in ways that benefit educators, parents, and students. If problems are viewed as insurmountable or if community members find it difficult to identify and address points of conflict in diplomatic yet authentic ways, then there is little hope that a community will grow and survive. The same holds true if the community is afraid of problems, or if problems are seen as being somehow "bad" or something to be avoided at all costs. Finally, if the community sees problems within a narrow framework, the teachers may not be able to handle all problems that might arise. Problems are almost always connected to and influenced by people, things, and conflicts outside the community.

Once again, our vignette provides a very good example of how your answers to the above questions will influence the success of your collaborative community. Through their problem-solving approach, these educators were able to restructure the master schedule to allow Latisha to co-teach with her general education colleagues each day. However, this solution led to another problem: Bill found it difficult to meet the needs of all the students when Latisha was not in the room. At the end of the vignette, these three educators were gearing up to revisit and evaluate prior decisions and activities to determine what alternatives might be implemented to address the latest conflict. This conflict could not be addressed at the school level.

However, central office and state guidelines were in place that regulated special education class sizes and teacher-student ratios. Even though central office workers Stacy and Kim provided assistance through seminars, courses, and sharing what was happening across the county, they had no control over enforcement of special education regulations. This reality rendered these educators powerless when the learning disabilities roll dropped below the number needed to maintain a full-time special education teacher.

Based on this situation, you can see clearly that conflicts with a collaborative community never go away and that continual, cyclical problem solving is necessary. Now that we have provided these three guiding principles, we provide more specific information about this process.

What specific processes can be used to implement and evaluate collaborative work?

A Collaborative Framework.   As we mentioned in the beginning of this chapter, when groups come together to engage in collaborative work, they often think that each person's definition of the work, the targets, the goals and objectives are the same or at least similar. Not too long after the work starts, individuals and clusters within the community realize that definitions of common terms are *not* the same. In fact, they may be extremely incompatible. This in turn gives way to tensions and conflicts among community members. For instance, it did not take Bill and Latisha long to determine that their ideas about instructional models were very different. In their case, however, the time spent observing and talking minimized the emergence of insurmountable problems. Often, however, this may not be the case.[13] Sometimes members of a collaborative community never address incompatible visions and beliefs and end up either disbanding or implementing their programs in contrived and superficial ways.

Before beginning collaborative work, community members really need to establish a mutual understanding of how the three principles of context, history, and problem solving will be applied in their setting. After this stage, it is time to develop a cyclical problem-solving framework that will guide the work of the community. This framework is not stagnant. In fact, it should always be changing and evolving as a deeper understanding of the patterns that lead to growth or deterioration of their community emerges. The following questions must be answered continually as the community engages in collaborative problem solving:

- Who are we and why are we here?
- Who are we trying to help?
- What are our outcomes for those we are trying to help?
- What tools are we going to use to accomplish our outcomes?
- What are the rules that will guide our work?
- Who, within and outside the classroom, might help us accomplish outcomes?
- Who is going to do what?

Figure 7.1 provides a graphic representation of how the framework might be applied. Once again, we use the vignette to help make the connection between the theoretical framework and actual application. First, we see that the collaborative community is made up of the teachers and administrators who represent the group that is attempting to make a difference in the lives of students with and without disabilities served in general education classrooms. Some of the outcomes of the collaborative group include being able to (1) serve students with disabilities to the fullest extent possible in classrooms with their nonlabeled peers, (2) improve social and academic skills of all students, (3) create ways to include others who might contribute to accomplishment of goals, and (4) develop collaborative processes that promote trust and growth for everyone involved. Tools used to accomplish these outcomes include (1) strategy instruction, (2) social skills instruction, (3) direct instruction, (4) process-oriented instruction, (5) frequent discussion, and (6) frequent evaluation of the process and student outcomes. So far, one can see that two of the rules of the community are honesty and confidentiality. Those who might contribute to accomplishment of goals and outcomes include (1) state department of education staff, (2) lower- and higher-level central office administrators, and (3) parents. The higher-level central office administrators made top-down decisions with little input from Stacy and Kim. However, it appears that members of the collaborative community at Du Bois engaged in more lateral and dynamic decision.

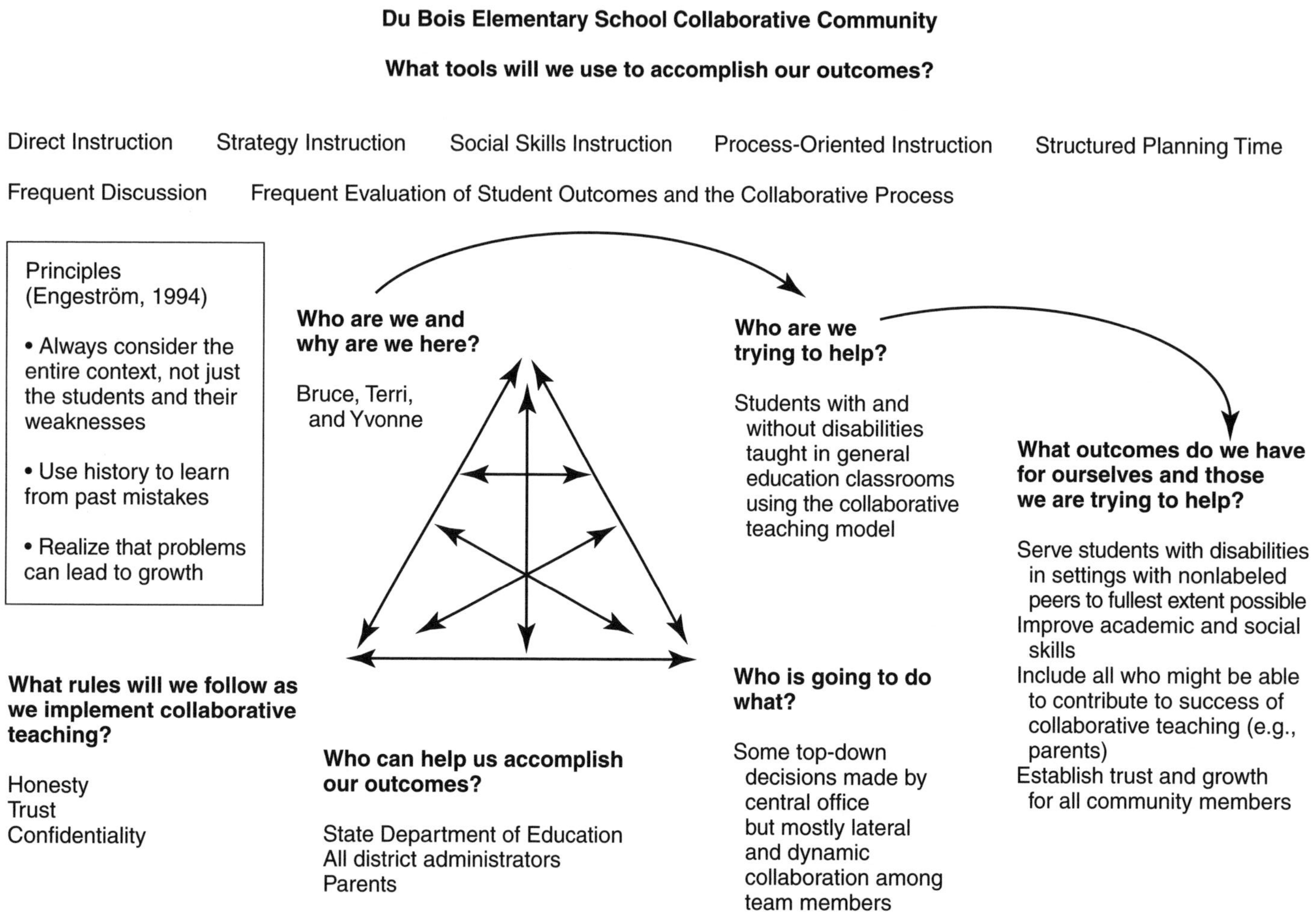

Du Bois Elementary School Collaborative Community

What tools will we use to accomplish our outcomes?

Direct Instruction   Strategy Instruction   Social Skills Instruction   Process-Oriented Instruction   Structured Planning Time

Frequent Discussion   Frequent Evaluation of Student Outcomes and the Collaborative Process

Principles
(Engeström, 1994)

• Always consider the entire context, not just the students and their weaknesses

• Use history to learn from past mistakes

• Realize that problems can lead to growth

Who are we and why are we here?

Bruce, Terri, and Yvonne

What rules will we follow as we implement collaborative teaching?

Honesty
Trust
Confidentiality

Who can help us accomplish our outcomes?

State Department of Education
All district administrators
Parents

Who are we trying to help?

Students with and without disabilities taught in general education classrooms using the collaborative teaching model

Who is going to do what?

Some top-down decisions made by central office but mostly lateral and dynamic collaboration among team members

What outcomes do we have for ourselves and those we are trying to help?

Serve students with disabilities in settings with nonlabeled peers to fullest extent possible

Improve academic and social skills

Include all who might be able to contribute to success of collaborative teaching (e.g., parents)

Establish trust and growth for all community members

FIGURE 7.1   The Collaborative Community

Once again, one mark of a successful collaborative community will be constant revision of these original components in ways that contribute to accomplishment of goals. The example, in this instance, is the continual focus on grouping arrangements. At the end of the vignette, the community was engaged in problem-solving to address the issue of too many students with disabilities in one classroom.

Now that we have provided a framework to guide collaborative work, we end this chapter with a four-step, cyclical problem-solving approach that will further contribute to the success of a collaborative community.

A Cyclical, Iterative Approach to Problem Solving.   The following four-step process can be used in a cyclical, iterative manner to solve problems more effectively within a collaborative community. We present the process in Figure 7.2 and also provide explanations of how the process works.

1. *Make past and current practices visible.*   As they engaged in problem solving, the collaborative community in the vignette was constantly engaged in identifying successes and failures. As they discussed their circumstances regularly, they identified the patterns in thinking and behavior that either helped or detracted from accomplishment of outcomes. This may be done using flowcharts and diagrams that show the history of the community in linear progression.

2. *Try to identify past patterns that have either contributed to growth or stifled collaborative work and accomplishment of goals and outcomes.*   As they worked to accomplish goals, Latisha and her colleagues realized that putting all the students with disabilities in one classroom provided more time for her to work with all students. Another pattern that

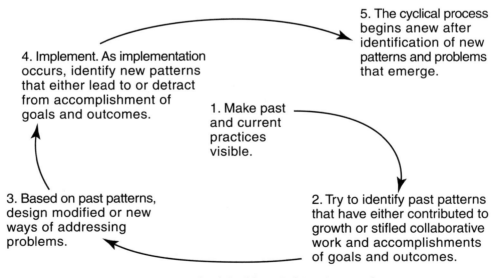

FIGURE 7.2   The Four-Step, Cyclical Problem-Solving Approach

stifled growth was failure to include higher-level central office administrators in the implementation of *every* phase of design and implementation.

3. *Based on past patterns, design revised ways of going about collaborative work.*   However, another problem emerged. The general education teachers were not nearly as effective when Latisha was not in the room. Rather than continuing this pattern, by the end of the vignette the team was engaged in problem solving to address this new concern. Unfortunately, they did not think about how outside forces might affect the sustainment of their work.

4. *As implementation occurs, identify new patterns that either lead to or detract from accomplishment of goals and outcomes.*   We do not know how this community addressed the new grouping problem that emerged. However, we see that, unfortunately, failure to address the expanded communication and input resulted in discontinuation of this successful program. We leave you with this question: What could the team have done that might have resulted in continuation and growth of their collaborative model?

Summary

Teachers possess expertise and knowledge that make them well suited to work collaboratively with one another to solve problems they encounter in the classroom. However, collaborative work at the classroom level cannot be viewed in isolation from outside factors that will influence effectiveness. Teachers may be able to solve problems while implementing inclusive education models without outside assistance, but there will come a time when they will be unable to address certain roadblocks to effective practices. Researchers have determined that it is best to examine collaborative outcomes within the framework of school and school district outcomes. In so doing, practitioners must develop processes derived from their needs, including the needs of their students, when engaged in collaborative work.

Within this realm, educators should look closely at the total context (not just students in isolation), study the patterns from the past that affect accomplishment of outcomes, and develop cyclical approaches to problem solving. As the vignette showed, this framework will not ensure success and sustainment of a collaborative community. However, it can increase the likelihood that outcomes will be achieved. In this way, not only will students make gains but also adults in the community will learn to collaborate in ways that promote integration of knowledge and skills, supported practice, and sustained professional development. Within each of the models described, care must be taken to include administrators, parents, and students in the development and implementation stages. Moreover, *none of the models should be used as administrative structures that are created to deny special services to students who are disabled.*

Finally, teachers, consultants, and administrators must realize that, to a large degree, program effectiveness will depend on the amount of time allocated for planning, the resources provided by administrators (e.g., fiscal, material, human), and continual evaluation. Also, all members within the collaborative community must realize the importance of analyzing thinking and actions historically and iteratively, and understand that problems can lead to growth.

REFERENCES AND RESOURCES FOR FURTHER STUDY

The following references provided the basis for many of our statements in this chapter. You may wish to consult selected references for additional information on specific topics.

Ainscow, M. (1999). *Understanding the development of inclusive schools: Studies in inclusive education.* Philadelphia, PA: Falmer Press.

Baker, E. T., Wang, M. C., & Walberg, H. J. (1995). The effects of inclusion on learning. *Educational Leadership, 52*(4), 33–35.

Baker, J. M., & Zigmond, N. (1995). The meaning and practice of inclusion for students with learning disabilities: Themes and implications from the five cases. *The Journal of Special Education, 29,* 163–180.

Bauwens, J., & Hourcade, J. J. (1995). *Cooperative teaching: Rebuilding the schoolhouse for all students.* Austin, TX: Pro-Ed.

Bruskewitz, R. (1998). Collaborative intervention: A system of support for teachers attempting to meet the needs of students with challenging behavior. *Preventing School Failure, 42,* 129–134.

Chalfant, J., Pysh, V., & Moultrie, R. (1979). Teacher assistance teams: A model for within-building problem-solving. *Learning Disability Quarterly, 2,* 85–96.

Cheney, D. (1998). Using action research as a collaborative process to enhance educators' and families' knowledge and skills for youth with emotional or behavioral disorders. *Preventing School Failure, 42,* 88–93.

Engeström, Y. (1994). Teachers as collaborative thinkers: Activity-theoretical study of an innovative teacher team. In I. Carlgren, G. Handal, & S. Vaage (Eds.), *Teachers' minds and actions: Research on teachers' thinking and practice* (pp. 43–61). Washington, DC: Falmer.

Fleming, J. L., & Monda-Amaya, L. E. (2001). Process variables critical for team effectiveness: A Delphi study of wraparound team members. *Remedial and Special Education, 22*(3), 158–171.

Friend, M., & Cook, L. (2000). *Interactions: Collaboration skills for school professionals* (3rd ed.). New York: Longman.

Fullan, M. (1999). *Change forces: The sequel.* Philadelphia, PA: Falmer.

Gerber, P. J., & Popp, P. A. (1999). Consumer perspectives on the collaborative teaching model: Views of students with and without LD and their parents. *Remedial and Special Education, 20,* 288–296.

Hargreaves, A., & Wignall, R. (1989). *Time for the teacher: A study of collegial relations and preparation time use among elementary teachers* (Final research report funded by Transfer Grant No. 51/1020). Toronto: Department of Educational Administration, Ontario Institute for Studies in Education.

Heflin, L. J., & Bullock, L. M. (1999). Inclusion of students with emotional/behavioral disorders: A survey of teachers in general and special education. *Preventing School Failure, 43,* 103–111.

Heron, T. E., & Harris, K. C. (2001). *The educational consultant: Helping professionals, parents, and students in inclusive classrooms* (4th ed.). Austin, TX: Pro -Ed.

Huberman, M. (1993). The model of the independent artisan in teachers' professional relations. In J. W. Little & M. W. McLaughlin (Eds.), *Teachers' work: Individuals, colleagues, and contexts* (pp. 11–50). New York: Teachers College Press.

Hudson, P., & Glomb, N. (1997). If it takes two to tango, then why not teach both partners to dance? Collaboration instruction for all educators. *Journal of Learning Disabilities, 30,* 442–448.

Idol, L. (2002). *Creative collaborative and inclusive schools.* Austin, TX: Pro-Ed.

Little, J. W., & McLaughlin, M. W. (Eds.). (1993). *Teachers' work: Individuals, colleagues, and contexts.* New York: Teachers College Press.

O'Shea, D. J., & O'Shea, L. J. (1997). Collaboration and school reform: A twenty-first-century perspective. *Journal of Learning Disabilities, 30,* 449–462.

Pugach, M. C., & Johnson, L. J. (2002). *Collaborative practice, collaborative schools* (2nd ed.) Denver, CO: Love.

Rogoff, B., Baker-Sennett, J., Lacasa, P., & Goldsmith, D. (1995). Development through participation in sociocultural activity. *New Directions for Child Development, 67,* 45–65.

Safran, S. P., & Safran, J. S. (1996). Serving "students at risk": Training professionals to collaborate in teams. *Journal of Learning Disabilities, 6,* 363–369.

Salend, S. J, & Duhaney, M. G. (2000). Parental perceptions of inclusive education placements. *Remedial and Special Education, 21*(2), 121–128.

Sawyer, R. K. (2004). Creative teaching: Collaborative discussion as disciplined improvisation. *Educational Researcher, 33*(2), 12–20.

Tharp, R. G., Estrada, P., Dolton, S. S., & Yamauchi, L. A. (2000). *Teaching transformed: Achieving excellence, fairness, inclusion, and harmony.* Boulder, CO: Westview Press.

Trent, S. C. (1992). *Collaboration between special educators and regular educators: A cross case analysis.* Unpublished doctoral dissertation, University of Virginia, Charlottesville.

Trent, S. C. (1998). False starts and other dilemmas of a secondary general education collaborative teacher: A case study. *Journal of Learning Disabilities, 31,* 503–513.

Trent, S. C., Artiles, A. J., Fitchett-Bazemore, K., McDaniel, L., & Coleman-Sorrell, A. (2002). Addressing ethics, power, and privilege in inclusive classrooms in urban schools: A cultural-historical approach. *Teacher Education and Special Education, 25*(1) 11–22.

Trent, S. C., Driver, B. L., Wood, M. H., Parrott, P. S., Martin, T. F., & Smith, W. G. (2003). Creating and sustaining a special education/general education partnership: A story of evolution, change, and uncertainty. *Teaching and Teacher Education, 19,* 203–219.

Zigmond, N., & Baker, J. (1995). Concluding comments: Current and future practices in inclusive schooling. *The Journal of Special Education, 29,* 245–250.

ENDNOTES

1. See Fullan (1999) and Little and McLaughlin (1993) for further discussion.
2. See Fullan (1999).
3. See Trent (1998) for further information on consultative relationships.
4. Heron and Harris (2001) provide further details.
5. See Friend and Cook (2000).
6. See Fleming and Monda-Amaya (2001), Hargreaves and Wignall (1989), Pugach and Johnson (2002), and Trent et al. (2002) for more discussion on collaborative teaching.
7. See Safran and Safran (1996).
8. Teacher assistance teams are discussed by Chalfont, Pysh, and Moultrie (1979).
9. See Safran and Safran (1996).
10. See Safran and Safran (1996) for further discussion.
11. Rogoff et al. (1995) discuss collaborative communities.
12. Engeström (1994) gives details on predicting the outcomes of collaborative initiation.
13. See Huberman (1993).

CHAPTER

8 Working with Parents and Families

Parents and families play a critical role in the education of students with disabilities. Some make it their business to remain actively involved in their child's education; others appear to relinquish control to educators. In any case, as a teacher, it is your responsibility to make every effort to involve parents in the education of their children. "The involvement of parents in the education of their children is of unquestionable significance. Scores of studies indicate that student achievement increases as parents become more involved in their children's education."[1] You *can* help students improve their behavior in school, but without parent support and collaboration in the intervention, the behavior changes will be school-specific and will not generalize to other settings.[2] Consider the experiences of teachers Sadie and Marie in the vignette.

There is general agreement about the importance of involving families of students with disabilities, but there are few guidelines for accomplishing this goal. This transitional, multicultural nation often demands that teachers and parents from different ethnic backgrounds, different races, different socioeconomic backgrounds, or those with vastly different values collaborate for the improvement of students. "We either don't know how or don't consider it important to admit to and examine our prejudices about these many differences. Without this self-realization, we may inadvertently make a mess of our attempts to collaborate with parents."[3] No wonder some teachers would rather perform odious chores than meet with parents. One colleague who was to meet

135

Sadie

Mrs. Hecht had three boys, all of them kids with mild mental retardation and every one of them a serious behavior problem in school. Roger, the youngest, was in my class. I was pretty successful in dealing with his behavior in my classroom, and I didn't feel a particular need to get his mother involved, other than through the usual notes home and an occasional phone contact. I knew she herself had had serious problems in school, and my guess was that she had about the same level of intellectual ability as her sons. She was a single parent and very hard working. When I arranged to meet her in my classroom at 7:45 one morning (the only time she could come to the school because of her work) so that she could sign Roger's IEP, I had no idea what I was in for. As soon as I put the IEP in front of her, she started sobbing uncontrollably. This took me completely by surprise, and I had no idea what she was crying about until, after a few minutes, she pulled herself together enough to say between sobs, "I just don't know what I've done, I just don't know how I've hurt my boys so. They're all so messed up, and I know it's my fault, but I just don't know what I've done. . . . " She really went on and on about how guilty she felt for having three boys with such terrible problems—not able to get along with other kids, failing in school, driving her crazy at home, and so on. I ended up feeling terribly sorry for her, crying along with her, and trying to reassure her that it wasn't her fault. But I really didn't think it was fair for me to have to deal with this. I mean, I'm not a psychologist or a counselor, I'm just her kid's teacher! Besides, I don't know how she might have actually contributed to her boys' problems. Maybe reassurance wasn't what I should have offered. I don't know. It was really an upsetting experience for me.

Marie

Rusty Farmer was one of the most violent young students I've seen in my 15 years of teaching. At age 8, he exhibited very serious aggression in my classroom. He hit other children, he hit me, he threw things—I was concerned about other children in the class being hurt seriously by him. Since the beginning of the school year, I had dealt with his taunting of classmates until they hit him and then pummelling them in return; his attacking me with his fists and feet; his sweeping everything off other children's desk and throwing such items as books and pencil boxes; his overturning desks and throwing chairs. I had not been able to engage Rusty's mother in a serious conversation about his behavior, partly because she seemed to have a sullen disposition and partly because she cared for several neighbors' young children and didn't seem to have time to talk. However, Mrs. Farmer, who was 24, seemed quite approachable to me and to be seriously concerned about Rusty's behavior. I thought I'd have a good chance of getting her help in dealing with Rusty's aggression. When I finally reached her and explained my concern about Rusty's violence toward adults and other children, her exact words to me were, "He don't give me no problems like that at home. I don't know why you folks let him do that to you at school. He don't try none of that kind of stuff with me no more. Don't you let him rear up like that on you, no ma'am! I don't put up with none of that at home, and I don't want you to put up with it at school neither. You just knock him on his ass. That's what I do with him, I just haul off and knock him right on his ass if I see him doublin' up his fist or somethin'. He deserves it when he acts like that!" What could I say? I was dumbfounded. And what was I to do now?

with a difficult parent commented that she would rather clean the toilets in the boys' bathroom than meet with this parent! When asked why, she remarked that even though cleaning toilets was nasty, she knew that she could do it competently. She said she wasn't sure whether she could have "the collaborative, supportive parent/teacher conference the school system expects with the reincarnation of the Wicked Witch of the West." Depicting a parent as a witch during lunchtime conversation is something we don't recommend, but we also know that this parent had a reputation in the school system for antagonizing school personnel, and that the administration had not offered any guidelines and precious little support for dealing with this parent. (Even the principal was afraid of the parent, called the WWW!) This parent had fought hard and long to get some of the needed special education services for her child. She came to school ready to rumble, and we're not sure that we blame her.

Questions for Reflection

Clearly, you might consider a wide variety of questions about the most appropriate roles of parents and teachers and various strategies for working productively with parents. We have organized our discussion around these essential questions:

- Why should I involve parents and families?
- Who are the parents of my students?
- What are my prejudices?
- What is the reciprocity of parent-child interaction?
- What are the school guidelines for communicating with parents?
- When should I involve parents, especially parents of tough kids?
- In what ways can I involve parents and families?
- Why is it so hard to involve parents?

Why should I involve parents and families?

The Individuals with Disabilities Education Act includes provisions that require the involvement of parents. In what might be considered the Dark Ages of special education, there were no federal or state guidelines for determining how children qualified for services as a special education student. Special education class roles expanded as teachers decided they couldn't cope with particular students and made decisions— pretty much as individuals—that a student should be in special education. All that was needed to transfer a student from a regular classroom to a special classroom was verbal permission from the principal, and the act of removing a student's cumulative folder in the central office file from one teacher's class to another. You cannot imagine the fury and shock of parents who accidentally discovered that their child suddenly was in a class for students with disabilities when they had not been consulted or advised. We know that at least one angry parent of that era yelled at the teacher, "Who decided this? *You?*" Then, with even greater anger, the parent said to the teacher, "*No, I guess not. You're too young and too stupid!*"

Beyond the legal requirements, however, expert teachers realize that efforts to work most effectively with students include help from parents, as the emotional ties between parents and children are immeasurably more binding than those between teachers and students—even students whose parents are abusive. Neighbors of 5-year-old Abigail called the child protective services because Abigail and her 3-year-old sister were eating out of garbage cans and sometimes sleeping in the alley behind their apartment. Their hygiene was so terrible that they were infested with lice and had large oozing sores all over their bodies. Both girls were placed in foster care. At age 8, even though Abigail had not lived with her mother for three years, she remembered some of the horrors of her former life, and remarkably, these memories did not dim her desire to once again live with her mother. When one of us asked her why, she said, "She's my mom." One of us witnessed this extraordinary parent-child emotional bond as a volunteer for the court-appointed special advocate (CASA) program. We have observed these bonds between parents and their children repeatedly across different ethnicities, religions, and socioeconomic levels.

Also, a child's teacher holds only a limited number and variety of reniforcers for the student. Parents have a large number and variety of reinforcers they can employ with their children. Most important, parents know what will provide reinforcement for their children and what will not.

Another reason for involving parents is to minimize the chances that the child will be able to manipulate parents against you—or you against them. To be most effective in managing behavior, teacher and parent need to be united in their expectations and discipline, just as both parents need to present a consistent united front. The only way to avoid the problem of children manipulating differences between adults is to maintain close communication between home and school. Close communication does not guarantee that the child will be unable to play adults against each other, but it does make such manipulation more difficult.

There are no hard and fast rules for determining how to engage parents in a collaborative and supportive relationship, but we can avoid some of the pitfalls. First of all, who are the parents of your students? The twenty-first century presents different family configurations than in years past.

Who are the parents of my students?

Understanding Economic Stresses on Families.   According to the Bureau of Labor Statistics, in 1940, less than 9 percent of all women with children worked outside the home. In 1997, 76.5 percent of women with children between the ages of 6 and 13 were employed outside the home (http://stats.bls.gov). There are many reasons why mothers work, but one is that it's an economic necessity. It's more and more difficult to support a family on one income.

Child care often consumes a large share of the resources of families who live in poverty. The U.S. Bureau of Census reports that poor families with an employed mother pay roughly three times as much of their budget on child care as families who are not poor—20 percent versus 7 percent, respectively—and 36 percent of poor families had *no* regular arrangement for child care (www.census.gov). You might ask your-self this: *How many mothers of my students are single?*

In 2001, one in three American babies was born to a single mother due to the increase in the divorce rate and women giving birth out of wedlock (Annie E. Casey Foundation, 2003). In many instances, the income of single women is barely above pov-erty level, so that the role of single parents, the only caregivers for their children, becomes both an economic and an emotional stress. Recent studies by social services indicate that the number of fatherless children has reached 17 million, and this absence of fathers produces profound problems for our schools (Connecticut Department of Social Services). "In fact, children from fatherless homes have been found to be both less productive in school and responsible for a high percentage of criminal behavior."[4]

The statistics from the Department of Social Services of Connecticut demon-strate the problems with fatherless children. Did you know that children who live with-out contact with their biological fathers, when compared to other kids are:

- Five times more likely to live in poverty;
- More likely to bring drugs and weapons to school;
- Twice as likely to commit a crime;
- Twice as likely to drop out of school;
- Twice as like to be abused;
- More likely to run away from home (boys 63 percent more);
- More likely to commit suicide;
- Twice as likely to abuse drugs and alcohol;
- Twice as likely to end up in jail;
- Four times more likely to need help for emotional or behavioral problems; and
- More likely to become pregnant as a teenager and start the welfare cycle all over again. (Connecticut Department of Social Services, www.dss.state.ct.us)

Another economic stressor on single-parent families is the uncollected child sup-port, which may account for the statistics reported by the U.S. Bureau of Census in 1999 that 41 percent of families headed by single mothers lived in poverty. For example, presently 361,000 parents owe their children more than $2 *billion* in child support in the state of Virginia (www.dcse.dss.state.va.us).

Another possible result of poverty is homelessness. The National Center for Homeless Education reports that in 1998, there were over 615,000 homeless children in the United States, and 45 percent of these homeless children (K–12) did not attend school regularly (www.serve.org/nche/SEASdata.htm).

Parents who live in poverty are often overwhelmed with worry about how to pay the rent, put food on the table, buy clothing, and provide medical care for their chil-dren. The issue of providing the daily necessities for their families becomes consuming, which means that many parents may not have the energy or the time to collaborate with schools. Single mothers who work several part-time jobs probably won't volunteer to bake cookies for the class party or to chaperone the next field trip. But this doesn't mean that these parents don't care for their children. They may be working several jobs and not have the time or the transportation to come to school for a conference. But they still love their children. For example, the visiting teacher at one school insisted that the father of a very aggressive fourth-grader come to school every time his son was violent, which was often. This father was a custodian who took the bus to work, had no sick leave, no vacation time, and no health care. The first time this dad came to school, he spoke with affection about his son, even though he also revealed that his son embarrassed him and that he felt helpless to change his son's behavior. He said, "I want my son to get an education. I'll help however I can." After the third time in a week that the visiting teacher yanked this father off his job and dragged him to school, he angrily told teachers to handle his son's problems at school and to stop bothering him. He said, "I don't get no money if I'm not pushin' the broom. They dock my pay for every hour I'm gone. I live too close to the bone as it is." Sometimes the necessities of life—food, clothing, and shelter—override parent collaboration with schools.

Even though teachers often view these parents as not attentive at best, or neglectful at worst, most parents care deeply for their children. Some are overwhelmed, and often their apparent lack of attention to their children covers a more troubling problem.

Understanding Parents from Different Cultural or Ethnic Backgrounds.   One of us can say this: "With the exception of my fourth-grade teacher, all my teachers, kindergarten through high school, either taught my parents or went to school with them. For better or worse, teachers and students occupied the same economic, racial, and cultural background in my hometown. Not so today, and sometimes these differences become a quagmire to negotiate."

We cannot offer a book on multiculturalism, nor do we wish to stereotype any ethnic groups; however, it is important to grasp the fact that most of the views we hold about ethnicity and race are based on what we have learned from our families and from the media. And sometimes these views are distorted.

Ask yourself: *Do my students come from ethnic and cultural backgrounds that are different from mine?* A teacher acquaintance of ours remarked on the culture shock she experienced when she moved to a rural school in the South from an affluent suburban school in the Northeast. She said, "It's been hard to adjust. For example, some of my students' families hunt and eat squirrels! Can you imagine?" She was ready to scuttle back across the Mason Dixon line when one of us told her that we grew up eating squirrels and that our grandmother liked to fry up the heads, crack them open with her knife handle, and pick out the brains! It's interesting to note that this teacher was of the same Irish American heritage as that of the coauthor to whom she was speaking.

But regardless of where one teaches, it is clear that the demographics are changing in the United States. Presently, approximately 35 percent of the students in the United States are from ethnic/racial minorities; however, the 100 largest school districts in the country, which teach one in every four public school students in the nation, already serve populations that are 68 percent minority.[5] It is projected that by 2050, minorities will *collectively* account for 57 percent of the student population, and although the numerical majority of poor children in the United States is white, a larger percentage of minority populations than of white children experience poverty. This trend is particularly alarming. "Because a student's academic achievement is highly correlated with his or her socioeconomic status, the recent growth in poverty among children is of serious concern to educators."[6] And who is teaching most of the students from diverse backgrounds?

Most of our nation's teachers continue to come from a rather homogeneous group; approximately 88 to 90 percent are European American and middle class. Indeed, the profile of the teacher education student that emerged from Zimpher's study in 1987 has not changed appreciably: "the typical teacher education student is a monolingual white female from a low-middle or middle-class suburban or rural home who wants to teach children who are like herself."[7]

You might think about the ethnic or cultural identity of your students. For example, you might ask: *Are any of my students Asian?* According to the report from the White House on Asian Americans and Pacific Islanders, Asian Americans and Pacific Islanders are the fastest growing racial/ethnic population in the United States—a 95 percent increase from 1980 to 1990, and a 43 percent increase from 1999 to 2000 (U.S. Census Bureau, 2000). They come from nearly 50 countries and ethnic groups, each with distinct cultures, languages, and traditions, and they occupy almost every socioeconomic level from the very rich to the very poor.

Although these groups have wide diversity in religion, culture, and language, there are some similarities to consider. "The concern for maintaining the interdependence of the family and individuals' loyalty to the family is seen in child-rearing practices. Behaviors of the individual are seen as reflecting on one's ancestors and one's race."[8] Because teachers in Asian cultures are accorded a higher status than teachers in the United States, Asian American students may be confused by the informality between American teachers and students. This higher status granted to teachers in the United States by many Asian Americans may also contribute to an area of potential cultural confusion for teachers who expect parents to be actively involved in making suggestions for their children's education. Because many Asians view the teachers as experts and authorities on education, they believe that teachers will have all the resources to guide them properly.[9] Finally, some think that Asian American students function better in a quiet, ordered environment.[10]

You might ask: *Are any of my students Hispanic?* Hispanics comprise the majority population in some areas of the United States, and by 2010, Hispanic students will be the largest minority in the country. Again, a reminder that this chapter is not a course in multiculturalism, and that making generalizations can be dangerous. However, we offer a few generalities that *may* guide today's teachers.

"To be Hispanic is to value children."[11] A Latino acquaintance told one of us how much he enjoyed his children and how he hoped to have more. "The house is so happy with children, even when they cry." This is not to say that other cultures don't value children. But there is a different emphasis on family and children than in U.S. competitive society, which may be confusing and cause conflict when collaborating with Latino parents. For example, Hispanic children may seem babied and overindulged by some teachers' standards. It may not be unusual for a Latina mother to tie her 6-year-old children's shoestrings, or for preteens to sit on their mothers' laps, or for preschoolers to still drink from a baby bottle.[12] This potential conflict has been described as follows:

> In brief, schools tend to reflect the values of the so-called mainstream, which are highly individualistic—teaching students to become independent and take care of their own needs. In contrast, immigrant Latino families tend to be collectivistic—teaching children to be interdependent with others and to attend to the needs of the family.[13]

And, similar to the attitudes of many Asian parents, Latino parents may *not* view their job as teaching their children academics. "Seeing the functions of teacher and parent as clearly distinct, they may believe that academic instruction should be restricted to school. They may believe that their primary responsibility is to socialize the child, not to teach academics."[14] The preceding may mean that a request for Latino parents to drill their child on a list of vocabulary words you send home may not receive the attention that you hoped for.

You might ask: *Are any of my students African American?* In 1995, African American students accounted for 14.7 percent of school-age children; however, by 2050, it is predicted that African American children will account for 16 percent of our student bodies.[15]

"While all minorities experience racism to some extent, none is so profound in the United States as the discrimination experienced by African Americans."[16] Because of the overt and incipient racism, many African American parents encourage independence, assertiveness, and individualism in their children so they will be able to cope and survive in a racist society. We've heard white teachers complain that African Americans view everything through the prism of racism. "They're all paranoid!" one teacher lamented. What mainstream society may view as paranoia, African Americans historically view as necessary for their survival. African Americans have survived under harsh economic and social restraints and have developed:

- Strong kinship bonds among a variety of family households
- Strong work, education, and achievement orientation
- High level of flexibility in family roles
- Strong commitment to religious values and church participation values
- A humanistic orientation for perceiving the world and relationships[17]

African American children are typically encouraged to learn self-help skills—walking, eating, dressing, and bathing—early, and are expected to take on household chores earlier than in most mainstream families. This independence, paired with academic achievement, is also a tool for combating racism.

Parallel with teaching children how to survive racism are (1) the value placed by many African Americans on relatives and friends and (2) the high level of flexibility in family roles. "Reliance on this extended kinship system has important survival value for African American families."[18] This reliance on others, the philosophy that it takes a whole village to raise a child, means that friends and relatives may feel responsible for disciplining children. It also means that there may be multiple caregivers for some of your African American students, and this is often a worry to mainstream teachers who are concerned about lack of predictability in their African American students' environments and the possible lack of consistency regarding discipline.

Discipline is also an area where African American parents may differ from most of society. African Americans parents tend to be more authoritarian than most parents, and many are not opposed to corporal punishment. "If your background reflects a preference for nonauthoritarian, relatively permissive discipline practices, be aware that this difference is a particularly difficult one with which to deal unemotionally."[19]

You might ask: *Are any of my students Native American?* American Indians constitute approximately 1 percent of U.S. school-age children, and that statistic will probably remain stable for the future.[20] There are over 500 tribes in the United States, half of which live west of the Mississippi River. These tribes speak over 200 different languages, which require teachers to become familiar with the cultural practices of the American Indian children they teach.

But there are some similarities among the tribes. First, as in the Asian and Latino communities, many American Indians are collectivists who not only emphasize the extended family but also the tribe and the community. This means that parents may identify a friend as spokesperson or as a source of information about the child. A typical teacher with little or no knowledge of the culture of her or his American Indian students may be unnerved that someone other than the parents—aunt, uncle, grandparent, or sibling—is responsible for disciplining the children, or providing pertinent health information.[21]

Often, American Indians encourage their children to manage themselves and to operate independently when the children are very young, which most teachers may view as overly permissive or neglectful. However, even though there is an emphasis on self-sufficiency, many American Indian parents do not encourage competitiveness, and this independence must never be at the expense of the family or the community. "Attempts to convince Native Americans to be competitive (such as being the first, best, fastest, or smartest) are incompatible with their cultural values."[22]

Finally, you may ask: *Are any of my students biracial or multiracial?* A growing number of students are biracial and multiracial, and their families may have different preferences about how they wish their children to be recognized. Some parents of biracial or multiracial children prefer to think of their children as "just children." Others acknowledge both backgrounds and have definite wishes about how their children should be treated. Still others may embrace fully the cultural identity of one of the parents.

Be careful! With regard to all of the information we have provided about different cultures, we urge you to be careful. It is imperative that teachers conscientiously not only study the *cultures* of their students but also have enough contact with their students to understand that they are *individuals* with crucial differences. They may or may not conform to the generalizations we have made about their culture.

What are my prejudices?

Before you begin communicating with parents, you must be aware of *your own* views regarding the following:

- How do you view different ethnic and racial groups? Are your views stereotypic?
- How do you view families who are poor? Do you blame them for their poverty?
- How do you view same-gender partners as heads of household?
- How do you view religious differences?
- How do you view single parents?

School systems in the United States serve diverse ethnicities and religions—cultures that all educators may not understand. Unfortunately, most of the views people hold about these differing cultures are based on what they learned from their own families and the media, and sometimes these views are distorted. Therefore, it is essential to examine your personal values and beliefs about these differences. "This does not mean that we scrap our value system and subscribe to those of others, but it does mean that we understand our beliefs, how our beliefs might cause us to judge others, and how these judgments might interfere with collaborating with parents."[23] For example, when one of us was a court-appointed special advocate (CASA) volunteer, her director requested that she advocate for a little boy named Martin. In Martin's eight years, except for a two-year stay with a family friend, he had been shifted among over a dozen homes, and most of his caregivers had been either abusive or neglectful. Needless to say, by the time Martin was 8 years old, he was angry, defiant, noncompliant, and generally difficult. Social services had difficulty placing him, and Martin was having a good time controlling a lot of folks. In the CASA volunteer's first conversation with Martin, he said that he liked "scaring adults and keepin' 'em jumpin'." He was good at it too!

But life had not always been one of shifting families for Martin. One of his first caregivers was a single woman, Miriam, who had kept him from birth to age 2. At that time Miriam was diagnosed with a terminal illness that carried the prognosis of a long and painful death. Miriam sadly relinquished Martin to his relatives, sold her home, and prepared to die. Six years later, the diagnosis was amended, she discovered that she was not going to die, and she wanted Martin back. The Department of Social Services thought that this was a great idea. However, by this time, Martin had run through all his abusive relatives and was successfully getting banished from one foster home after another, as well as routinely suspended from schools. So the idea that someone actually wanted this extremely difficult child was an answer to a prayer. But there was a problem. Miriam was gay and had a partner. The social worker wanted to know if the CASA volunteer would have trouble advocating for a child to be placed with a gay couple. The advocate asked what a person's sexual orientation had to do with parenting skills. The agency then asked if the advocate would write a report that would reject the fallacy that if a gay couple raises a child, the child is bound to be gay. The state was very conservative and some of the folks involved with the case also thought that to be raised by a gay couple was "unnatural," or "a sin against God," or "unlawful."

Miriam successfully adopted Martin, but the volunteer advocate's interaction with professionals and other volunteers while working on this case was unnerving. Many spoke of being uncomfortable placing Martin with a gay couple, but they could not explain their discomfort. They said things like, "I'm just uncomfortable, that's all." And one of the professional witnesses who had written most of the definitive studies about children raised in homes with same-sex partners said that she would not testify as an expert witness if Martin's family contested social service's decision to place Martin with a gay couple. At other hearings at which she had testified, her life and that of her family had been threatened, and she was not willing to risk her family's safety.

Recently, an acquaintance of ours from a southwestern state bemoaned the fact that the Indians were a lost cause in her state. "You have no idea how much money they squander on alcohol." In her eyes, they are "lazy drunks." But she had no knowledge of the nineteenth- and twentieth-century boarding schools that were organized in an effort to assimilate the American Indians. Indian children were forcibly removed from their parents and shipped long distances on trains so that the children could learn English and a marketable skill and thereby "assimilate" into mainstream society. Perhaps the motives of the authorities at the time were good (sometimes people are simply misinformed, not mean), but the boarding schools were harsh. The Indian children were routinely punished for speaking their language or practicing their traditional customs. Consequently, because some of these children did not return home for years, and because they were not allowed to speak their native language or practice their customs, they forgot them. Many blame the boarding schools for the increase of alcoholism among Native Americans, who were robbed of their culture but who did not fit into mainstream society either. Our acquaintance didn't know about boarding schools, nor did she know that one of this country's founding fathers couldn't decide whether the nation should "assimilate or annihilate" its Native Americans. She also did not know that many health professionals think that Native Americans have a physical predisposition for diabetes and alcoholism.

As a teacher, one of your jobs—perhaps the most important job for collaboration with parents—is to listen to parents so that you can help your students. That is going to be difficult if a teacher thinks that a single mom who has to commute an hour on a bus to and from work, while child care sucks up one-third of her salary, could come for parent-teacher conferences if she *really* wanted to. Or if the teacher thinks that gay parents are objectionable and make her feel uncomfortable. Or if she thinks that illegitimate children are a sin against God. Or she is nervous around those of a different race or culture. Perhaps the hardest part of teacher-parent collaboration is determining how you think and feel about those who are different from you. But it's the first step to forming a collaborative relationship with parents.

What is the reciprocity of parent-child interaction?

Expert teachers also realize that parents of students with behavior problems are not always the cause of their children's problems. Researchers in recent years have confirmed what many parents have contended for a long time: Some children are born with temperaments that make them more difficult to parent and teach. Many parents of more than one child will tell you that almost from the moment of birth they noticed distinct differences between their children. For example, one baby was happy and easy to soothe, the other was irritable and hard to please. Research has now shown that different temperaments can have a powerful influence on how parents deal with their babies and children. Difficult babies can place a great deal of stress on parents. For many years, the dominant child development theorists viewed child-parent interaction as a one-way street running from parent to child. Experts now know that the relationship is reciprocal. Parents can and do influence children, but it is also the case that children can and do influence parents.

That parent-child interaction is reciprocal has important implications for how teachers view parents, especially parents of children with behavior problems. Keep two things in mind. First, parents of children with behavior problems are not necessarily to blame for their children's behavior. Second, even if you witness poor parenting of children with behavior problems, it may not be entirely the parents' fault. Some of the most intelligent and well-intentioned parents can easily get caught up in an interactive pattern that results in their exhibiting inappropriate parenting behaviors. It is instructive to keep in mind your own interactions with intractable students. Given that on occasion you have found it difficult to maintain your professional composure with particularly nasty and ill-mannered students, think of having to contend with such behavior daily over the course of several years.

Just as you should not be quick to blame parents, neither should you deny that they can at times be culpable. Poor parenting, especially abusive parenting, can directly cause behavior problems in children. And some parents indirectly contribute to the behavior problems of their children by consistently responding in a maladaptive manner to their children's misbehavior. We caution here that you should not assume that parents do not care about their children if they are poor parents. Nearly all parents are concerned for the welfare of their children, even if they abuse them. Parents who have poor parenting skills may want to be good parents, but they may simply not have the knowledge of alternative ways of rearing children or have not learned the self-control required to discipline their children humanely.

What are the school guidelines for communicating with parents?

After you have examined your values and your prejudices, you need to understand the school guidelines for communicating with parents—particularly if you are a new or transferring teacher.

- Do written contacts with parents need principal approval?
- Should you have someone from the school accompany you on parent visits?
- What are the school's expectations for how many parents you should meet within a year? If you are teaching 150 students in high school, are you expected to conference with all of them sometime during the year?
- If the parents are divorced, do the records indicate who has custody and with whom you should share the student's progress?
- If the records or teacher talk indicate that the child has a guardian, do you share information with the parents also?
- What should you do if a parent's expectations are unrealistic? For example, if they are:
  Visiting or calling everyday?
  Contacting you by e-mail every day?
  Demanding that they move their child to a higher academic group before the child is ready?[24]

When and how should I involve parents, especially parents of tough kids?

One of us was told by a fellow teacher on our first teaching job, "You'd better trot right on down to Jake's house and introduce yourself, because you are going to need this grandma. Yes, sir!" This teacher had looked at the class role and pointed to one of the names.

The Sooner, the Better. The sooner you contact parents, the better. We hope you will have done your homework about your class—read the folders, talked to other teachers—and know the names of the students who will in all probability present problems. Call the parent. Begin by apologizing for disturbing him or her.[25] Usually, it is wise to contact parents of tough kids in the following manner:

> Mrs. Smith, I'm sorry to bother you at work (or at home). My name is Alice Jones, and I'm going to be Tommy's teacher this year. I hope Tommy can have good year, and I wonder if you have any suggestions about how I can help him have a good year."

Even if you don't glean any important information from the parent, she or he knows that you're interested in Tommy, that you want parental collaboration, and that you're focusing on the future, not past mistakes. Concentrate on the future! Make the conversation brief, but also tell the parent that you will check back after school starts to make sure that Tommy isn't experiencing any problems of which you are unaware. Give the parents your phone number. Availability is important. But even more important is listening to the parents.

If parents don't work or don't have a home phone, make a home visit. Although this is controversial, many have had success by visiting parents of tough kids before they come to school. But follow these guidelines:

- Make sure that you have examined your prejudices and won't judge the parents or home harshly when you go.
- Find out your school system's policy about home visits.
- Don't go alone. Try to find either someone the family knows to go with you or someone who is familiar with the area.
- If you know that the family has a social worker, the social worker is usually happy to make an appointment for you, and might even accompany you. If you don't know the social worker, apologize to the parents for disturbing them and ask if it would be better if you made an appointment to see them at another time.
- If the parents ask you in, don't sit down unless they ask you to.
- Use the same message you would use if you had phoned the parents—you are looking to the future, want a good year for their child, and want suggestions from them.
- Also discuss how you will communicate in the future—perhaps a home-note plan.

As a first-year teacher, one of us didn't follow the colleague's advice who directed us to visit Jake's home until his behavior was beyond control. Here is that experience as one of us remembers it:

After whining to my mother about the perils in the classroom in general and Jake in particular, my mother directed me to visit Jake's guardian, his grandmother, Augusta. Mother said that Augusta had a hand in raising my cousin Jeff. She went on to tell me that Augusta did not tolerate foolishness from anyone, "whether they be black, white, orange, big, or small." Jake's home had no phone, and when I took Jake home, his grandmother gave me a cool reception, mumbling something about "teachers all time complaining about Jake." She did not ask me in but stared at me through the screen door until in desperation I asked her if she knew my mother. "I reckon I do," she smiled, and asked me to come in. I told her that I thought Jake had a lot of potential and could probably learn a whole lot more if I could get him to behave. She agreed. I didn't elaborate any more than that on his behavior. I didn't have to. Augusta told Jake that he better do what I ask him. "Period! Do you understand me?" Jake wasn't a model student after that, but his behavior did improve dramatically. My only regret was that I didn't follow the teacher's advice and visit Augusta *before* Jake set foot in my classroom—*before* any problems arose. When I left Augusta's house, she said, "The only time I ever saw Jake's other teachers was when he acted up in class. Hope that's not the case with you." I listened to Augusta.

Letters.   Introductory letters home before students start the school year can be valuable in establishing contact with parents. There are some restrictions, one of which is money. Sometimes neither the school systems nor the teachers can afford the postage to send letters home to parents. If that is the case, then an introductory letter should be sent home the first day of school. Introductory letters to parents should be brief, be simply written, and give information about how to contact you at home and at work. You need to be available so that you can listen. For example:

> Dear Parents,
> My name is Jeffrey Jones, and I'll be your child's teacher this year.
> Home phone: 555-1111
> Work phone: 555-2222
> I don't have a phone in my classroom, so I may have to call you back. But I shall return your call as soon as I can. I'm looking forward to meeting you. I need you!
>
> Sincerely,
> (Signature)

You might delineate some the behavioral and academic goals with which you will begin the year. However you choose to contact parents, the first contact should be positive. Remember Augusta. *Don't wait until there's a problem before you contact parents.*

Parent Conferences.   Successful conferences take preparation. The following are a few guidelines for a successful parent conference:

- *Have you done your homework?*
  1. Reviewed the student's cumulative records
  2. Consulted with other professionals
  3. Documented the student's academic and behavioral progress
  4. Established rapport with the parents before the conference
  5. Familiarized yourself with the student and family's culture

- *Have you involved the parents **before** the conference?*
  1. Discussed the goals of the meeting with the parents and solicited their input
  2. Involved the student, as appropriate
  3. Scheduled a mutually convenient day and time for the meeting
  4. Provided written notice prior to the meeting

- *How do you involve the parents **during** the meeting?*
  1. Welcome the parents and speak informally with them before beginning
  2. Reiterate the goals of the meeting
  3. Begin with a discussion of the student's strengths
  4. Support your points with specific examples and documentation
  5. Encourage parents to share insights
  6. Ask open-ended questions
  7. Avoid jargon
  8. Practice active listening. Remember, one of your big jobs is to listen to parents
  9. Review the main points of the meeting and determine a course of action
  10. Provide additional resources (e.g., support groups, family resource centers, websites)

- What do you do *after* the meeting?
  1. Document the results of the meeting
  2. Share results with colleagues who work with the student
  3. Follow up with the parents as needed to discuss changes.

There are other points to consider before a conference. Ask yourself this: *Am I able to avoid blaming parents?* One of the least helpful things a teacher can do is lay the blame on parents for the misbehavior of their children. Parents will already be on the defensive because you have called them to have the meeting. Weigh your words carefully so as not to give the impression that you think they are the culprits. Even if you are convinced that they are the cause of their children's problems, you should avoid accusations. If they are at fault, it is better to let them arrive at that judgment on their own.

An acquaintance of ours, an immigrant from Great Britain, angrily asked if all teachers in America were bossy or just her 8-year-old daughter's second-grade teacher. This mother was very worried about her daughter, who insisted on taking a nap as soon as she got off the school bus and then wanted to go to bed immediately after supper. The pediatrician assured this mother that her daughter was just small and tired easily and that there was nothing wrong with her. The mother was considering changing pediatricians for a second opinion when her daughter's teacher called and brusquely demanded that she put her daughter to bed on time on school nights because she was sleeping during the day. This mom asked us, "Couldn't the teacher have asked if we've seen the same behavior at home? She just decided that we were awful parents who kept our child up late every night."

Here's another question to ask yourself: *Am I willing to admit it when I'm wrong?* Some teachers, especially those who are relatively inexperienced, feel that it is a sign of weakness to acknowledge to parents that they have made mistakes. We don't think you need to see the meeting as an opportunity to reveal all of your shortcomings, but if you have doubts about how you have handled the student, it is a good idea to concede this point.

Another question: *Am I willing to admit it when I don't know the answer to parents' questions?* Again, be careful not to fall into the trap of feeling that you need to answer every question posed by the parents. Confident teachers are more than willing to say that they are not all-knowing. In fact, teachers should view the parent-teacher conference as an opportunity to learn more about the child from the parents.

Can I accept the family as it is? Some teachers view parent-teacher conferences as quasi-therapy sessions in which they should try to influence family dynamics. Your focus should be on what the student is doing in your classroom. To be sure, you will want to talk about how the child behaves at home, and you may want to suggest that parents carry out certain procedures in the home to back up what you are doing at school, but you should not see yourself as a family therapist.

Am I attuned to cultural differences between myself and the parents? It is important that you respect the cultural backgrounds of parents and not misinterpret their behavior or offend them because their customs vary from yours.

Can I find something positive to say about the child and something positive about the parent that I can support? It is very important that you try to find something positive and supportive to say about the child and the parent in every parent contact. Sometimes this may be difficult. A first-grade teacher where one of us worked began a parent conference with the parents of a very violent and noncompliant child by reporting that Johnny eats his lunch every day. Sometimes you have to really dig to find a few positives to share with the parents. Nevertheless, if all the parent receives is negative information, you are not likely to get very far in resolving the problem. Dishonesty about your feelings and perceptions is not helpful. Going out of your way to find something—anything, regardless of how small—that you can be positive about or support will make your attempts to work cooperatively with a parent more likely to be successful.

Meeting with parents about a student's misbehavior demands a delicate balance between providing an objective account of the misbehavior and demonstrating that you are an advocate for the child. Even though you need to be sensitive to the possibility that the parents are going to be unreceptive to what you have to say, it is important that they hear what you have to say about their child's problem behavior. At times it is tempting to spare parents the anxiety caused by information that will likely prove disheartening. Conveying only good news skews their perspective, however, just as much as conveying only negative information. If a serious incident arises, then they have no sense of background or warning. Filling them in at this point may lead them to conclude that you are withholding information and provoke a sense of mistrust. When telling parents unpleasant information, it helps not only to be as objective as possible but also to state the case in a way that clearly conveys your advocacy of the student. It is paramount that you focus on the future—how you and the parents can help the child behave appropriately. When it is obvious to the parents that the teacher is angry or upset with their child, parents become apprehensive about the treatment the child may receive. A common response to this sense of dread is a defensiveness that polarizes parent-teacher relationships.

Abusive Parents. Some teachers are lucky enough to have long careers without experiencing an angry or verbally abusive parent. When a parent does become abusive, it can be unnerving or frightening. The following are some guidelines for facing an angry parent.

- Remain calm.
- Do not make angry responses.
- Speak softly.
- If you are in error, admit it. (It's best to contact the parents with the error before they find out from their child.)
- Maintain eye contact.

Sometimes teachers feel sandbagged by explosive parents, and it is not always possible to determine why they're so angry. Parents might feel guilty about their child's lack of achievement, feel overwhelmed by poverty, or have had a bad experience with schools in the past. Whatever the reason for the abuse, remember that you *need* them. And you don't want to give them the ammunition to take to your principal or superintendent. *So keep your cool!* Don't hang up the phone, or walk away, or scream, or respond defensively or angrily. Some consultants suggest that you handle abusive parents in the following manner: "Mrs. Smith, please don't talk to me that way. I will never speak to you like that, and I will never speak to your child like that."[26]

Of course, this means that you know yourself and know that you never would speak to a student that way. And remember that delivery is everything. You must be calm, speak softly, maintain eye contact, and not get into the back-and-forth of an argument that you can't win. If you have made a mistake that has infuriated the parents, admit it, and tell them how you will prevent this from happening again. Try to focus on the future and how you can prevent this problem from erupting again. Restate that the purpose of the meeting is to help the student in the future.

In what ways can I involve parents and families?

Home-Note Programs. *Home-school plans*, sometimes known as *home-contingency plans*, can be very effective in helping students to control their behavior. With a home-note plan, *you* evaluate the student's behavior, but the parents deliver the consequences. The teacher fills out a brief report on the student's behavior, the student takes it home, and the parents deliver the reinforcement. Although home-notes are not a panacea, research indicates that they can be highly effective. They are palatable to most parents and students and require a minimum of teacher time. They also provide a means by which parents and teachers can work together in a constructive way. But home-notes should not be used in the following situations:

- If you suspect abuse
- If you think that the parents may not consistently implement the program

There are several other things to keep in mind in setting up a home-note program. Most important, of course, is that you meet with the parents to work out the features of the program. In this meeting, you should leave as many choices as possible up to the parents, especially with regard to the types and amount of reinforcers as well as the schedule of reinforcement (i.e., how many "good" notes it takes to receive a reinforcer). The more they feel they are working with you in the development of the home-note program, the more likely parents are to carry it out consistently. You should also consider the possibility of including the student in on the planning at some point. It is usually best to meet with the parents first and then decide whether to include the student in another meeting.

Although you should be as precise as possible in defining the criteria you will use in judging the occurrence or nonoccurrence of behaviors, the note home to parents need not be detailed. In other words, the feedback to parents need not be lengthy or complicated. Unless they request it, all you need do is inform them that the child has or has not engaged in the desired behavior. Perhaps you will leave space for teacher or parent comments, but you might use this option only occasionally.

Most researchers suggest that teachers begin by using the home-note system on a daily basis. Once it has been working successfully for a couple of weeks, you can begin to wean the child from the system by going to a once-a-week note. In the early stages, especially, you should check frequently with parents. Even at later stages, you should make periodic checks with parents to see how they think the system is working. Figure 8.1 is a copy of a home-note used for a third-grade student who refused to complete any seatwork.

If the parents are abusive or won't consistently implement the plan, it is often effective to use a mentor in the school to reinforce the student: another teacher, an aide, the principal, a secretary, or anyone who will show an interest in the student and implement the plan consistently. One student in the school where one of us taught was very fond of the physical education teacher who shot baskets with this student on Friday afternoons if the student had successfully met the terms of the plan.

Why is it so hard to involve parents?

The seeming contradiction—that parents hold a great deal of influence over their children but should not be automatically blamed for the behavior problems of their children—is perhaps what makes it so very difficult for novice teachers to work constructively with parents, especially parents of students who misbehave. You need to maintain a very delicate balance between recognizing that parents are important to the educational process and not immediately pointing the finger at them when their children misbehave.

Name _____

Date _____

Completed reading follow-up

    Neatly   Yes   No

    Accurately   Yes   No

Completed math follow-up

    Neatly   Yes   No

    Accurately   Yes   No

Teacher Comments:

Parent Comments:

_____   _____

Teacher's signature   Parent's signature

FIGURE 8.1   Sample Home-Note for Third-Grader

Summary

The ability to work with parents is often the critical difference that divides good teachers from those who are truly excellent. Possessing skills in instruction and behavior management in the classroom can serve teachers well with many students, but they are often not enough. In order to achieve excellence, teachers must be able to communicate effectively with parents. By so doing, they can enhance their behavior management techniques by leveraging the influence that some parents have over their children. Although working with parents does not come naturally to all teachers, those who take the time and effort to develop such skills will be rewarded handsomely.

REFERENCES AND RESOURCES FOR FURTHER STUDY

The following references provided the basis for many of our statements in this chapter. You may wish to consult selected references for additional information. Our endnotes for this chapter refer to sources in this list.

Bordin, J., & Lytle, R. K. (2000). The IEP meeting: All together now . . . ? *Exceptional Parent, 30*(9), 74, 76–77.

Brice, A. E. (2002). *The Hispanic child and speech, language, culture, and education.* Boston: Allyn and Bacon.

Cushner, K., McClelland, A., & Safford, P. (2000). *Human diversity in education, an integrative approach* (3rd ed.). New York: McGraw-Hill.

Educational Research Service. (2003). *Culture and learning.* Alexandria, VA: Author.

Individuals with Disabilities Education Act Amendments of 1997, Pub. L. No. 105–17 (1997). Available online at: http://www.ed.gov/offices/OSERS/IDEA/the_law.html.

Kelley, M. L. (1990). *School-home notes. Promoting children's classroom success.* New York: Guilford.

Kerr, M. M., & Nelson. C. M. (2002). *Strategies for managing behavior problems in the classroom* (4th ed.). Upper Saddle River, NJ: Prentice-Hall.

Klein, M. D., & Chen, D. (2001). *Working with children from culturally diverse backgrounds.* Delmar, CA: Thomson Learning.

Kroth, R. L. (1985). *Communicating with parents of exceptional children: Improving parent-teacher relationships* (2nd ed.). Denver, CO: Love.

Lambie, R. (2000). *Family systems within educational contexts: Understanding at-risk and special-needs students* (2nd ed.). Denver, CO: Love.

Manning, M. L., & Baruth, L. G. (2000). *Multicultural education of children and adolescents* (3rd ed.). Boston: Allyn and Bacon.

Mathews, R. (2000). Cultural patterns of South Asia and Southeast Asian Americans. *Intervention in School and Clinic, 36,* 101–104.

Morgan, D. P., & Jenson, W. R. (1988). *Teaching behaviorally disordered students: Preferred practices.* Columbus, OH: Merrill/Macmillan.

O'Shea, D. J., O'Shea, L. J., Algozzine, R., & Hammitte, D. J. (2001). *Families and teachers of individuals with disabilities: Collaborative orientations and responsive practices.* Boston: Allyn and Bacon.

Patterson, G. R., & Forgatch, M. S. (1987). *Parents and adolescents living together.* Eugene, OR: Castalia Publishing.

Pianta, R. C., Marvin, R. S., Britner, P. A., & Borowitz, K. C. (1996). Mothers' resolution of their children's diagnosis: Organized patterns of caregiving representations. *Journal of Infant Mental Health, 17,* 239–256.

Pullen, P. L. (2004). *Brighter beginnings for teachers.* Lanham, MD: Roman and Littlefield Education.

Rodriguez, G. (1999). *Raising nuestros ninos: Bringing up Latino children in a bicultural world.* New York: Fireside.

Rothstein-Fisch. (2003). *Bridging cultures, teacher education module.* Mahwah, NJ: Lawrence Erlbaum.

Schnieders, C. A., & Tafoya, A. T. (1998). Teaching families to collaborate: From a mad hatter's tea party to effective program planning. *Special Services in the Schools, 13,* 47–61.

Springate, K. W., & Stegelin, D. A. (1999). *Building school and community partnerships through parent involvement.* Upper Saddle River, NJ: Prentice-Hall.

Villegas, A. M., & Lucas, T. (2002). *Educating culturally responsive teachers: A coherent approach.* Albany: State University of New York.

Walker, H. M., Ramsey, E., & Gresham, F. M. (2004). *Antisocial behavior in school: Strategies and best practices* (2nd ed.). Pacific Grove, CA: Brooks/Cole.

Whitaker, T., & Fiore, D. J. (2001). *Dealing with difficult parents and with parents in difficult situations.* Larchmont, NY: Eye on Education.

ON-LINE RESOURCES FOR FAMILIES

Ability Online Support Network: www.ablelink.org/
Annie E. Casey Foundation   www.acf.org/kidscount/databook/summary/suumary12htm
Connecticut Department of Social Services: www.dss.state.ct.us
The Council for Exceptional Children: www.cec.sped.org/
Family Education Network: www.familyeducation.com/
The Family Village School: laran.waisman.wisc.edu/fv/www/education/pti.html
Internet Resources for Special Children (IRSC): www.irsc.org/
National Center for Homeless Education: www.serve.org/nche/SEASdata.htm
National Parent Network on Disabilities: www.npnd.org
Parent Advocacy Coalition for Educational Rights (PACER) Center: www.pacer.org
Parents Place Co.: www.parentsplace.com
The Technical Assistance Alliance for Parent Centers: www.taalliance.org
U.S. Department of Labor Statistics: stats.bls.gov
U. S. Census Bureau: www.census.gov

ENDNOTES

1. Quoted from Whitaker and Fiore (2001, p. 15).
2. See Walker, Ramsey, and Gresham (2004, p. 280).
3. See Pullen (2004, p. 31).
4. See Whitaker and Fiore (2001, p. 18) for more discussion on fatherless families.
5. See National Center for Education Statistics, *Characteristics of the 100 Largest Public Elementary and Secondary School Districts in the United States: 2000–2001* (p. 5).
6. Quoted from Villegas and Lucas (2002, p. 8).
7. Quoted from Cushner, McClelland, and Safford (2000, p. 12).
8. See Springate and Stegelin (1999, p. 107).
9. Mathews (2000, pp. 101–104) discusses this in greater detail.
10. See Springate and Stegelin (1999, p. 108).
11. Quoted from Rodriguez (1999, p. 3).
12. See Brice (2002, p. 202).
13. Extracted material from Rothstein-Fisch (2003, p. ix).
14. From Educational Research Service (2003, p. 74).
15. See Villegas and Lucas (2002).

16. See Klein and Chen (2001).
17. This list is based on Springate and Steglin (1999, p. 106).
18. Quoted from Klein and Chen (2001, p. 82).
19. Quoted from Klein and Chen (2001, p. 83).
20. See Villegas and Lucas (2002, p. 4).
21. See Klein and Chen (2001).
22. Manning and Baruth (2000, p. 186) discuss competitiveness and Native Americans.
23. See Pullen (2004).
24. See Pullen (2004, p. 41).
25. Whitaker and Fiore (2001) discuss the scenario of calling students' parents.
26. See Whitaker and Fiore (2001, p. 119).

PART TWO

Cases for Analysis, Discussion, and Reflection

What You Don't Know Can Hurt You!

JOHN McCULLUM

When John, a student teacher, thought about his seventh-period class, his breathing became shallow and a radiating knot of anxiety formed in his stomach. This class, the only one that proved to be troublesome, consisted of 15 eighth-grade students—7 very high-achieving students and 8 who performed considerably lower academically. Of these 8, 5 talked, laughed, and attempted to dominate the class and him throughout the period. Although John had managed to cope with these problems on a more or less passable basis, doing so had taken a great deal of energy. John had a difficult time concentrating on his lesson delivery as he was constantly distracted by the students who seemed to want to set up a situation in which either he or they won control of the class. He braced himself daily to confront this group. He thought he was familiar with the problems and potential pitfalls in this class. But John was soon to learn that it is easier to fall prey to the dangers of the unexpected, and that they often hold the most dire consequences. He was to learn this lesson from a usually quiet student in this seventh-period class.

One afternoon, John planned to conduct a test review in the form of a quiz-show game. On this particular day, his clinical instructor was absent and a substitute teacher was in his place. The clinical instructor seldom if ever attended class, so this day was much like any other for John. He was accustomed to having complete freedom to plan for and instruct this class as he deemed best. Because he was given this autonomy, he chose to take a different approach with the class than that of the clinical instructor. The clinical instructor had usually given the students individual written assignments to complete and he used very little direct instruction or group work approaches with them. John felt that it was important to use a variety of instructional techniques for these students.

After directing the students to form groups of their choice, he began the game with the expectation that although the class would be rowdy, the game would prove to be an enjoyable and effective review technique. Very little time had elapsed before John realized that the students had selected themselves into groups along racial and academic achievement lines. Six high-achieving white students formed two groups of three each. Only one black female was a high achiever. Of the low-achieving students, seven were black and one was a white male. These remaining nine students formed three groups of three each. John knew that the white students also came from upper-middle–class neighborhoods, whereas the other students came from relatively poor homes. Although he was aware of these factors, he was yet to appreciate the potential volatility of the situation.

When an argument erupted between one of the students from a high-achieving group (Chris) and one of the low-achieving students (Richard), John immediately rose and stepped between them. Ignoring the obscenities being exchanged, John moved quickly to separate them because they had already begun pushing and shoving each another. After separating the students, he was able to recommence the game, which continued more or less successfully until the end of the class period. As the class was dismissed, however, the two students resumed their hostile exchange at the door.

Again, John moved to intervene, calling both students back to the classroom. Only Chris complied. Richard ran down the corridor and turned the corner. Because Chris did not start the argument, and because John thought that it would have been fruitless to discuss the issue with only one of the students involved, he released Chris to go home.

In the empty classroom, John reflected on the incident. Despite Richard's academic difficulties, he had not been, up to this point, a behavioral problem in class. In fact, John knew very little about him beyond the fact that he was an academically weak student and had been retained several times. Consequently, Richard was much older and larger than his classmates. John felt that he should not allow Richard's flagrant disobedience to go unaddressed. He decided to go look for Richard. Finding Richard at the bike rack just outside the building, he approached him and said that he wanted to talk. Richard responded by jumping on his bike and stating, "I don't got time for this," as he rode away. John, stinging with indignation, immediately went to the office and submitted a disciplinary referral.

Upon Richard's arrival at school the following morning, John presented him with the referral notice and walked with him to the office for a conference with the vice principal. On the way, John explained that the referral meant an automatically assigned afternoon detention period in his classroom for refusing to stop when he called. Less than half an hour later, John went to the office to complete some copying and noticed Richard still waiting outside the office for his conference with the vice principal. As he went about his chore, Richard began to make comments in a somewhat staged whisper to the student next to him. These comments amounted to threats directed toward John, such as, "I'm going to break his jaw." At this point, John decided to ignore the remarks.

As he was leaving, he once again encountered Richard, who had gone to the hallway water fountain. John glanced at him as he walked by, and Richard retorted sharply, "Don't be looking at me, boy." John was becoming increasingly angered by Richard's exhibition in front of another student. Although he thought it best to ignore the remarks, he wheeled around and faced Richard. Taking a deep breath to catch himself, he slowly hissed through clenched teeth, "Go in, sit down, and don't make anything worse on yourself. Just sit down and shut up and wait for Mr. Roberts to see you." After mumbling a few unintelligible remarks, Richard complied.

Although Mr. Roberts had agreed to keep Richard in the in-school suspension (ISS) rather than sending him to John's class that afternoon, Richard showed up in class. Obviously, Mr. Roberts had bungled the ISS schedule somehow, and now John had to deal with Richard in spite of the tensions created by the situation. Fortunately, Richard remained quiet and low-key throughout class.

When John reminded him of the detention that afternoon, Richard declared that he had to catch his bus or he would have no way home. Doubting that this was the case, John told Richard that he could go home as long as he made arrangements to stay the following day. He also warned him that failure to do so would result in a rereferral and possible suspension.

John's difficulty with Richard escalated the next day during the suspension period. Ironically, John had not seen Richard in class because he had been kept in ISS. He couldn't help feeling a little resentful that Mr. Roberts had failed to keep Richard the day before and then kept him when it no longer mattered. At least, he thought, they could give me a little support downstairs. How hard could it be, after all, to keep a simple ISS schedule straight?

Upon arrival for his afternoon detention, Richard announced, "The only reason I'm staying this detention is because Mr. Roberts said I had to." When John attempted to explain to him exactly why he was given detention, Richard's behavior became erratic. A sickening knot formed in John's stomach as he realized that he was losing control of the situation.

Because Richard refused to be seated, and walked around the room striking the computer, walls, desks, and other objects with a yardstick, John was forced to ask students who had remained after school to complete a project to go to the library. John told him several times to be seated and tried to explain to him why he had gotten the referral. Each time, Richard retorted, "How come Chris didn't get a referral?" John attempted to explain several more times that the referral was not given for fighting, but for running away and refusing to return. Several times during John's explanations, Richard covered his ears and began singing a rap tune. With each explanation, he repeated the same refrain, "How come Chris didn't get a referral?"

Soon, Richard began performing a rap song with graphic lyrics that detailed his plan to beat up Chris. Several times he told John that he was going downstairs to tell the vice principal that "you were trying to beat me up, that you were trying to hit me with the yardstick, and that you were trying to slit my throat." He called John "stupid" and "peanut-head," declared that he hated him, and asked him why he didn't go back to the university. John began to sense that the differences in race and backgrounds had something to do with the animosity he was receiving from Richard.

At intervals, Richard pulled a small bottle from his jacket pocket and drank from it. The contents looked like water, but he called it his "beer" and "wine." Twice during this period, Richard wandered outside of the classroom. Both times, John followed him, reminding him that during detention he must stay in the room. When Richard decided to return to the classroom, he preceded John inside, pulled the door closed, and held it so that he could not get in.

Once inside the classroom, John attempted to get some work done, but Richard's singing was too loud for him to concentrate. When John delivered a stern look in his direction, Richard leaped from his chair and confronted him. "You staring at me? Don't be looking at me. Have you got a problem?" Implicit in this confrontation was a physical threat. John sensed that Richard was soliciting a fight. His pulse quickened and, much to his chagrin, John found himself sizing up Richard's physical bearing, comparing it to his own, inch by inch, pound by pound.

At that moment, John saw a student walking down the hall. Slipping out of the room, he asked the student to get the teacher next door. The teacher, who happened to be Richard's English teacher, was quick to grasp the situation. Stepping inside the classroom, she ordered him in a stern tone of voice to sit down. Richard retaliated with several sharp remarks. It was clear that he was ready to take her on as well. Realizing this, she went downstairs to the vice principal, who told her to release Richard from detention.

Before he released Richard, John told him that he intended to report his behavior and to rerefer him. Initially, Richard refused to leave until he had completed his detention because he thought that John would not be able to rerefer him if he stayed for the duration of the period. Finally, John told him that he could stay if he wanted, but he would still get rereferred. Richard insisted on remaining for the entire period.

John left school that afternoon with an abysmal sense of failure. He mentally reviewed the events leading up to this afternoon like a bad song that he could not get off his mind.

Two days later, during a discussion with the English teacher and a special education teacher, he discovered that Richard had been attending classes for students with behavior disorders for the past two years. Still, Richard had not been a problem before during this class, and John blamed his own ineptness for creating the situation. If only he hadn't...

Grandma's Boy

HELEN JAMISON

Part A

"I was totally unprepared to deal with those people." Helen Jamison took a sip from the apricot tea that Cindy, her roommate, had just brewed. "All I could think of was poor Justin and how awful it must be for him to live with such a dysfunctional family. I just hope we can come up with something at school that will help this kid."

Helen was a second-grade teacher at C. E. Conners Elementary School. Just two months into her first year of teaching, she had encountered the first rift in what had otherwise been a smooth and gratifying beginning. As a novice in the profession, she had hit the ground running, and her innovations had caught the eye of the central office supervisors, building-level administrators, and parents. For the most part, her 27 second-grade students got along well with one another, and she was excited about the cooperative spirit that she had managed to cultivate in this average-ability group.

At the beginning of the year, Helen had encouraged the students to select a name for the class—a name symbolizing strength, honor, and cooperation. The students had decided to call themselves the Spartans, and at Helen's request, the art teacher had drawn a picture of a warrior on horseback to post on the wall just outside the classroom. Helen had then cut the backgrounds from students' photographs and meticulously positioned and glued each picture over the silhouette of the warrior, creating a beautiful collage. Across the body of the horse, in majestic red, was a salutation: WELCOME TO ROOM 204: HOME OF THE SPARTANS.

Helen tried to perpetuate a theme of cooperation throughout the course of each day. She took time during each week to teach, model, and have the students role-play social skills that would encourage cooperation and citizenship. She praised students when she "caught them being good," and she routinely coupled this social praise with "Caughtcha!" stickers that they could exchange for prizes from her treasure chest. She presented "Spartan of the Week" awards to students who worked hard to improve their grades in an area of weakness. Of course, there were times when curiosity and mischief spawned misbehavior and minor noncompliance, but for the most part Helen believed herself capable of using basic behavior management techniques to handle such occurrences.

And so it was that after just two months of teaching, Helen was quite pleased with her performance and the performance of almost all of her students. She was greatly concerned about one of her little "munchkins," however. Justin E. Richardson II had transferred from another school in the county, and he was not keeping up with the rest of the students in the class. He daydreamed constantly, and he completed virtually no assignments. Against the advice of a colleague, Helen had scheduled a meeting with Justin's father, hoping to develop a home-school behavior management program that would motivate the child to increase his productivity. The meeting had been a complete disaster, and now Helen sat in her apartment, totally flustered by her first encounter with irate parents. She was glad that Cindy was home, for she really needed to vent her frustrations, anger, and disappointment about what had just happened. She curled up in her recliner, gazed straight ahead, and began recounting her experience.

"After the first month of school, I reread Justin's cumulative folder and discovered that a confidential folder had also been sent from his old school. Justin's first-grade teacher, Judy Cole, had written on the referral form that Justin's behavior had started to deteriorate toward the end of the year. He daydreamed constantly, was inconsistent in his work habits, and refused to comply with her instructions. She also said that Justin was not an acting-out child, but that he was difficult to deal with because of his passive-aggressive personality. No one at Conners knew anything about this kid, so I called Judy, hoping she could tell me about some 'trick' that worked last year. I can still remember her response after hearing who I was: 'Oh, so you're the lucky one this year!' She told me she felt as if she was on a treadmill with Justin, his father, and the grandmother last year. It's really sad. Judy didn't think she could do anything to help Justin. She believed nobody would be able to help the poor kid until they eased up on him at home."

"Exactly what was happening at home?" asked Cindy as she kicked off her shoes, sat Indian style on the sofa, and began munching an apple. Cindy was an elementary school guidance counselor and a masterful listener. She interjected very little, but she frequently nodded her head and gestured to Helen to continue. For this, Helen was extremely grateful. Having a live-in therapist was great!

"Well," responded Helen, "I questioned Judy further about the home situation and discovered that Justin's parents had just divorced last summer. After the divorce, Justin and his father had moved in with his paternal grandmother, Ann Richardson—better known to school personnel as 'Brunhilda.' Judy also warned me that this grandmother was a real 'busybody' and would make herself a part of every interaction that took place between Mr. Richardson and the school.

"She told me that I'd 'really have to watch that lady.' Apparently, Judy's child study team recommended that Justin undergo a full evaluation, but his father refused to grant the school permission to go through with the testing. Judy didn't believe for a minute that the refusal came from Mr. Richardson. His mother has such a dominating influence over him that Judy was convinced that she's the one who blocked the testing. Grandma came to all the meetings with Mr. Richardson, and she was adamant that Justin's problems in school were all caused by his mother—'his no-good, cheating, lying mother.' "

"Boy, it sounds like this Mrs. Richardson's a real charmer," Cindy concluded, rising to refill their mugs. She reclaimed her spot on the sofa and asked, "Is what she said about Justin's mother true, or did Judy give you conflicting information?"

"Actually, Judy wasn't aware of the causes leading to the split-up of Justin's parents, but she did know that the mother had relinquished custody of Justin and had left the state shortly after the divorce. No one at Judy's school knew exactly where the mother had moved to, and this 'mystery woman' had made no attempts to contact any school personnel. Judy finally told me that because the mother was no longer in the picture I should follow her strategy from last year and try to get help from my school psychologist or guidance counselor. She told me to stay away from the father and grandmother because they're the ones mostly responsible for what this child is going through.

"I now realize that Judy couldn't have been more accurate in her assessment of the situation," continued Helen. "As far as I'm concerned, this meeting was a waste of time. Granny Richardson, even though I didn't invite her, came with her son to the conference and immediately started to blame Justin's mother for all of his problems. I couldn't believe it when she bad-mouthed her 'low-life' ex-daughter-in-law. The way she sat straight up in her seat reminded me of a drill sergeant, and the way she barked at me made me feel like I was a recruit!"

Helen sat bolt upright and proceeded to imitate Mrs. Richardson. Her voice took on a different timbre, and for a moment Cindy actually felt that she was being lectured by a sergeant. "'No matter how hard I try to make that boy realize that he has a no-account for a mother, he still wants to see his parents back together again. He wants them to be a threesome again, so he stages these little games and hopes that Jus will contact his mom.' 'Jus' is what grandma calls Mr. Richardson."

Helen stood, pointing her finger at Cindy, and continued her impersonation. "'Well, the last time he showed off like this, I whipped his ass good and took away his bike, and I know he shaped up for a while. I guess I'm just gonna have to do it again.'"

Helen took her seat, folded her arms, and nodded her head matter-of-factly. Cindy applauded this electrifying performance, concluding that this role-playing was just the thing Helen needed to relieve some of the tension that she was feeling. She motioned for her counselee to continue, and they both giggled as Helen resumed her story, now somewhat more relaxed.

"Cindy, I could not believe what I was hearing or seeing! Just as Judy had told me, Mrs. Richardson monopolized every moment of the conversation. Mr. Richardson occasionally nodded and affirmed what his mother reported, but he contributed little else to the conference. I tried to direct questions his way, but every time I tried, 'Brunhilda' jumped right in. More and more, I realized that, because of his home situation, Justin was in jeopardy of developing some serious emotional problems."

"So, what did you suggest?" asked Cindy as she slid to the floor and rested her back against the base of the sofa.

Helen sat on the edge of her chair and shared her game plan. "At one point, I had decided to suggest that the family seek counseling, but after just a few minutes I realized that that recommendation would go over like a ton of lead. Also, I'd been warned previously by my assistant principal that such suggestions were frowned on by the school division, because if Justin was found eligible for special education, then the system could be forced to pay for this as a related service. So, when I wasn't able to think of anything else, I decided to push for my idea of a home-school management program. I also tried to make these people understand that finding a solution to Justin's problems would require much more than spankings and scoldings. I described Justin's behavior, hoping that this would provide me with a lead into my management proposal.

"'Justin,' I said to them, 'sits and stares most of the time. He doesn't interact with the other students in the class. In fact, if they initiate a conversation or ask him a question, he usually refuses to even acknowledge their existence. He looks at one of his books or writes in one of his skillbooks, pretending to be hard at work.'

"I also explained that Justin didn't respond to either praise or criticism, rewards or punishment. He hasn't completed any assignments. He's failed every section of every unit criterion test in reading. On one occasion, I watched him complete the comprehension subtest by merely going down the list and selecting answers at random. He hadn't bothered to read any of the passages in the section, and he failed the test miserably. After this, I thought that Justin was preoccupied and unmotivated. Later, I realized that, on the few occasions when he did try, Justin found it extremely difficult to decode unfamiliar words, and his oral reading was choppy and labored.

"Well, for what it was worth, I shared this information with Justin's father and grandmother. I practically begged these people to understand that we all needed to work together to help Justin. Unfortunately, after hearing my concerns, Mrs. Richardson held on to her notions about what was best for her grandson. When I tried to ease into my proposal, I was interrupted abruptly."

Helen resumed Mrs. Richardson's position and voice. "'Justin don't need no kind of home-school program.' That was Mrs. Richardson's response to my plan. 'You deal with him your way here, and we'll deal with him our way at home. Like I already said, if push comes to shove, we'll just have to beat some sense into him. Once we help him get that woman out of his system, he'll be all right anyway. Just you wait and see, he'll be all right.'

"There was no need for any further discussion," sighed Helen. "After this outburst, I thanked the Richardsons for coming and ended the meeting. As they were leaving my room I think I may have managed a half-hearted smile, but I couldn't help feeling sorry for Justin. This child is constantly being bombarded with negative information about a mother that he apparently loves, and he's being punished severely when his behavior and feelings are in conflict with those of his grandmother and father. I tell you, Cindy, I was exhausted and depressed after that meeting, and even though talking about it has helped, I just don't know what my next move will be."

Cindy broke the silence that followed with the suggestion that they identify the most salient problems and rank them. The two then spent the next half hour trying to identify possible strategies that might improve the situation.

Lenny

SARA OLSON

Part A

Sara Olson had been a teacher at Cross Lake Elementary School for 11 years, and for the past 5 years had been assigned the kindergarten classroom. Cross Lake was her first teaching job and would probably be the only one she ever had. She loved the Cross Lake community and was active in community clubs and activities. For the past 3 years she had served as chair of the summer water carnival and was an ardent and active member of the Cross Lake Garden Club. She and her husband, Jim, a state game warden, had bought a house on Bad Medicine Lake just west of town. Their two children, Justin and Katy, were well adjusted and active fourth- and sixth-grade students at Cross Lake Elementary School.

Sara enjoyed her students, and it showed in their affection for her. It showed after school each day when she would say good-bye to them as they got on their buses. Usually, they gave her a big hug. She always hugged them back, though she clearly remembered the warnings she had received during in-service training about the dangers of touching students. Her students' affection for her also showed as they got older and went into secondary school. The only cafeteria in Cross Lake was in the elementary school, and the secondary students walked a block from the high school to eat at the elementary school each day. Sara always saw some of her former students as she brought her students in from recess, and invariably they greeted her with a happy, "Hello, Mrs. Olson."

For the most part, Sara really enjoyed her job. There was a good comradery and support among the teachers and with the principal, Jean Ollerud. The school felt comfortable to her, and it certainly didn't have the kind of racial polarity, staff morale, and discipline problems known to be issues at the Cross Lake High School.

Cross Lake was a reservation border town, lying on the western edge of the Forest County Ojibwe Reservation in the northern area of the state. Sara had lived in the community long enough to have seen the transition of the community during the past several years. When she had taken her first teaching job as a fourth-grade long-term substitute, the majority of the students were "town children." Only a third of them were "reservation children." That had changed in the past 10 years; now the majority of her students came from the reservation. Although most of them still came from poor families, there seemed to be a small and growing American Indian middle-class, who, unlike the American Indian families Sara had previously known, participated more often in school activities. The middle-class American Indian parents came to parent-teacher conferences, whereas those of lower socioeconomic status rarely came to the school. Several of the middle-class Indian parents served on the school board and the Indian parent committee and were demanding changes in the curriculum to better reflect their Ojibwe heritage. They also were insisting that the school district hire Indian teachers, and, indeed, several Indians had been hired. More recently, Dale Bird, an Ojibwe from Minnesota, had been hired as the high school principal.

For the most part, Sara tried to change with the times by having reservation elders come to her class several times a year to tell legends and stories. Even though some schools had quit decorating during the Thanksgiving holiday, Sara continued to decorate her room and the area outside her classroom. During this time of the year she featured her Indian unit, teaching the children the contributions Indians made to America. Three years ago she had taken a summer school course at Mt. Scenario College called Teaching the American Indian Pupil. Although none of her close friends was Ojibwe, she felt she harbored no prejudice against Indian people.

With the start of the new school year, Sara was busy getting to know all the children and trying to assess how well prepared they were, both socially and emotionally, for kindergarten. But one of the children, Lenny, was having a difficult time.

Lenny was one of the reservation children from Bull Club, a small community south and east of Cross Lake. From what she had found out by asking one of the Indian teacher aides, Madeline Wind, Lenny had attended Forest County Ojibwe Head Start. Both of his parents worked for the tribal council and had recently built a new home out in the "Mission" area of Bull Club, so called because an Indian Bible camp was located in the area. According to Madeline, Lenny was "hell on wheels" and had given the Head Start staff fits in trying to deal with him. According to her, Lenny didn't listen to anyone.

"I heard that last year he even bit the Head Start bus driver," Madeline had told Sara. She also indicated that Lenny may be hyperactive.

During the first week of school, Lenny seemed to be adjusting well. Although he was quite active, he seemed to be making an adequate social adjustment.

When Secrets Disable

CATHY SCHROCK

I never thought I would see Kate Morrissey sitting with a group of girls and boys laughing and talking. The change in her had been remarkable. In a little more than a year, she had gone from a sullen, introverted, unpopular fifth-grader to just another good kid.

Looking back, I remember thinking how confident I was starting the school year. I had been teaching for two years, I still loved teaching despite the long hours it demanded, and I had handled several difficult situations successfully since I left college—I was ready for anything, or so I thought. I looked at my roster of new students and wondered what surprises would be in store this year. In the first two years there had been challenges, but so far none that I couldn't handle. Had I known what was ahead, I probably would have taken a leave of absence. This class would require strength and energy I didn't even know I possessed.

It started with a note from the resource teacher telling me the names of the six students with learning disabilities who would be in my room. Our school had been using an inclusive model for resource help for several years now, so I knew I would have these students in my room most of the day. This didn't bother me because I had been successful in the past working with students who had both behavior and academic problems.

I decided to read the green files before meeting the students, so I could make preparations for their arrival. I made a list that included students' names and disabilities. Most of them were having difficulties with reading and math. A couple had behavior problems as well as academic problems, but still I thought I could handle these issues with help from the special education teacher. I must admit I did become concerned when I discovered that one of the students had severe emotional disturbance and had been violent in the past—punching a hole in the wall, breaking a window with his fist, and dislocating the principal's shoulder. It was definitely going to be an interesting year!

After school began I noticed there were many student issues I had not expected—two students were identified for the gifted program, one student had been diagnosed with ADHD but was not on medication, one student had behavior problems stemming from sexual abuse, another student's mother was terminally ill, and then there was Kate. With everything else I had to do, how would I ever find the patience to deal with the tantrums, screaming, stubbornness, and neediness of Kate? I knew teachers were supposed to be able to do it all, but this seemed overwhelming.

I had never run across a child like Kate. I knew from the moment I met her that she was incredibly bright. Unfortunately, her appearance and behavior put people off so quickly that most never took the time to get to know the "real" Kate. There may be more diplomatic ways to say it, but she was dirty, "smelled like a dog" (as a fellow student described her), and was totally unsociable. She always had her nose in a book—at lunch, at recess, and any time there was a break from structured activities in the classroom. I had to hand it to the other kids in class—they didn't tease; not much, anyway. Some of the children I had known through the years would have been unmerciful. Most of the students in the room ignored her—there was little interaction between Kate and the rest of the class.

It was obvious that Kate loved to read, but still I was somewhat surprised by her score on the reading assessment—her instructional level was seventh grade. Her spelling inventory, however, showed she was a level-one speller. The disparity was stunning. Any kind of writing, even the unstructured variety in her journal, was extremely frustrating for her. Every Monday morning I had a battle with Kate when it was time for word study. The task was to use each word from the word list in a sentence. She hated to write. She would whine and mope, and often when I insisted she do the work, she became belligerent—she simply refused to write. The other children observed these episodes, of course, and sometimes they were frightened by Kate's actions. On more than one occasion Kate screamed at me and pushed her book off the desk.

"OK, Kate, take your word study journal out of your desk and begin your sentences for this week," I said one morning. Kate just sat there staring defiantly at the floor. "Kate, it is time to start." Kate blurted, "I'm not going to do it, and you can't make me."

The mornings I could not cajole Kate into participating, I would give her a choice of going to time out in the room to do her work or going to the office. Once, when Kate chose not to work or go to time out, I called the office and asked the assistant principal to come to my room, which was actually a trailer outside the building. The assistant principal arrived and told Kate that she must go to the office to finish her work. Kate held on to her desk and would not move. I sensed that Kate was on the verge of an emotional explosion, so I had all of the other students line up to go to the library. Kate lined up too. As we walked to the library the assistant principal followed the group. When we passed by the office the assistant principal told Kate to go into the office, and Kate complied. I felt lucky that the strategy to get Kate to the office had worked without having a violent confrontation in our classroom.

Kate was puzzling. She could be so difficult. It was almost impossible to get her to do anything she didn't want to do. She would dig in her heels psychologically and simply refuse to cooperate. You could see her resistance in her posture. She folded her arms tight against her chest and looked off into space. What seemed totally incongruent and very surprising to me was Kate's sophisticated sense of humor. Early in the year she had begun to bring in cartoons from *The New Yorker* and show them to me. The two of us would howl as we read them. The other fifth-graders looked on in confusion, trying to understand what was so funny.

When I met Kate's mother and her mother's boyfriend at Back-to-School night, I didn't form much of an impression for good or ill. Her mother looked fairly plain. "Please tell me, Ms. Morrissey, do you work in the home or outside?" I asked. She replied, "I recently completed my master's degree in social work. I am a caseworker for the county social services department." Apparently she put in long hours, because she did not spend much time at home. "I'm glad to be finished with the long, frequent drives to night school. For several years I have been unable to spend much time with Kate in the evenings. I gave her so much independence in those days, that now she resents it when I tell her what to do."

Ms. Morrissey's boyfriend was a little rough around the edges—short, chubby, a couple of days' growth of beard, and remarkably odoriferous. He wore a hunter's cap and his shirt and pants had the kind of gray cast that my family's clothes get when I use cheap detergent. What little he said was virtually inaudible, because he mumbled.

Ms. Morrissey asked some good questions about Kate. She expressed some concerns about her friendships, or lack of them. When I broached the topic of Kate's uncompleted homework assignments, Ms. Morrissey remarked, "That is Kate's responsibility. She knows what she is supposed to do. If I make suggestions she either acts as if I'm not there or refuses to do it." I also summoned up my courage to tell Ms. Morrissey about Kate's body odor. Her response was essentially the same: "That's her job too. She knows she is supposed to bathe every night. When I tell her to shower, she usually responds by throwing a tantrum that may last as long as half an hour."

Time might have passed with only minor rough spots in our classroom had I not decided to visit Kate's home. That visit set us up for what turned out to be a tense, troubling, and fairly long-lasting confrontation. It was in February after I had developed what I believed was a mutually caring relationship with Kate, even though I was beginning to discover that Kate was tight-lipped, even secretive, about her life outside of school.

I was becoming increasingly concerned because Kate had confided reluctantly that frequently nobody came home until 11:00 or 12:00 at night. Many nights, she was in the trailer-home all by herself, except for Sandy, her pet rat, and Rover, her beloved dog. She boasted that she could take care of herself and was not afraid, even though her trailer was in an isolated area. On these nights she fixed macaroni and cheese and treated herself with bags of Oreos—in fact, her reliance on sweets had begun to be apparent. She also told me about how messy things were at her house. She seemed quite pained to tell me these things. Kate would say things like, "You wouldn't believe what a mess my house is. You wouldn't want to come to my house."

When I looked back over my own journal, I realized that I had actually been building a case for making a home visit. Or, more accurately, my letters to myself seemed to compel me to visit Kate and her mother in their home. The opportunity for making a home visit fell into my lap when Kate sneaked her pet rat to school on the bus. Students are not allowed to have animals on the bus, so that evening I offered to give Kate a ride home and to take Sandy the Rat with us. In fear of what I might find, I invited the assistant principal to go with us.

When we arrived at the house, I discovered there was good reason to be concerned. The trailer was down a long, bumpy driveway, nowhere near any other houses. The trailer was old, the front steps sagged, and the storm door, hanging from its hinges, had a broken pane. The yard looked like the local junkyard and included an old refrigerator that had been used for target practice. But the worst was yet to come. Inside, half of the living room was piled from floor to ceiling with trash. A spot had been cleared on the couch just large enough for Kate to sit and watch TV. I could see how Kate might be overwhelmed by the enormity of the task of cleaning up the mess.

Kate had been assigned a Big Sister through a program at the university. Ms. Morrissey had told Kate that she couldn't see her Big Sister until the house had been cleaned. With the three of us working together—Kate, the assistant principal, and I—I figured we could at least take care of Kate's room. It didn't take long to discover that it wasn't possible. Her room was covered with trash, books were on the floor, all of her clothes were scattered around the room—not one piece of clothing was in her closet. We started to pick up the trash, but soon stopped when I picked up a book and found dog feces on it. I looked down and realized I was standing in dog poop! Kate was right. The problem was just too big.

All of this happened on a Friday. I did not see her until the following Monday. When Kate arrived at school she was very angry with me. She gave me the cold shoulder. "Hi, Kate!" I said as she walked in the door headed toward her desk. Kate did not respond.

I should have known not to press her, but she had made me angry too—she had been rude all morning. Once again, it was time to collect the sentences for word study. Kate would not hand in her notebook. I gave her an ultimatum and told her she must hand it in now. She looked at me and yelled, "This is my book. You can't have it. This is all your fault!" She threw the book at me, continued screaming, and started tipping over desks.

It took both the assistant principal and me to calm Kate. When she finally settled down, I was so emotionally exhausted that I could have walked out the door and never returned. Following the confrontation, the assistant principal and I agreed that what we needed was an all-out program to bring Kate into the mainstream of life in school, and somehow this effort had to include her mother. We had the will, and we hoped we had the energy, but what we didn't have was a strategy.

They Failed Derrick

MELINDA SMITH

Part A

I watched through my classroom window as Derrick and his mother got into their car and drove away. I tried not to cry as I gathered up Derrick's textbooks and returned them to the book room. I walked back to my classroom, sat down at my desk, and tried futilely to work on my reading lesson for the next day. I couldn't concentrate. Each time I tried to read something from my teacher's manual I couldn't help but think about Derrick and what I feared was going to happen to him.

And as for that placement team—that wonderful group of concerned educators—well, I was furious with those guys! The decision to transfer this child to a middle school and place him in a class for children with behavioral disorders was the worst possible thing that we could do to him! Even though he had taken me through some real challenges since the beginning of the year, Derrick had made a lot of progress, and I really didn't feel that placing him in a special education class would improve his behavior. You would think that my previous experiences with children with disabilities would have counted for something, but it didn't. We simply didn't give this kid enough time. I will always believe the we moved too early on this one.

I came to know Derrick my first year back in a regular classroom after teaching children with mental retardation for over 15 years. Now that my own two kids were grown up and off in college, I felt that I was losing touch with how normal kids think and operate. I also believed that I was doing a disservice to my little kids who have disabilities. You see, because many of the classes for students with mental retardation were being phased out, my class had become a regional program. Students from all over the county were bused to my school to receive services. I was teaching some of the same pupils for up to five years, and it finally dawned on me that this was not in their best interest—nor in mine. I considered myself a good teacher and I really cared about these students, but at the same time I felt myself becoming too routinized. I needed a change, and so did the kids. So, I decided to take the plunge. It was time for me to return to the regular classroom.

There were regular classroom vacancies at my school, Essig Elementary, but after considering my options I decided that I needed to make a clean break. Even though I got along very well with the faculty and staff at Essig, I just couldn't imagine watching my kids walking down the hallway with another teacher. So I talked with an old partner in crime, Greg Rodgers, who was the principal of Helmsley Elementary School. Greg and I worked together during my first five years as a teacher, and over the years it seems our paths always managed to cross. After he became an administrator, we were assigned to assist with the development of several countywide in-service projects. I also served as his assistant principal during a few summer school sessions. Greg was a professional in every sense of the word, and I thought that it would be very rewarding to work under his leadership on a full-time basis. After taking care of all of the formalities, Greg offered me the position as the teacher of high-average and gifted fifth-grade students. I looked forward to this change and challenge, and though it was difficult for me to walk away from what had been a major part of my life for 15 years, I packed up boxes of books, ditto masters, teacher-made games, presents collected over the years, and, yes, even my drawer full of confiscated toys.

I started out on my new venture with a feeling of interest and optimism. During the summer, I enrolled in a course on teaching gifted children, and I read related books and journal articles whenever time permitted. I also spent a lot of time just thinking about my experiences and skills as a special educator and wondering how I could transfer these skills to my new situation. I was so excited! I wanted to be ready in September when those kids stepped off the bus and entered my classroom.

Well, even though I would be teaching higher-functioning kids, and even though I was in a new school, I found that I had been typecast. I don't know of any other way to put it. Other special education teachers who had returned to regular classroom positions often told me about their experiences. "Once a special educator, always a special educator," they'd say. It didn't take me very long to understand what they really meant. During the first day of teacher work week, Greg called me into his office and asked if I would consider taking a child who had some real emotional problems.

"This kid has shot holes through almost every teacher in this school," I remember him saying. "If there's anyone in the world who can make a change in him, it's you. Will you please consider taking him until we can get the paperwork done to have him placed in special education?"

"Flattery will get you nowhere," I replied. But in the end, I agreed to take on this kid. When I thought of having a student with emotional problems and academic deficits in a class with gifted learners, I felt a tingle in my spine. This would be a real challenge indeed, I thought.

The student was none other than the infamous Derrick Yates. He was 12 years old and functioning at about a third-grade level in all subjects. He had developed a notorious reputation around school. None of the teachers could handle him during the one year he had been at Helmsley. In fact, I found out that last year he hadn't even been able to stay at school all day. Greg had made arrangements with Derrick's mother to have him picked up after lunch until such time that his behavior improved. Greg had also written a contract with Derrick that outlined student, teacher, and administrator responsibilities. The contract also specified the conditions that would allow Derrick's time at school to be extended. Unfortunately, Derrick never made it past lunchtime. He defied and frightened faculty and staff members on several occasions. He never lasted longer than five minutes in physical education, art, or music because he would disrupt the class, curse or threaten a teacher, and be sent to the office.

Honestly, I hardly had time to hang my bulletin boards during in-service week because my room was buzzing with teachers who wanted to give me the low-down on Derrick. The other fifth-grade teachers talked about how their nerves had been frazzled all summer long because they feared that their worst possible nightmare might come true—that Derrick would be assigned to their classroom. Needless to say, they were quite relieved to know that moi—Melinda Smith, the new kid on the block—was also certified in behavioral disorders and fit all the qualifications to be the "chosen one."

"He has terrorized everyone," Karen, one of the fifth-grade teachers, told me. "His mother has absolutely no control over him at home, and so he thinks that he can also be the man in charge here. The weird thing about it is that . . . I think he's right."

At this point, I began to wonder what I had gotten myself into. The stories I heard about Derrick's home life were totally unbelievable. Derrick's father and mother were divorced, and Derrick was living with his mother and a younger brother and sister. He was angered by his parents' separation and the divorce, and he blamed his mother for the failed marriage. Apparently, he idolized his father, but these feelings weren't mutual. Unable to deal with this rejection, Derrick took out his frustrations on anyone and everyone with whom he came in contact. This included his mother, brother, and sister. Barbara Cole, the school social worker, told me stories that gave me goose bumps.

"This child actually butchered and killed the family dog with a knife. He cut off the poor dog's head and extremities and lined them up in a neat row in the backyard. His mother had locks installed on the kitchen drawers because she was afraid that he would use the utensils as weapons against her and the other children. She's also installed a double-bolt lock on her bedroom door, and she lets the two younger children sleep in the room with her at night. Some people would consider this absurd, but she was wise to take this action."

To say the least, Barbara had aroused my curiosity. "What do you mean?" I asked.

"Well, on one occasion, Mrs. Yates reported that Derrick was angry with her because he was convinced that she had not allowed him to speak with his dad on the phone. Actually, Mr. Yates had called about child support payments and had expressed no interest in speaking to any of the children. That night, Mrs. Yates awakened to the sound of Derrick jabbing a large butcher knife against her bedroom door. After she threatened to call the police, he finally stopped his terrorizing and returned to his room.

I tried, but I couldn't get a word in edgewise. Barbara continued to share her experiences with Derrick.

"Shortly after that, I was sent to the Yates's home to conduct an interview with the mother. I found Derrick home alone that day. For no apparent reason, he was absent from school. Now, Derrick is a large kid for his age, and coupled with those bucked and crooked teeth, and that uncontrollable sick kind of laugh, he really looks like something scary. To see this kid in action is like watching a scene from an Alfred Hitchcock movie. Anyway, Derrick opened the door, stared at me, and asked in a threatening voice, 'What you want, bitch?' Honey, I just politely turned, walked to my car, and got out of there."

As I listened to these horrendous stories, I realized that this would be the case of all cases. But still, I wanted to give this one a whirl. I had a few tricks up my sleeve that I hadn't even tried yet, and from the way everybody described Derrick, I figured that I would finally have the chance to use them. And so my special education training and my natural inclination and desire to work with troubled children prompted me to accept Derrick Winslow Yates into my fifth-grade classroom.

On the day the students arrived in September, it didn't take me two minutes to realize which one was Derrick. Aside from the descriptions that my colleagues had given, one could not help but feel this child's presence. There was a certain "looseness" about him. From the way he moved about the room, I could tell that he knew he could frighten people, and as I told the class to sit down and get settled I could feel his eyes on me. He took his time getting to his seat, and I had the feeling that he was trying to let me know that he expected me to fear him, too. Just as the other teachers told me, I could see that "look" in his eyes. So, I realized the very instant I met Derrick that I would have to handle him with kid gloves. Even though I had a little fear, I was determined that I would not let him see or even sense this fear. As usual, I tried to think positively, but I also made plans to expect the worst.

Well, to my surprise, the first three weeks of school went by without any major hassles. In fact, Derrick was not really a problem at all. He was talkative, restless, and obviously frustrated because the work was way over his head. I modified his assignments, however; and I kept a careful watch on him when I assigned independent work or work in cooperative learning groups. I also used proximity control, and sometimes, if he was getting restless or starting to harass one of the other children verbally, I would simply walk over to him and calmly put my hand on his shoulder, and he'd straighten up. Still, he maintained the "look," and I resigned myself to the fact that I could not let down my guard—that I had to watch him every minute he was in the room.

I don't think Derrick knew how to take it that I was not yelling at him, isolating him, or sending him to the office. He really tickled me one day when he walked up to me and asked, "You don't know about me, do you?" When I asked what he meant, he stated that he had a bad reputation and that he had stayed in the office more time last year than he had stayed in the classroom. He told me that the principals, teachers, and the kids were all afraid of him and that he liked to do mean things. Boy, did he lay it on the line! I had to think quickly before I responded.

"Why, thank you, Derrick," I replied. "Thank you. I appreciate that you told me special things about yourself that will help me plan for you." I also told him that I was pleased with his behavior so far, and that I looked forward to having a good year with him in my class. With that, he looked at me as if to say, "No such luck, Lady!" and returned to his seat with one of his eerie chuckles.

A few days later, his mother called me very upset because she said that things were getting worse at home and she didn't know how long she could keep dealing with Derrick. He was driving her crazy, and she was still very much concerned about the safety of her other children. Well, I felt that Derrick, by coming to me and exposing the negative side of himself, was letting me know that our little hiatus was about to come to an end. It was as if he was saying, "Now you know, I've talked to you and my mother has talked to you, and now I'm going to let it all hang out." This is precisely what he did.

I'll never forget the very first major incident. The kids knew about Derrick's reputation, and they came in really upset and a little nervous to tell me that he had a pocket knife on the bus. Joey mustered up enough nerve to make the report. He was shaking like a leaf when he came up to me. He looked over his shoulder constantly to make sure that Derrick wasn't in the room.

"Mrs. Smith, Derrick had a knife on the bus, and he was waving it in all of our faces, and he dared us to tell the bus driver!"

Poor thing, he was gasping for breath by the time he finished, so I used an old tried-and-true trick—"antiseptic bouncing"—to help him get himself under control. This little technique had been a real life saver during my years as a special educator. I sent Joey to the office with a note to the secretary requesting that she send him back with some bond paper after letting him sit and calm down for a few minutes. Just as he left the room, Derrick entered as if nothing out of the ordinary had occurred. He walked over to the browsing table and started thumbing through a motorcycle magazine. As usual, I told everyone to sharpen pencils and prepare for work. Then, I breathed a deep sigh and walked over to Derrick.

Stealing Time

ROBERT CARTER

Part A

Robert's seventh year of teaching began like most of the others. As a fourth-grade teacher, he had learned the value of setting his standards early in the year, letting students know in no uncertain terms the range and limits of acceptable behavior in his classroom. He felt strongly about strict but fair enforcement of rules, and he found that his students soon conformed to the standards he administered. He believed that if he was fair with students, they would be fair with him. As a result, his classroom became like a small community where everyone knew what to expect and how to behave at all times. Robert found that even his most unusual or troubled students soon fell in line with his expectations, and he believed that his classroom management benefited these difficult students as much, perhaps even more, than the other students. In his classroom there was a comfortable predictability based on the mutual understanding of, and adherence to, the ground rules.

Fall semester progressed just as he had assumed it would. He had worked hard to set his "precedents" and, before the conclusion of the first six-week grading period, his students had settled in. He was pleased that Andy and Martin, both children from very deprived, troubled backgrounds who also had behavior and academic problems, had shown much improvement in their ability to fit in. Kara, a mainstreamed student with behavior disorders, also appeared to be progressing nicely with the help of her special education teacher, as did David, a student from the self-contained learning disabilities classroom who was mainstreamed for short nonacademic periods of the school day. David came to Robert's class for morning homeroom period, which included roll-call, lunch money collection, the pledge of allegiance, and the like. David also went to art, music, and physical education with Robert's class. With the exception of minor and infrequent student transgressions, all was well.

Shortly after Christmas vacation, David's special education placement in the self-contained learning disabilities classroom was submitted for the reevaluation required every three years. The eligibility committee decided, based on his recent assessment results, that David should now be placed in the regular education classroom for at least

51 percent of the day. In other words, he was to receive special education services in a learning disabilities resource room, but more than half of his instruction was to take place in the regular classroom. Robert now had David for mathematics, a subject in which David possessed relative strengths, as well as for science and health. In addition, David ate lunch with Robert's class and attended the regular fourth-grade social studies class with Ms. Gleason across the hall. Because David's participation in his class had not presented a problem before, Robert had no apparent reason to anticipate what was to come.

Within a few days Robert sensed the beginning of the end of what he had considered a pleasant school year. In mathematics, David did not turn in assignments and was soon far behind in his work. While Robert instructed the class, David alternately made strange noises and interrupted Robert and other students by blurting out declarations such as, "I know that," or "Let me do that." He dropped books loudly and deliberately on the floor, banged his pencil rhythmically on his desk, and probed noisily in his desk for lost objects. When Robert requested that he stop these disruptive and highly annoying behaviors, David ignored him. Robert considered David's behavior a relentless onslaught of interruption and rudeness aimed at him and the other students. He reasoned that David was attempting to regain the attention he had been accustomed to in the special education classroom. After all, in there he had been one of only five or so students with one teacher and a teacher's aide; he had been spoiled by receiving so much individual attention. Robert was certain that he was capable of successfully completing his assignments and that he was simply choosing not to do so, just as he was choosing his outrageous misbehavior. Whether David had taken his Ritalin, or had taken it at the proper time, did not seem to make much difference as far as Robert could see. Robert felt that David did what he wanted to do; and, most of the time, he wanted to show off and interrupt the class.

As both David's work and his behavior continued to worsen, Robert's loathing and resentment of him grew. This one student was ruining everything he had worked so hard to accomplish. To add insult to injury, David often stated loudly that he wanted to go back to his "real" class and to his "real" teacher. He was not even giving Robert a chance to be his teacher. He did not like Robert, and he did not like the other students. Robert felt that somehow he had failed to gain David's respect, but he was at a loss to explain why. In the meantime, David's relationships with the other students were deteriorating.

Because Robert's mathematics class was set up in a cooperative learning format, the students were compelled to work together in small groups, the success of which depended on each member's productive contributions and hard work. David's refusal to complete assignments naturally lowered the average of his group. When some of the other students tried to help him, he rebuffed their efforts. Soon, his classmates began to complain. Robert began keeping David in from recess when he refused to complete his assignments, but he continued to neglect his work.

The day David took an assignment that Robert had just distributed and "chucked" it immediately into David's desk, deliberately signifying that he had no intention of completing it, Robert went to his desk to declare sharply, "That's not what we do in here, that's not what's expected of you in here, and I've had just about enough of it." David retorted that he wanted to go back to his old class and that he did not like the way the other students looked at him. Robert replied that the other students looked at him because of the way he was acting. He went on to explain that these kids had never seen anybody act like this before, and that if he didn't want them to look at him, he would just have to change his attitude and change what he did in the classroom. At this point, Robert dismissed his class for lunch.

After lunch, David's behavior reached extreme proportions. When he reentered the classroom, he was "bouncing off the walls." He began making noises, pulling on the window blinds, and telling his classmates to "shut up." Robert had planned to have the class prepare some answer sheets for the upcoming standardized testing. Because David was not to be tested with the rest of the class, Robert told him to go to the back of the room (to the time-out seat) so that neither he nor the class would disturb each other. David picked up his materials and went to the designated seat; however, when he reached his destination, he slammed his things onto the desk with such force that his pencil bounced off the wall. Robert seized him briskly by the arm, informing him, "You are not going to throw things in this classroom." David replied, "It didn't hit anyone." He was anxiously repeating this assertion for the third time when Robert jerked him up by his arm, pulled him down the hall, and placed him forcefully into a student desk in the principal's office.

After instructing David not to return until he had completed his work, Robert returned to his classroom. David remained in the office until late afternoon. Because school rules dictated that students were not to be kept in from P.E. during formal instruction from the physical education teacher, David was to attend. Before leaving the classroom for P.E., David commissioned a classmate to tell Robert that he wished to talk with him. When Robert received the message, he told his class that David would just have to wait until the rest of the students went out for P.E.

When the others had left, Robert went to the back of the room where David waited. David said, "I hear you wanted to talk to me." Robert replied that he had understood that David had wanted to speak with him and that he was willing to listen to what David had to say. David's response to this was to tell Robert, "Forget it." After sitting quietly in the back of the empty classroom for a while, David approached Robert's desk and explained that he was sorry for his behavior but he didn't like the other kids in the class staring at him. Robert reiterated the previously offered reasons for their staring. He went on to ask David if he might work better if the other students were told not to stare at him. David allowed that this would help him work better, and Robert followed by inquiring whether he or the class could do anything else to help him. David said that it would help if Kevin did not fuss at him in math groups. Robert explained that Kevin wanted his group to do well and that he fussed at him because David was bringing the group's average down. Finally, David agreed that it might be all right if Kevin fussed, but that it would be much better if he did it quietly. During these negotiations, David agreed to bring his materials to class, to treat Robert and the other students with respect, and to complete his assignments. After this discussion, David's behavior and schoolwork improved for the next several days. The following week, however, the situation regressed to its previous state.

Once again, David behaved as if he were angry with everyone. Robert kept him in from recess for not completing assignments, and he spent more time sitting in the principal's office. As Robert explained it, "He was just angry at everything, and the other kids in the class are just so angry at David, and I'm angry at David, too, because of what he's doing with us. He's just pushing my buttons, and it's just like a power struggle between the two of us. He wants his way, and I want my way. As long as I'm the adult in the classroom, it's going to be my way, because it benefits the rest of the class. I can't have David disrupting everybody else in their work just because David's special. Well, as far as I'm concerned, I have 25 other kids who are special, who want to learn, and David has shown me so far that David just wants to learn when he feels like it; when he doesn't, he wants to disrupt everybody else."

While David was out of the classroom one day, one of Robert's students broached the subject of David's behavior. Several of the others joined in, asking such questions as: "Why is he disrupting our classroom? Why isn't he doing his work? Doesn't he know he's going to fail if he doesn't do his work?" They told Robert that the day he had jerked David out of the classroom, they had laughed. Robert responded by admitting to the students that it must have looked "pretty comical." When they inquired, "Why did you have to do that?" Robert replied, "I don't think it's fair to you for David to sit in here and disrupt you." He followed this statement by asking, "Do you think it's fair?" The class concurred with his conviction. He went on to explain that he did not understand what made David "tick." By holding this discussion with the other students, Robert felt that he was being honest and "up-front" with them. Robert could see that the class was beginning to see David as a renegade and a social outcast, as many of them made statements such as, "We don't like David to come in here." David was to provide further fuel for this opinion in a few weeks.

One afternoon, Robert did not allow David to attend recess because he had not completed his assignments. As David was working on one assignment in the empty classroom, Robert stepped out for three or four minutes to copy a worksheet David had not completed. When the class returned from recess, Bob, whose desk was near David's, reported that his watch, which he had left on his desk, was missing. Robert instructed Bob to check his locker and his desk. He had the other students look for the missing watch, too, but no one found it.

The following morning, David immediately rushed up to Robert's desk and announced, "Look at this watch that my daddy gave me!" Robert asked David to take the watch off so he could see it. As Robert examined the watch, he felt his anger, hurt, and suspicion growing. He was virtually certain it was Bob's watch.

The Truth about Alice

JANET LANE

Janet Lane often found her Algebra 1a and 1b courses a challenge. These courses were designed for ninth- and tenth-graders who were comparatively slow to grasp the fundamental concepts of the subject. Janet noticed that this course sequence—Algebra 1a (pre-algebra) first semester in preparation for Algebra 1b (regular algebra) second semester—was generally selected by lower-performing students and that she often had particular difficulty managing students' behavior in these classes.

Janet had dealt with her share, or more, of low motivation, inattention, and overt attempts to disrupt the class. In her 16 years of teaching, she felt that she had handled these problems more or less successfully. She had never encountered a problem that, over time, she was unable to resolve—until recently.

During the first semester in Algebra 1a, Janet's class consisted of the usual mix of students. One student, however, distinguished herself from the others on the basis of appearance alone. When Janet looked at Alice, she could not help thinking that she was the most unattractive child she had ever seen. Although she was not from a poor home, Alice wore a pair of baggy dungarees (rolled up at the ankles) and a polo shirt to school every single day. She apparently had three sets of this "outfit," but she always looked the same. To magnify the frumpy style of her apparel, Alice's physical shape was, well, unusual. From the waist down, she was proportionally much larger than she was above the waist, giving her a peculiar pear-shaped appearance. The way she turned her feet in when she walked made her look almost as if she had an orthopedic deformity. Very thick glasses; dental braces; stringy, oily hair; and a general unkempt appearance all added to her misfit look.

If only Alice performed well academically, Janet thought, her odd appearance could be somewhat compensated for; but, in fact, Alice was also a weak student. Her parents had recently decided to remove her from the learning disabilities program because they did not want her to be in special education in high school. No one had brought this fact to Janet's attention. But she did not customarily seek such information, choosing instead to "let the kids tell me what they are." As it turned out, there was a lot Janet didn't know about Alice.

Alice had been in Janet's class only a few days when she approached her and stated, "I'm going to have to be late for class." This soon became a frequent occurrence. Because the class met directly after lunch, the first several times Alice was late Janet didn't see it as a problem. After all, she reasoned, Alice had been nice enough to tell her each time she was going to be late.

When Alice's lateness became consistent, however, Janet became concerned and decided to have a talk with her. When she told Alice that her tardiness to class was becoming a problem, Alice became quite agitated and repeatedly insisted in a squealing voice, "I have to be late for class." Deciding that she must be firm, Janet replied, "I don't care if you're late occasionally, but you can't be late every single day. We have a class to run, you know."

Perhaps she should have expected the earnest flow of tears which ensued, but, in fact, Alice's weeping caught her off guard. At the moment, all she could think to do was to tell Alice not to worry, that they would discuss it later.

That afternoon Janet decided to seek some information and advice concerning this situation. Noticing Martha Keys, the sophomore guidance counselor, in the main office, she greeted her and began an account of the problem she was having with Alice. Almost immediately, Martha began to laugh so heartily that Janet felt a mild surge of confused annoyance. Noting the bewildered look on her face, Martha managed to ask mirthfully, "You don't know?" Janet shook her head "no" while Martha proceeded to direct her toward the guidance office. After closing the door, Martha explained the situation. Alice, she recounted, had attracted a great deal of attention last year as a result of an incident in the girls' restroom that had become, in a short time, almost legendary.

It seems that Alice's mother had insisted that she brush her teeth after lunch daily and had sent her to school with a neat little kit with which to accomplish this task. Too embarrassed to brush in front of other students, and too compliant to disobey her mother's orders, Alice solved her dilemma by brushing in the toilet stall. By all accounts, Alice was observed by another student using the water in the toilet to carry out her dental hygiene.

Word of this "incredibly grody act" spread quickly among the students, and when Martha got wind of it she called Alice into her office to discuss the matter. They resolved the problem by allowing Alice permission to be late for class after lunch so that she could brush her teeth at the sink after the other students had gone to class. Unfortunately, the incident had resulted in tremendous social damage and now presented Janet with some unusual behavior problems in her Algebra 1a class.

Janet had been aware that Alice's late arrival to her class caused some disturbance among the other students; yet she was unable to fully grasp the situation until she had discovered the reason for Alice's tardiness. It seemed that everyone had been in on the joke except Janet. When Alice entered class late, she was met with greetings such as, "Hello, Alice!" or "Watcha been doing, Alice?" These remarks were conveyed in ironic tones which held, for the informed listener, thinly veiled reference to Alice's past bathroom misadventures.

Now that she understood what lay behind these "greetings," Janet became increasingly aware of the disruption instigated by Alice's late arrival. The problem had grown to the point that three of the boys were so consistently ugly to her that Janet was compelled to go to the assistant principal and say, "I want those three boys, myself, and you to sit down and have a little talk." The "little talk," however, didn't amount to much. Just the usual, "I can't believe you are picking on this girl! Leave her alone! Act your age! Pretend she's not there . . . " During the meeting, Janet decided that she would definitely have to separate these three and Alice in class, surrounding her with a shield of nice kids. This worked well—for about a week.

Having decided that the boys were the instigators, it came as quite a shock to Janet when she discovered that notes were being passed between these boys and Alice. The particular "love note" that came to her attention was written to Alice by Mitch, the ring-leader of the boys who were entertaining themselves at Alice's (and Janet's) expense. The note consisted of a simple message: "I like you, Alice. Would you like to go out sometime?" Alice had replied affirmatively and enthusiastically, and the note was on its way back when Janet intercepted it. Several students exchanged meaningful looks as Janet returned to her lesson.

Disgusted and frustrated, Janet took both Mitch and Alice to the office after class and had them assigned to in-school suspension. She tried to reason with Alice that she was guilty for having participated in the note-passing. How could she get Alice to understand that the boys were making a joke of her without hurting her feelings? Alice just didn't seem to "get it," and this made Janet worry even more. Alice, believing that the boys really liked her, could be played for the fool by them. In the back of her mind, Janet also worried about the possibility that the boys might easily take sexual advantage of Alice. There seemed to be no way out of this situation that would avoid Alice's eventual humiliation or further loss of social status.

One Bad Apple

ELAINE BROWN

After 26 years of teaching, Elaine Brown had developed a guiding philosophy that helped keep her goals as an educator in perspective. She believed that, as a teacher, she should get to know each student's distinctive blend of abilities and set her expectations accordingly. As she expressed it, "My expectations are different, not only for different students, but for every subject. If a student has trouble in math, but is extremely gifted in English and reading, I don't expect As from him in math, but he'd better give them to me in English and reading because that's his field." As she began her 27th year in the classroom, this year teaching fifth grade, she already had a working knowledge of most of her students' strengths and weaknesses because she had taught this group as fourth-graders last year. She had only two new students, William and Eddie.

William had moved to Pine County from a nearby city because his mother had withdrawn him from the class for children with behavior disorders and sent him to live with his father. From the little information Elaine could gather, William's parents had divorced when he was a toddler, and his mother was employed sporadically. Often, she and her three children slept in their car or floated from one friend's home to another between jobs. When she enrolled him in Pine County Public Schools, William's mother made one thing clear: She did not want him placed in a class for children with behavior disorders.

Elaine had serious misgivings about William being so abruptly and completely mainstreamed, but she felt she had little choice but to make the best of it. So she approached the task with the same philosophy she applied to the other students—determine what is reasonable to expect, and then uphold those expectations while always aiming higher. With William, she found that she had to set her expectations far below the average. Although he liked to read, William's reading was approximately two years below grade level. During the first week of school, he absolutely refused to do work in mathematics. He simply would not pick up his pencil. As the first several weeks of school elapsed, it was also apparent that he was not accustomed to attending school on a regular basis. In fact, he was absent two or three days a week.

Elaine reported this attendance problem to the visiting teacher (school social worker), Jerry West, who went to William's home on several occasions when William did not come to school. When Jerry had knocked on the door, no one answered, and everything seemed quiet and still. Jerry spoke with several neighbors who told him that as soon as he left, William—who had been home—opened the doors and windows and resumed watching television. These neighbors also explained that Mr. Payne, William's father, left for work at a pipe-fitting factory at 6:30 A.M. and did not return home until 7:00 P.M. Jerry then went to Mr. Payne's place of employment and spoke with him during a work break. Mr. Payne, a small man who looked to be in his fifties, explained to Jerry in a soft voice that he wanted William to go to school. He told Jerry that he awakened William each morning; but, because he left for work so early, William was able to go back to bed and skip school. "I'll lose my job if I stay home to make sure he gets on the school bus," he explained.

When he did attend school, William was dolorous and withdrawn except when someone did something he did not like, and then he became explosive. Sometimes these temper tantrums came with no detectable provocation. It was through repeated tantrums that William cultivated his teacher's apprehension and classmates' fear of him. One such incident occurred on a warm September afternoon. The class was subdued from the stuffiness of the classroom and the heaviness of the school lunch. Elaine, perspiring and weary, nevertheless carried on with her lesson on the exploration of the New World. Without warning, William rose from his desk. Wielding the large fifth-grade social studies textbook far over his head, William slammed it forcefully on Chuck's desk, who sat directly behind him. Chuck reflexively jerked his hands from the surface of the desk and pulled his torso as far back as the orange plastic chair would allow before the book struck the desk with an explosive impact.

The class froze. The second hand on the plastic wall clock ticked laboriously before the spell of the moment was broken by William who, glowering at the class with malevolent intensity, shuffled to his seat and faced the front of the classroom defiantly. Elaine realized—and she knew her students also realized—that William had had no intention of altering the direction or velocity of the textbook even if Chuck had not removed his hands with such quickness. Her mind struggled against numbness in an effort to decide what to do. At four feet, eleven inches, she was not prepared for a physical encounter with William, and she was unwilling to risk further violence toward the rest of her students. Besides, she reasoned, although William had disrupted the class, he had not actually caused harm. Her instincts told her that it was best to let the moment pass, deciding that any immediate intervention on her part might send William completely out of control.

Because William was frequently absent from school, Elaine had the opportunity to discuss his behavior with her students, which she did on two occasions. During these exchanges, she acknowledged their fears and apprehensions, and as a class they agreed to treat William carefully so as to avoid provoking his anger. They would not tease him, touch his belongings, or correct him in class if he made a mistake. These were all things for which he seemed to have a very low tolerance. Elaine also asked the class to give William as much encouragement as possible by doing simple things such as nodding affirmatively after he read aloud. She had noticed that he seemed heartened by such approval, and she wanted to take advantage of this to make him feel a part of the class and feel better about himself.

Elaine took comfort in the trust she was able to achieve with this group of students. The bond she had established with them last year now stood them in good stead. This is not to say that the students became less frightened of William; they did not. What they did become, however, was much more astute in reading him and knowing when and how to hide their fear. Elaine quietly observed these developments with a mixture of pride and sorrow. However, she felt that they were all doing the best they knew how under the circumstances.

The only exception to this cooperative effort was Eddie, a small, spare boy who seemed unable to resist attracting William's attention. Elaine believed that, in his own way, Eddie was at least as troubled as William. In fact, his records showed that he had been referred repeatedly to his previous school's child study committee because of behavior problems. His parents had refused to allow a formal evaluation by which the school could establish eligibility for special education services.

Because he was small, his behavior, although erratic, was more of an annoyance than a real problem, except when it came to William. Elaine's students were growing accustomed to Eddie's unexpected bids for attention. At almost any given time or place, Eddie would poke, slap, or punch classmates much larger than himself, apparently without heed of possible consequences. Any opportunity to get out of Elaine's eyesight provided him an occasion to provoke other students. Elaine remembered the day that, returning from lunch, she found Eddie crawling around on the floor biting his classmates on their ankles. Reprimanding him for such behavior usually brought a blank smile to his face. Although she had attempted to provide meaningful consequences for his behavior, she had yet to find either a positive consequence or a negative one that really seemed to mean anything to him.

As with William, the class demonstrated more patience with Eddie than Elaine felt she could rightfully expect from a group of fifth-graders. To be sure, some students had more patience than others. On occasion, a less tolerant student would reciprocate Eddie's most recent annoyance with a sound slap or a decisive shove against the nearest wall. Because these retaliatory acts appeared neither to faze nor to hurt him, and because they rendered at least momentary results, Elaine usually ignored this vigilante form of justice.

It was when Eddie picked on William that Elaine could not ignore the repercussions. Unlike her other students, Eddie simply did not seem to understand that he should not provoke William, nor did he seem to realize that she could not guarantee his safety when he chose to incite William's ire.

That she could not ensure Eddie's safety was clearly illustrated on a crisp November day as she led her class in from their midmorning recess period. She had established the routine of having her class line up for water before returning to the classroom. After each student had gotten a drink, he or she was to proceed to the classroom to prepare for the upcoming lesson. On this particular day, Eddie, who appeared to be bursting with energy from the preceding kickball game, left his place in line. Escaping Elaine's notice, he whizzed past William, giving him a playful push on his way to the end of the line.

Eddie's piercing scream caused Elaine's stomach to lurch and brought her rushing past the fine of wide-eyed faces. There she found William on top of Eddie with his right knee planted squarely in Eddie's spine. His powerful arms were pulling Eddie's frail shoulders toward him, and his contorted features conveyed the full force of his anger and rage. Within that crystallized split second, Elaine could almost hear Eddie's spine snap. Forcing a sense of quiet confidence, Elaine reached out, gently placed her hand on his taut shoulder, and whispered, "William." Almost instantly, William's muscles relaxed. He released Eddie's shoulders and slowly rose to his feet. His glaring eyes refused to meet Elaine's as he stated matter-of-factly, "I'm going to hurt him." Eddie rose to a sitting position and sat sobbing on the floor as the rest of the class stood in silent observation.

Turning her attention to Eddie, she asked him if he could stand. He nodded affirmatively, quickly got up, and wiped his tears on the ragged cuff of his blue flannel shirt. Watching William out of the corner of her eye, she reformed the line and directed the students to the classroom. No one spoke.

Arriving at the classroom, Elaine went to Katherine Ellis, the teacher next door, and asked her to watch the class while she made arrangements to have William taken home. She was hesitant to do this because she did not want to compound his truancy problem, but he seemed unable to compose himself. He continued to mumble threats, and his rigid bearing led Elaine to believe that he might explode again at any moment. She did not want to risk a second outburst in one day.

Upon returning to the classroom, Elaine noticed that Eddie's tears had long since dried and his memory of the incident seemed to have faded almost as quickly. She, on the other hand, would relive those moments frequently in the days to come as she grew increasingly aware of her tenuous control over the situation. She did discover, however, that she could protect Eddie from William's assaults by making sure that she was the first to intervene when Eddie misbehaved.

Although she did not believe in paddling, Elaine found that if she took Eddie out into the hall, borrowed a paddle from Katherine Ellis, and at least created the appearance that she was paddling Eddie for his misbehavior, William would leave him alone. "It was really easy," she explained. "I would take Eddie out in the hall, take the paddle and come somewhere near him [hit him very lightly], and he would scream like someone was killing him. And William thought I was doing my duty. I'd go back in the classroom, and William would be nodding, and he'd leave Eddie alone." Although she felt that this was less than an ideal solution to the problem, her main objective was to protect Eddie from actual physical harm. This tactic seemed to work better than anything else. Therefore, Elaine resigned herself to getting along the best way she could, but she yearned for the school year to end without a tragic incident.

Where to Now?

CONNIE BALLARD

Connie had always been a diligent student, and her commitment to academic success was very strong. At the beginning of her college career she had decided she could best serve her future students and teaching career by obtaining both an elementary education teaching degree and a special education license to teach students with emotional and behavioral problems. She wasn't daunted by the extra year's worth of coursework the extra license entailed. Now, close to graduation, Connie knew that she had made the right decision. Not only had she been consistently named to the dean's list, but she had even managed to take a few extra electives in areas she thought might someday be helpful in her own classroom.

With the end of her college preparation now clearly in sight, Connie enjoyed another sense of accomplishment knowing that she would not begin her first teaching job deeply in debt, as was the case with many of her friends. From her first year at McNair State University, she had worked in a busy branch of Smith's Discount World, a large regional store whose merchandise included clothing, sports equipment, household goods, and furniture. She smiled as she remembered her first few hectic days at Smith's—trying to learn her work routine as quickly as possible, making mistakes that sometimes embarrassed her, all the while doing her best to balance her work with her equally weighty responsibility of being a college freshman.

Connie's efforts had all converged in substantial success. Her academic record reflected a 3.98 GPA, and at Smith's she had been promoted from a stocker to being in charge of the store's security detail. By late fall, Connie was looking forward to the end of her final year. She anticipated that she would continue excelling at her college courses and that her work at Smith's would result in a fine letter of recommendation. Connie was well liked by the six security personnel she directed. She was able to apply many of the collaborative techniques she had learned in her teacher preparation program in managing the workers. All in all, things were going very smoothly.

On the Saturday before the start of the spring semester, Connie went to work feeling especially buoyant and optimistic. Over the hectic Christmas season there had been relatively few security problems, and she had been voted one of the two Smith's employees of the year. She was also delighted that she had just received word of her assignment to a plum student teaching placement at Harrison Junior High, a school noted for its excellent services to students with emotional and behavioral problems.

The store was unusually busy, even for a Saturday afternoon. As usual, Connie had two of her security personnel, Steve and Nancy, walking the store floor while she attended to some paperwork. Connie had developed a plan that allowed each security employee to circulate through the entire store in just over an hour. Their task was to monitor the aisles for any signs of illegal activity, usually shoplifting. It was common knowledge that the store lost a substantial amount of money each year to shoplifters, and Connie's patrolling plan had proved remarkably effective. Since implementing her plan, shoplifting had fallen by almost 75 percent.

Not long after her she began, Steve knocked at her office door and entered quickly.

"Connie, looks like we've nabbed a shoplifter. I passed her twice in the jewelry department after I saw her stuffing some merchandise into her coat pocket. I alerted Nancy when our security routes crossed, and she saw more of the same. I'm sure we've got it on the security videos, too."

Connie had dealt with this situation many times before. Most often, the culprit would confess to stealing the items and produce them in short order. Jewelry was one of the most popular targets of shoplifters. If the thief was 18 or older, company policy dictated that the police be called and the suspect booked on suspicion of shoplifting. After making statements to the police, the matter was referred to court as a misdemeanor charge of theft. When the suspect was younger than 18, however, it was store policy to interview the culprit, obtain detailed identification information, warn that such behavior was legally prosecutable, and then contact a parent to remove the minor from the store. Second offenses by the same person were referred to the juvenile justice system.

"OK, so, what do we have this time?" Connie inquired.

"Female, about 13 or 14, I'd say. She's in the waiting room with Nancy. She's denying that she took anything. All we've done so far is ask her to accompany us to the waiting room."

"OK, let's take a look," Connie sighed.

They walked into the small "waiting room" adjoining her office. Beside Nancy, a girl slouched in a chair—sullen, disheveled, and sporting bright pink and green hair, rows of earrings up both of her earlobes, and a large silver nose stud. Before Connie had a chance to speak, the girl interjected a preemptive strike.

"I don't need this shit, man. This is, like, harassment, you assholes! Why don't you, like, get a life? All you do is pick on kids because we choose to look different instead of frigging nerds like you all . . ." Her voice got louder the more she spoke. She was clearly angry.

"Hi, we need to sort some things out . . ." Connie began.

"Screw you, bitch! I'll make sure YOU get sorted out!" came the reply.

"Hold on, no one's accusing you of anything, so just chill out so we can send you on your way, OK?" Connie kept her cool. The girl, still angry, hesitated.

Nancy played a supporting role. "Hey c'mon, if there's nothing going on you'll be on your way in a minute."

Steve chimed in, "Sure, we're just doing our job, so . . . "

"You call this stinking treatment WORK? How piss-poor pathetic!" The girl turned her face to the wall and began kicking the side of her chair.

Connie tried again. "Let me tell you what happened. Nancy and Steve are security officers for the store. It's their job to walk around and make sure nothing illegal is happening. Most of the time it's pretty boring work. If they see anything happening that looks suspicious, they have to investigate."

"Oh, yeah, like, guilty until proven innocent, right? Are we, like, in Bosnia? What you gonna do? Take me out behind the store and shoot me before putting me in the dumpster? I don't need this crap."

"Easy, easy now," Steve said sympathetically, "There's no need to get this blown all out of proportion."

"Let's just start with your name," Connie suggested.

"Jenna."

"Jenna who?" Connie thought she'd made a good start.

"None of your goddamn business, that's who!"

Connie dodged that challenge. "OK, Jenna, how old are you?"

"Two hundred and fifty-seven, slut—in fact it's my birthday today. I'm like, immortal, get it?"

"Well, I'd guess that you're about 13 or 14 . . ." Connie felt she knew how to deal with bluster.

"So what if I am?"

"Well, we need to see some identification, or you can tell us who we can call."

"I'm Satan's wife, so go ask him—it's 1-800-GoToHell!" Hmmm, thought Connie, whoever Jenna is, she's getting pretty creative.

Nancy tried again. "Jenna, please . . . let's try to be reasonable about this. We just want to be sure you're not involved in something illegal here in the store. We think you lifted some jewelry and put it in your coat pocket . . . "

"See? I'm friggin' guilty! Here, string me up. I confess, I confess! Oh Lord, take thy wayward servant quietly to the stake! Send me to hell, O Lord!"

Exasperated, Jenna jumped from her chair with such force that it startled Connie. Jenna's sudden movement also ejected several boxes of jewelry out of her pocket and sent them clattering to the floor. The room was deathly quiet. Jenna, resigned to her fate, slumped in her chair, tightly folded her arms, and closed her eyes. Nancy retrieved the items from the floor. Along with the jewelry was Jenna's school ID card.

Nancy was matter-of-fact in summarizing what she found. "OK . . . So, you're Jenna Morris. You're in the eighth grade, and you live at 324 River Course Drive. Here's your home phone number, too . . . "

"WHATEVER!" shouted Jenna.

Connie continued, "You understand that shoplifting is a crime, Jenna, I'm sure. Here's what's going to happen. Because you're under 18, and this seems to be your first offense, we'll let you off with a warning, but we'll keep your ID on record. That information will be kept private and confidential here in my office to protect you. However, if this ever happens again, we'll refer you to the juvenile authorities. "

"SO F- - -ING WHAT? You think I can't screw them over as well? Geez, like, you don't know who you're dealing with, babe! I have a lot of connections, so watch out when you're driving down the street, like, know what I mean?"

Steve, Nancy, and Connie had heard this kind of thing before and were adept at ignoring such threats.

"I'll call your home right now for your mom or dad to come get you," Connie informed Jenna.

By the end of the shift, Connie had all but forgotten the incident. It was, unfortunately, one of many that blurred together quite quickly. Jenna's mother had come to pick her up, and all three employees were somewhat surprised that, unlike most parents, Jenna's mother seemed neither embarrassed nor angry, simply even more sullen than her daughter.

By the time Connie arrived at Harrison High the following week, she was excited and ready to teach. This was her final student teaching experience, and she was elated, knowing that after this practicum the next students she would teach would be in her very own classroom. Gillian Frontera, the school secretary, walked her down the hall.

"I'm sure you'll love it here, Connie," Gillian told her. "These seventh- and eighth-graders are a tough bunch, but your supervising teacher, Martha Seeger, is excellent. She's been teaching EBD kids for years and really does a good job. I'm sure you'll learn a lot from her."

Gillian opened the classroom door. Martha, just returning to her desk after checking students' work, smiled and came right over.

"Hi, you must be Connie. Welcome! Thanks, Gillian. I'll take Connie off your hands."

"Thanks, Martha. It's nice to meet you after only having spoken with you on the phone. I'm really looking forward to this."

"I'm sure it'll be fine, too!"

Connie admired Martha's energy and positive attitude. She looked around the room. Eight students were seated, two to a table.

"These are the seventh-graders. The eighth-graders will arrive after lunch," Martha informed Connie.

Connie spent the morning familiarizing herself with the classroom. She discovered where many teaching materials were stored, and, in snatches of time between lessons, Martha filled her in on the classroom routine, rules, and a host of other details that Connie tried to remember. Lunch was pleasant enough. Returning to the classroom with Martha, Connie was looking forward to meeting the eighth-graders.

As the eighth-graders arrived, Connie was preoccupied with some paperwork. She heard Martha giving rapid, clear instructions as the students got settled, but she was not prepared for what she saw when she looked up from her work. Seated in the front row, close to the door, was Jenna Morris. Connie caught her breath as a surge of adrenaline made her heart thump and her head throb. What would this mean? She quickly tried to determine whether Jenna recognized her. Connie hoped she looked quite different dressed for school than she did in her Smith's uniform.

"Class, this is our new student teacher, Connie Ballard," said Martha by way of introduction.

Connie smiled as best she could. Jenna's face grew increasingly cloudy. Ah, Connie thought, she remembers me.

The lesson passed quickly, and the eighth-graders were soon gone.

"Well, what did you think?" inquired Martha.

Connie knew she sounded much better than she felt, but she needed time to regroup and decide what, if anything, she should do about her dilemma.

"I think they'll be fine. I like teaching this age group, so I'm ready to jump in whenever you want me to."

"OK, why don't you plan on teaching the eighth-graders tomorrow? They'll all be bringing work from their regular math class. Here's the teacher's manual. They're reviewing Chapter 9, so be sure to look over it tonight and be ready for them tomorrow."

That night, Connie didn't get much sleep. The next day, she caught herself trembling slightly as she waited for the eighth-graders to appear. Martha had already left the classroom to make some phone calls to parents. As the students approached the classroom, Connie could tell that Jenna was being very noisy and disruptive. Taking a deep breath, Connie began to assert her authority.

"All right, everyone, time to settle down before we get to work. Quietly, now, come on in and get out your math books, we have a lot of ground to cover."

The students filed in, Jenna last. As Jenna walked past Connie, she whispered, "Hey, it's Ms. Connie *Smith*, ain't it? Still working that loser's job?"

Connie did her best to ignore the remark and began giving instructions to the class. Everyone complied reasonably well—except Jenna. Flopping into her seat, she stretched apathetically and yawned. Looking directly at Connie, Jenna didn't wait a moment longer.

"Ooooohh, it's our loser student teacher! Hey, Ms. SMITH, whaddya gonna do to us?"

"I'm Ms. Ballard. Please address me by my last name," Connie said calmly but firmly.

"No it ain't, it's SMITH, get it guys? As in SMITH's DISCOUNT WORLD over on 12th Avenue. This loser works over there. Whassa matter, you can't get no friggin' teaching job? Know what she does, guys? She's the store GESTAPO! I swear, goes around hasslin' little kids and being really nasty. It's a wonder anyone shops there! She tried to mess with me one time, but me and my mom took care of her sorry ass. Ain't that right, SMITHIE? Checked your car tires lately? How about your apartment? That dog of yours still alive and kicking?"

Connie hesitated. She knew that venting her rising fury was not going to be effective, but this was the first lesson of 15 weeks of student teaching . . .

The Contract with Parrish and Son

REBECCA PHILLIPS

Frustrated and helpless isn't a good way to feel, Rebecca thought. It seemed such a long time since she had first met Bob Parrish, and she wasn't really sure that the strain was worth the investment of emotional energy she had put into trying to get through to him during the past three weeks. But there he was in her class, in her face, tearing at her heart, and the end of the school year seemed years away.

Rebecca Phillips had been teaching students with learning disabilities for six years. She felt confident now with her teaching techniques and with the progress of most of her students. She had learned the hard way, through trial and error, about discipline. She now understood the importance of setting up a consistent structure for behavior management from the very beginning of the school year.

This year, Rebecca had switched to a new behavior management program to enforce the rules that she and the students had decided on together. It entailed positive reinforcement in the form of free time or time to engage in preferred activities. She had set up a group contingency with which she was quite satisfied. The class or workgroup began every period with 10 minutes of free time "in the bank." She kept a chart on the board reflecting the current allotted time. If students followed the rules, the group had a chance to earn additional time at Rebecca's discretion. She was careful to award additional time intermittently so that her students could not anticipate when their good behavior might pay off. If a student was not following the rules, however, Rebecca simply pulled out her stopwatch and timed the student until he or she complied. She did not say anything to the student, nor did she stop her instruction. When the student complied, Rebecca stopped the watch and wrote the amount of time it had taken the student to get back on task in a "time lost" column on her chart. The total minutes and seconds lost would then be subtracted from the group's accumulated minutes of free time.

Rebecca felt her group contingency worked very well because she didn't have to interrupt her instruction with reprimands or reminders. Her students began urging each other to stay on task, a kind of peer pressure Rebecca judged to be effective and appropriate. When she started her stopwatch, one or two students always seemed to notice and either let the offender know that he or she was not behaving as expected or helped the misbehaving student comply. For instance, another student might give the offender paper if he or she came to class unprepared. Even chronic offenders began coming to class with needed materials, participating in class, and helping others behave as expected. Only one of Rebecca's students did not appear to be affected by the fact that he was losing free time for the group by misbehaving. As a matter of fact, Bob seemed to thrive on the negative attention he drew from his peers.

Bob was an uncoordinated, slightly overweight seventh-grader, what some might call "husky." He dragged a large book bag around from classroom to classroom, usually tripping over it at least once in each class. Rebecca wondered whether this was an attention-getting device or simply adolescent clumsiness.

Bob had moved into Monroeville in early January, bringing with him a confidential file indicating that he had previously received instruction in reading, math, and English in a self-contained class for students with learning disabilities. While reading through his file, Rebecca noticed that Bob had a history of frequent moves—five in his eight years of schooling. Almost every teacher had remarked on Bob's attention-getting antics—inappropriate comments, yelling at the teacher, and refusing to remain on task, for example. Rebecca had made a conscious effort not to prejudge Bob because of his history, hoping against hope that he might have learned some coping skills in his last placement. Her hopes were dashed the day she met him. In group situations from the beginning, he volunteered a running commentary on anything she said that could be twisted into a double entendre. In a class of eight adolescent boys, his comments inevitably created a commotion.

"No matter what the topic during my language arts class," Rebecca recalled, "Bob managed to twist the words around in order to get his classmates' attention. One time when we were discussing Prohibition, I asked for a definition of 'speakeasy,' and he said, 'Isn't that where people used to get sex in the 1920s?' The rest of the class responded with laughter to Bob's comments at first, then began to ridicule him as 'dumb' and 'stupid.' The more the class got upset with Bob for each 'stopwatch' episode, the more Bob seemed to continue and intensify his efforts to get everyone's attention."

Rebecca quickly realized that Bob should not be included in the group contingency, as he was both thriving on the negative attention and reducing the effectiveness of the program for the other seven boys in the class. After only one week, she pulled Bob out of the free time program and set up an alternative individual contingency for him. She also felt that his parents needed to be made aware of his problems in the classroom. Two weeks after he joined her class, she found herself calling Bob's home.

What she learned from her call led Rebecca to believe that Bob's home life played a significant role in his behavior at school. As far as Rebecca could ascertain, Mr. Parrish had obtained custody of his two sons, Bob and his younger brother, after a lengthy search to locate their mother and the two boys, who moved frequently. Bob's father had finally won custody a short time before their move to Monroeville. Mr. Parrish and the boys lived with Mr. Parrish's parents in an upper-middle–class neighborhood. Bob's grandmother had a history of mental illness and was frequently in and out of "rest homes." When she was home, she apparently did not get along well with her husband. It was in this setting that the boys had begun to build a relationship with the father they had never known.

Mr. Parrish had definite ideas about how Bob should be raised. He intended, as he put it to Rebecca, to "make him into a man." When Rebecca had called to suggest that they discuss Bob's misbehavior, Mr. Parrish had not hesitated to agree to a parent-teacher conference.

At their first meeting, Rebecca was struck with how much Mr. Parrish looked like Bob—an older Bob with a clear edge of toughness, she thought. Mr. Parrish was tall, tanned, and obviously lifted weights. It immediately occurred to Rebecca that this totally masculine father figure might present some problems for Bob. Mr. Parrish was cordial and appeared concerned about Bob. He told his story of recently obtaining custody of his sons, stressing how hard he had worked to get his children back from their mother. He informed Rebecca that he punished Bob's misbehavior with a belt—one with a buckle, of course. In addition, he gave the impression that he did not have much patience with either Bob or his younger son. Mr. Parrish felt that Bob's problems stemmed from being babied by his mother for 12 years. His parenting responsibilities, he explained again, included "making a man outta him." One step toward this goal, he believed, was to put Bob on the football team, adding that he attended a "few football practices to help the coach out and kick Bob's ass when he messed up."

Soon after her first conference with Mr. Parrish, Rebecca met with Bob and his father to set up a home-school contract involving Bob's homework and behavior. Bob seemed to want to please his father as much as his father wanted Bob to "act more like a man." Although she had some doubts about what would happen, Rebecca had hopes that the contract would work. She had no idea what the consequences would be. The day after setting up the home-school contract, Bob confronted Rebecca when he came through the door.

"How come you told my dad I was bad in class? He beat me when he got home, and it's all your fault." He stomped to his seat and flopped down, slamming his book bag down on the desk. Rebecca was stunned. Her heart went out to Bob. She was incensed with Mr. Parrish and his "macho" attitude. At that point, she decided that contacting Mr. Parrish about any of Bob's misbehavior would only result in a beating.

During class that day, Bob participated reluctantly for a short time. But he soon began tapping his pencil loudly on his desk. Rebecca reminded him of their contract. "It don't matter," Bob responded. "My dad don't think I can do it. He said so."

Rebecca felt her anger at Mr. Parrish growing by the second. How could he sit there in the conference and agree that the contract was a good idea and say he would encourage Bob, then go home and tell Bob he thinks he can't do it! Sighing, Rebecca tried to focus her attention on her work with the other students, hoping Bob would return to his work. He didn't. A few minutes later, she tried another tack, suggesting that he follow along with a student who was reading aloud from the literature book. His retort was swift and firm.

"I don't care where we are."

Rebecca chose to ignore this comment and went to stand near Bob's desk, cuing him to the sentence the student was reading. Bob continued to play with his pencil. Gently, Rebecca removed the pencil from Bob's grasp. He yielded, and turned his efforts to getting another student's attention. Rebecca did not say a word, but she felt that Bob was trying to upset her because he held her accountable for the previous night's beating. Although she felt guilty about this, she refused to let Bob get the best of her. She had worked hard to get the other students to work as a cooperative group, and she didn't want them thinking she was playing favorites by giving Bob more than his share of attention. As the other students finished their oral reading, Bob informed them of his evaluation.

"Man, you guys are the lousiest readers I ever heard."

Always priding herself on accepting each student at his or her individual level of ability, whatever it was, Rebecca responded immediately in a slow, even voice.

"Bob, I would like to talk to you out in the hallway. Please follow me." She began walking slowly toward the door.

"What? Me? What'd I do? It's the truth!" Bob complained.

Rebecca paused at the door, waiting for Bob to comply. A few seconds later, Bob ambled to the doorway. Rebecca struggled to contain her anger, her voice trembling.

"As long as you are in my class, you will not make comments about the abilities of other students. We are all in this class because we all have different strengths and weaknesses, and we are trying to find the best way for us to learn. If you continue to make these comments, I will have to call your father."

Bob stood against the wall, avoiding her stare. He said nothing, nor did he acknowledge her warning.

"Bob, did you hear me?"

Still no answer. Rebecca stuck her head in the classroom and asked her instructional assistant to come out into the hallway.

"Bob needs a little time to think about what I just told him," she explained. "Would you please stay out here with him for a few minutes until he feels he is ready to rejoin the class?"

Reentering the class, Rebecca was surprised to see that the other boys were simply sitting there, waiting. She thanked them for being so quiet and calm, and rewarded them with two extra minutes of free activity time. Bob tried to follow Rebecca back into the room almost immediately; she waved him back. When he returned several minutes later, he was compliant. He completed all his classwork and showed it to her. Perhaps, Rebecca thought, my troubles with Bob are over.

When Bob arrived the next day, he immediately searched for his writing journal. Rebecca's students wrote in their journals each day. Rebecca agreed with her students that their journals were confidential, so she read them only if they were intentionally left on her desk. At the end of first period, Bob's journal was on her desk. What she saw when she opened it sent chills down her spine. Bob had drawn an effigy of himself hanging from a tree. On another page, a knife was thrust deep into the head of his likeness. Another page contained a headstone with Bob's name and birth date. Under these scenes, in Bob's characteristic scribble, she read, "I hat life. I wish I wer ded." Rebecca caught her breath. Was this one of Bob's attention-getting ploys, or was he serious?

Realizing that in Bob's best interests she was compelled to break the confidence of his journal, Rebecca consulted the school psychologist, Mr. Moore, at her first opportunity. Mr. Moore suggested that she question Bob carefully to see whether she could determine the reason for his drawings and statements. He also encouraged her to keep anecdotal records of Bob's behavior. Together, after a few weeks of observation, he suggested, they could decide whether there was reason for referral.

Uncertain of how she should react, Rebecca did not write a response to Bob's entry as she usually did; she waited to see what would come next. The following day, Bob again immediately went to his journal. Rebecca watched him open it and quickly close it again. Later that morning, he chose not to write in his journal while the rest of the students did so. From across the room, where she was working with another student, Rebecca prompted Bob to get started.

"I don't have nothing to say," he grumbled.

Rebecca repeated her request and began to move toward Bob. He reacted immediately.

"Why do you always hafta come over here? I ain't doin' nothing!"

Irritated at the disruption of her work with a willing student, Rebecca responded, "That's why I'm coming over, because you're not doing anything."

As Bob's face reddened with rage, she regretted her words. Fearing an all-out scene, Rebecca quickly asked her aide to take over while she talked to Bob. The situation was escalating rapidly to a crisis.

"Why are you always picking on me? Hector doesn't always write in his journal, but you don't yell at him!"

Refusing to get caught up in a power struggle, she continued to move toward Bob. She heard him mumbling.

"I don't care, you can't scare me. I can't stand you anyway. I hate this f- - -ing class!

At the last comment, Rebecca became indignant.

"In my class, there is no profanity. You know the rule. I'll have to call your father."

"Go ahead," Bob retorted loudly. "Maybe he'll kill me this time and I won't have to worry about you and this f- - -ing class."

The other students stopped their work, staring at Bob and Rebecca. Rebecca was desperately trying to figure a way to get Bob out of the room, but she was afraid he was too angry to attempt any kind of move.

"Don't think the f- - -ing principal can help me!" Bob yelled. "Nobody can. Everybody hates me, especially my dad. And I hate you, you f- - -ing bitch!" With that, Bob pushed Rebecca's aide aside and ran out of the room.

Winnie

PATTY GRAY

Part A

8/27

Well, journal, it's my first day back at school. I'm beginning my second year of teaching and I think that this time I'm in for a real treat. This year, I'll be teaching a group of "at-risk" first-graders. When my principal first asked me about this class, I wondered, "What in the world do you mean by 'at risk'?" I'd heard so many different definitions while I was in college. Well, as he explained the situation, it didn't take long for me to understand. The students I would have had been in our pre-kindergarten program, our kindergarten program, and most of them had been retained in first grade. My goodness! I had taught a class of average students last year. This year, most of my kids would be 8 years old in first grade. Mr. Brown (my principal), the reading specialist, and the Chapter 1 teacher decided that instead of using the standard phonetic reading program, I'd use a basal series that combined phonetic and whole-word approaches. I was also told that I should contact the consulting teacher at our school to find out about supplementary materials and behavior management techniques that I'd probably need.

9/1

Wow, it's Friday already. I haven't had time to do much writing. We've been running from one in-service program to the next all week long. Boy, these work weeks are real killers! I'll get my bulletin boards up before Monday if I work all day on Saturday and Sunday. Fortunately, Mr. Brown will be here to let us in. Oh well, such is life in the fast lane.

    Betsy, the kindergarten teacher who had many of my kids last year, gave me the low-down on many of the students during lunch today. Man, I'm going to have a class full of boys—11 of them and only 3 girls. Half these guys are on Ritalin. With such an active bunch, at least I don't have to worry about being bored this year!

    Betsy also schooled me about one kid in particular. He's called Winnie. His real name is Winslow. He is 7 years old and the only student in the class who was not retained in first grade. He's really tiny for his age, but he's also a real pistol. Betsy shared that Winnie could be so obnoxious that last year he was passed around from one kindergarten teacher to the next. She could only tolerate him for so long and then she'd have to send him to another teacher for about 30 minutes just to catch her breath. Winnie followed her everywhere—even into the bathroom. Many times she would use the class bathroom so that she wouldn't have to leave the room. The door wouldn't lock, so Winnie would just walk right in. Betsy would be sitting on the commode and he'd just walk right in.

I kid you not, Bets had me in stitches when she told me about this. She would look at Winnie with an I-can't-believe-you're-doing-this stare on her face and say, "Winnie, I'm using the bathroom." This didn't faze him in the least bit. He'd just simply respond, "But Mrs. Thompson, I have to tell you something." And then he would just say what was on his mind, turn, leave, and shut the door behind him. That's just one of the things he did all year that almost drove poor Bets crazy. I hope that knowing all this will help me cope with these problems. I'm also hoping that Winnie has matured some over the summer. Well, must get back to making the nametags for the kids. I'll try to write again soon.

11/3

My, how time flies when you're having fun! Sorry, I know it's been a while. I must be more consistent with my writing. Someday, when I'm old and gray, I'll be able to look back at these entries and have a laugh or two. For now, though, let me fill you in on how things are going.

It's now been about two months since school started, and although I'm really enjoying my class, I've already had to get some help to deal with both their academic and behavioral problems. Everybody told me at the beginning of the year that I needed to talk with Jackie, the consulting teacher at our school, for help. And so I did. Jackie has a very interesting job. Unlike us regular classroom teachers, she is not assigned to teach a group of students each day. Instead, she's available to provide consultation to those of us who have students with academic and behavioral problems. We meet with Jackie on a one-to-one basis or with a group of teachers referred to as a teacher assistance team. Frankly, I've preferred working with her on an individual basis and you know what—she's really been great! We've been meeting, planning, and implementing for only a couple of weeks, and already I can see a difference in my group.

First of all, Jackie really helped me with the reading program. It didn't take me long to realize that the basal reading program I was given to use was not the answer for my children. I mean, my kids have such limited experiences and vocabularies that they simply can't relate to the material. I needed to make reading more relevant for them. So, I talked to Jackie, and she agreed to help me supplement my reading program with a whole-language component. We're going great guns with this approach.

For Halloween, for example, we made a witches' brew. This was really neat because we were able to build on what the kids already knew to increase their vocabularies. Jackie brought in this huge black pot and a long wooden spoon and I brought the ingredients for our brew. We had all kinds of nuts, raisins, yogurt raisins, pretzel sticks, malted milk balls, and—you know—the stuff you use to make granola. Both Jackie and I were dressed in witches' costumes, and we started the lesson by having the kids identify the ingredients and taste them. As they munched, we had them come up with words that described the taste—words such as *salty, sweet, crunchy, chewy*. As they sampled each ingredient, we poured that ingredient into our "caldron." As we stirred, we danced around the "caldron" and sang a tune about witches' brew. This continued until each student had "taste tested" all of the ingredients. Finally, we had them sample the brew to note the difference in taste after all the goodies had been mixed together. The kids thought this was great! They were having fun and they were building their vocabularies at the same time.

Jackie also helped me with behavior problems. In other words, she helped me with Winnie. From the very beginning of school, he would never raise his hand. Whenever he had something to tell me, he would just blurt it out. Jackie and I talked about this, and together we came up with a plan. We decided that we would try to modify Winnie's behavior by ignoring him when he did not raise his hand and wait to be recognized. Of course, we sat Winnie down and told him what we were planning to do. To draw attention away from him, we told the class that this was something that we were doing with everyone. We expected everyone to raise their hands when they wanted to speak. Jackie did a few demonstration lessons to show me how to react to different degrees and variations of the target behavior and then I followed through with implementation of the procedure. She was—and remains—available to observe and coach me when I'm trying a new teaching strategy and this really helps me refine my skills. I really do hope this plan will work. I'm already beginning to feel the way Bets did last year.

11/19

Well, it's been two weeks since I last wrote. We've been using our B-MOD plan with Winnie and it seems that things are getting worse instead of better. You won't believe this, but as I walk around the room, he continues to call out my name constantly. If he calls my name and I don't answer him right away, he forgets what he's planning to tell me. When I finally do acknowledge him he'll say, "Mrs. Gray," and then he'll snap his fingers and go "uhh, uhh, uhh." I guess that's why he feels he has to blurt out whatever he needs or wants to say—if he keeps quiet, the poor thing knows that he is going to lose whatever's floating around in his little head. The kids have started to pick on him when he does this. I really can't afford to let things get any worse, so I'll plan to meet with Jackie and develop a modified strategy. Will try to see her tomorrow if I have the time.

11/21

Boy, it's really nice to have someone around who is so readily available. Today, I met with Jackie after school and we modified Winnie's behavior management plan. In addition to ignoring his call-outs, we also came up with a chart system for Winnie. I made a chart and divided it into sections for reading, language, spelling, social studies, and science. If at the end of one of the blocks he hasn't blurted out an answer or called my name without acknowledgment, he'll get a plus (+). If not, if he does call out, he'll get a minus (–). If he's gotten no more than three minuses in a day's time, I'll let him do something special, like read to the class. He's coming along nicely with his reading and he really enjoys showing off his skills to the rest of the class.

12/30

I know, I know. I've been bad. I said that I would write every day. Things just got so hectic after Thanksgiving that I just could not get to you. I had a wonderful Christmas! Went skiing with some friends and had an absolute blast! Got some really nice presents, too! Jerry gave me a new compact disc player. I really love the sound. Will really enjoy it.

Well, I guess I'm writing because it's getting close to that time again. On Monday, vacation will be over and I'll be back at school with my class. I'm sure Winnie will be in rare form the minute he steps off the school bus. Honestly, you'd think he'd miss a day once in a while. He's the only kid in the class who has perfect attendance!

I mentioned on November 21 that we started using a chart with Winnie. Well, before we got out for Christmas break, it finally started working to where we could get him to raise his hand before he yelled out for help or just blurted out whatever was on his mind. But you know, with all the nervous energy that this kid has, the problem just started to manifest itself in other ways. One day the psychologist came into the room to observe another student. It seems that each and every one of them has some problem or another. Anyway, Winnie raised his hand, but I didn't call on him. Well, as loudly as he could, he just slammed his hands down on his desktop. I kept on ignoring him and the longer I ignored, the louder he got. He was tapping his pencil, kicking his desk, and he continued to slam his hands against his desktop. Finally, I just looked at him and said, "I simply refuse to speak to you while you are acting this way. When you can start to act like a 7-year-old, then I'll look at you." At that point, he was really angry. He put his head on the desk and pouted. He wasn't disturbing anyone else so I just let him sit there until he cooled off.

By our last day before the start of Christmas break, I wanted to SCREAM! I just wanted to change my name because even though he was raising his hand more often, now Winnie was really into the same act that he so artfully performed in Betsy's class last year. He was constantly out of his seat, following me around everywhere I went. He followed me to the office. If I left the room to get something from another teacher I'd look back and there he was behind me. I didn't dare use the class bathroom when he was anywhere in sight. One day, he called my name so much that I just started to count the times. By the end of the day, he had called my name 37 times without raising his hand. Can you believe it? It seems like this was an improvement over his performance before we started using the chart, but he also has regressed to the point where he can never be wrong. If you tell him that he has missed two words on a spelling test—TWO WORDS—he just loses it! He bangs his head against the top of his desk, he crosses his arms and pokes out his lips, or he'll simply sit and sob incessantly. Oh, what a kid! What a kid!

I tell you about all the problems I have with Winnie, but you know, this kid is no dummy. He is the sharpest reader in my class. He can sound and blend like a champ and his comprehension is not at all bad. In math, he's a little slow with word problems, but he's great with computation and he's learning his facts with no problems. I honestly don't think that he has a learning problem. He's the youngest kid in my class, but academically, he's the strongest. Well, I'll see how he's doing in just a few days. Give me strength.

Whose Class Is This?

JANE LEE

Part A

Jane's transition from the special education classroom to a regular fourth grade had been uneventful. After three years in a resource room, she welcomed the change. Teaching regular fourth-graders was just as challenging. Her confidence stemmed from the many hours of individualized work with her special education kids. She often joked that if she could handle what special education threw her way, regular class teaching was sure to be a breeze.

Sitting in her classroom this warm March afternoon, though, Jane wasn't sure where to go next with the surges of anger, frustration, and depression that washed over her. Her troubles had started only a few months ago, but it seemed like years. Ann Dean was not the problem; it was her mother, Belinda Dean. Jane turned it all over one more time. The battle was lost, and so was the war. She didn't want to deal with school politics, negative feelings, and emotional roller coasters. All she wanted to do was teach. But she felt she couldn't—at least not here at Eugene Field Elementary.

Jane hadn't thought it odd that Mrs. Dean had been somewhat irate during a parent conference before the start of the school year. Several parents had been dismayed that the county had changed the language arts curriculum without letting them know. Being a parent herself, Jane knew how they felt. She tried to direct their legitimate complaints to the district's central office. Belinda, tall and attractive, was a schoolteacher turned homemaker who served as a substitute teacher at Field School whenever she could, which was quite often.

Although she had felt safe in the answers she had given Belinda at that first meeting, their conversation had alerted Jane to the fact that Belinda seemed dissatisfied with a number of other things that were occurring outside of the classroom. Issues, Jane resentfully reflected, that were way beyond her control as a classroom teacher. Mrs. Dean's next complaint was not long in coming. Jane's substitute had mistakenly assigned classwork for homework, and Belinda's swift reply indicated another round of hassle. Jane reread the letter:

Dear Ms. Lee:

We spent far too much time on homework yesterday. I believe that when children are 9 or 10 years of age they should not be expected to spend more than one hour on homework. In order to assimilate, enjoy, and actually learn the meaning of some words, the task ought not to be overwhelming, frustrating, and tedious, which this homework undoubtedly was.

Sincerely,
Belinda Dean

Jane refolded the letter for the umpteenth time. She remembered making a quick call to Mrs. Dean to explain the substitute's mix-up. Belinda apparently accepted her explanation. Still, for some reason, Jane had the uneasy feeling that this scene would be repeated. Funny, thought Jane, there were no complaints from any of the other 18 sets of parents about the substitute's mistake. Jane tried to put the incident out of her mind.

Not long after Jane had received the complaint about homework, Belinda appeared as a substitute in the fourth-grade classes. In passing, Belinda made disparaging comments about the "chaotic" classes in which she was subbing, the clear implication being that the teachers were doing less than their best. Jane couldn't overcome her anxiety about Belinda's implied questioning of her fellow teachers' professionalism and, by association, her own. Knowing that Art Dean, Belinda's husband, was an editor for the local newspaper and a newly elected member of the school board didn't help Jane's feeling of uneasiness. Like most new board members, Art was keen on establishing a record of prompt attention to any problems in any school in the system.

Belinda's offhand criticisms escalated to the point at which the four fourth-grade teachers collectively asked Jim Black, the principal, to assign Belinda to other grades. On one of her days of substituting, Belinda crossed the thin line between professional teacher or teacher's aide and parent. Jane had seen this happen before. What perplexed her so about Belinda was the fact that she expressed her criticisms in the lunchroom for all the teachers and other school staff members to hear. Belinda appeared determined to voice her parental complaints to Jane right there at the lunch table.

"Jane, I think that Ann was treated unfairly last week when you held the fourth-grade reading auction. Ann never got to spend her tokens. I don't think this is a very positive way to deal with any child."

Belinda conveniently omitted the fact that Ann had been absent from the auction to attend a voluntary training program.

"Look, Belinda, why don't we set up a time for the two of us to get together, and I'll see if we can't work something out." It was all Jane could do to keep from screaming.

Belinda, however, was relentless. She aired other complaints: Why weren't the fourth-graders going on an extended field trip like they did last year? Was this a punishment for the whole fourth grade? If so, why were all the fourth-graders being made to suffer for the unruly behavior of a few?

Jane's logical answers fell on deaf ears. Belinda was hearing only what she wanted to hear. To this point, Jane felt that although Belinda was being troublesome, the barbs were not personal. Good communication and reciprocal understanding would, she assured herself, solve these problems over time. But a change in Belinda's tactics was soon to come.

The next meeting between Jane and Belinda was less gratifying. Indirectly, but clearly, Belinda let slip that Ann wasn't as happy as she had been the previous year. It didn't take a genius to establish that Belinda saw Jane as the reason for Ann's unhappiness. Jane reminded herself that Ann had had some problems the year before, too, but Jane's hurt and anger were on the rise.

"Belinda, I feel that we aren't achieving anything in going on like this. You are being very negative with me and very personal. Please try to see all the positive things we've done for Ann—for all the fourth-graders, as a matter of fact—like the reading auction . . ."

Belinda cut her off in midsentence. "Well, the reading auction really isn't Ann's thing."

Why, then, thought Jane, were you so upset that she missed the auction to attend her voluntary class?

Belinda leaned closer, as if to challenge Jane. Outraged, Jane nevertheless felt her intimidation by Belinda starting to show.

With barely controlled anger, Jane replied, "If all of this started with the change in the language arts curriculum, you should speak with the language arts committee. They made that decision. Really, it's hard to be expected to carry on, you know, instruction at everybody's level when you're the one in charge."

Jane knew this was crazy, but she couldn't help defending herself. Realizing that she was swiftly losing control of her anger, she abruptly ended the conversation. Nothing had been solved, and the gap between herself and Belinda had widened.

Two days later Ann handed a letter to Jane. Now more disbelieving than ever, Jane reread the neatly hand-lettered lines.

Dear Ms. Lee,

> After our talk the other day I wanted to encourage you to foster a more positive classroom environment. Children like to feel good about themselves, and I think that feeling good about oneself is very important for future development and growth. Perhaps I can help you. I would be willing to deliver treats or small gifts at random times to the students, a reward that will tell them that they are wonderful human beings just the way they are. I hope we can work together.

> Sincerely,
> Belinda Dean

Jane realized that she was in danger of losing her class. She was trapped between letting this situation escalate out of control, and of wanting to assert her authority as the classroom teacher. It was time to relay what was happening to Jim Black. Jane poured out her story. Jim was empathetic. He had had some problems with Belinda before. Belinda had complained about a situation with her son in the second grade. A day later several other parents who lived in the same subdivision as the Deans had complained about the same issue. Jim suggested that Jane no longer meet alone with Belinda, and offered to sit in on subsequent meetings.

For the next week Jane wrestled with her meager alternatives. She was sure, though, that she didn't want to start the random flow of noncontingent treats and repeated visits to her class by Belinda.

Two days after she received Belinda's last letter, Ann approached Jane's desk during homeroom period.

"My mother sent these," Ann said, handing Jane a pack of brightly colored pencils. Belinda was clearly serious about implementing her plan. The gauntlet had been thrown. Jane was adamant about not allowing Belinda to dictate what happened in her classroom. She put pen to paper.

Wandering in the Wilderness— The Ups and Downs of a Novice LD Teacher

JEFF HARRIS

Part A

Jeff Harris taught eight boys in a self-contained learning disabilities class at Indian Hills Elementary School in Hastings County, Georgia. Jeff had been born and raised in Hastings. After high school graduation, he'd attended a local university, earned a degree in special education, and landed a teaching position at Andrew Jackson Elementary School—just seven miles from where he'd been raised. Jeff was almost halfway through his fourth year as a special education teacher.

Things hadn't been easy for Jeff during his first three years. It wasn't that he was a poor teacher. Quite the contrary. He was quite conscientious, and he wanted to make a difference for children with disabilities. Parents, teachers, and administrators continually acknowledged his efforts and voted him Outstanding Teacher of the Year during his third year. Also, Jeff had been one of only five African American teachers at the school, and one of only two males. Several African American parents expressed their delight at having an African American male present in the school. "Our kids need to see positive black role models like you," he'd heard time and time again from parents happy to know he was in the building every day.

Still, Jeff felt a need to leave Jackson after three years. He was working himself to a frazzle trying to meet the needs of his resource students. He was assigned 24 students on a staggered schedule throughout the day. In addition, he was the school's educational diagnostician and permanent member of the child study team. In this role, he was required to administer individual norm-referenced achievement tests to students who were suspected of having a disability. The child study team also functioned as a prereferral committee, and each member was assigned to develop instructional interventions and management strategies for students who were experiencing learning and behavior problems but had not been diagnosed with a disability. This informal process was designed to decrease the number of inappropriate, formal referrals that were submitted to the child study team. Finally, Jeff—in all his naivete—was required to serve as a consultant to general educators who taught his students in general classroom settings.

To say the least, Jeff felt overextended, isolated, and overwhelmed, even after three years of teaching. In order to meet the demands of his job, he spent a great deal of time working during the evening hours and on weekends. He spent evenings outlining social studies and science chapters that were too difficult for his included students to read. He modified worksheets and tests. He taped reading materials. During any spare moments on weekends, he typed educational evaluations and developed lesson plans.

Jeff concluded that resource teaching was too cumbersome, too difficult to handle, so he jumped at the chance to move to a self-contained classroom. There, he'd have his own class, his own students, and wouldn't have to consult with as many adults. Only a couple of his students would receive services in general education classes. He'd also no longer have to serve as a diagnostician or member of the child study team. Jeff applied for the position at Indian Hills as soon as he learned of the vacancy. Based on his stellar performance at Jackson, Indian Hills administrators offered him the position on the spot. He was thrilled!

Now, in early December, as he stood once again before his self-contained class to begin what he called opening activities, he wondered if he hadn't—as his grandmother would've said—"jumped from the frying pan into the fire." He still felt isolated, and even though he continued to work late at night and on weekends, his kids just weren't making a lot of progress. Frustrated, Jeff concluded he'd been inadequately prepared to meet the needs of these students with learning and behavior problems far more severe than the kids he'd taught at Jackson. He was tired, worn out, and felt he was working his fingers to the bone for little or no payback. To make matters worse, he was beginning to believe that the problems were inside his students and there was nothing he could do to fix them. He was concerned that these beliefs were beginning to show in his interactions with the kids. As Jeff took attendance, he thought about his relationship with the students who sat before him.

At the first desk sat Buddie, a 12-year-old who had a severe reading disability, a quick temper, and mild seizures. No one had bothered to inform Jeff about the seizures, and he was totally unprepared the first time Buddie had one in class. Buddie was middle class and lived with his divorced mother.

Eight-year-old Asian American Hau was definitely one of Jeff's pets. He was a delight! He had been in a car accident when he was an infant and had suffered a brain injury, from which he had acquired speech and language disorders and physical disabilities. Also, he was functioning far below grade level in all areas. Still, he had a spirit and a zest for life that was contagious. He was good therapy for Jeff.

Demetri was another one of Jeff's pets. He was the only African American student in the class. He'd tested in the mildly retarded range, but the placement team believed the testing wasn't an accurate measure of Demetri's potential. He had cerebral palsy and for part of the day had to sit in a chair specially designed to stretch the muscles in his thighs. This kid had a heart of gold and was a good thinker. Still, this 8-year-old was at least two years below grade level in math and reading and was making only minimal progress. Demetri lived with his mother and five other siblings in a nearby housing project.

Sid was Jeff's upper-middle–class student. He was extremely intelligent and well informed about various topics and issues. Sid had a visual-motor problem that made his handwriting illegible. He performed at an average level in math and was above grade level in language arts. Jeff, along with other school personnel, believed most of Sid's problems were emotional. However, his parents had paid for an independent evaluation that identified learning disabilities as the primary label.

Jeff thought of 9-year-old Jimmie as the class "space cadet." He definitely marched to the tune of a different drummer. He daydreamed constantly and rarely came to class with completed assignments or the proper materials. He was a smart kid, but he just couldn't seem to pull it together in the classroom. This inattentiveness was beginning to irritate Jeff to no end. "If only he would pay attention," Jeff often thought after Jimmie botched an assignment. "He could be one of the highest achievers in this classroom." Jimmie's parents were divorced and he lived with his mother, a potter.

Jeff believed Justin was a budding sociopath and feared he was headed for trouble. This 10-year-old lived with his divorced mother and newborn brother in a trailer court five miles from the school. He lied constantly and always did the opposite of what he was told. Two years ago, he'd been diagnosed with ADHD and was supposed to take a dose of Ritalin before school each day. To Jeff's dismay, most mornings Justin's mom forgot to give him his medication, so it wasn't unusual to see him sitting in his chair with his head touching the floor, rummaging through his desk, rattling paper, flicking pencils, or roaring like a motorcycle. Like Buddie, he'd lose his temper in an instant and was always ready to fight anyone who so much as looked at him the wrong way.

Jonathan was 12 years old and from a middle-class background. He and Jeff had a rocky relationship because Jonathan revealed the first day of school that he didn't like African Americans. Jeff had managed to get Jonathan mainstreamed for everything except reading. He told himself he was mainstreaming Jonathan to prepare him for middle school next year, but deep down he concluded that the two of them were better off being separated as much as possible. He just didn't have the stamina to deal with the "race thing" on top of all the academic and behavioral problems he tackled every day.

And then there was David. Poor dumb David. He couldn't remember anything, and Jeff was convinced he was mentally retarded. David was from a large, lower-middle–class family. Several of his older brothers and sisters were attending or had completed college. It was obvious that despite their socioeconomic status, his parents had high expectations for their children and worked hard to ensure that they got a good education. They hadn't accepted the fact that David probably wasn't college material. Jeff had tried every strategy, every teaching approach that he'd learned during his college days, but he couldn't seem to discover techniques that helped David. He was on Ritalin, but this didn't seem to help either. Jeff concluded that it was time to pray for a miracle. He'd done all he could do for this kid.

Despite Jeff's frustrations, he continued working diligently, trying to find ways to motivate his kids. On this seventh day of January, he began what was called "opening activities," during which he attempted to build vocabulary through reading and discussing newspaper articles that students brought from home. David had brought in a newspaper article about New Year's resolutions. Jeff wrote the word *resolution* on the board and had the boys look it up in their dictionaries. After reading the definition and talking about it, Jeff asked about the two parts of the word, *re-* and *solution*. He then talked about prefixes, including what the word *prefix* means. Then he explained to the kids, "If you learn the meanings of prefixes and know the meaning of the root word, you can figure out the meaning of most words that contain a prefix and root word." They did a few examples using the prefix *re-*, and Jeff had students define the newly formed words. Everyone was into it and did quite well. "*Tres bon, mes enfants!*" Jeff shouted, letting the kids know he was very proud of their accomplishments. He only remembered a few phrases from his high school French classes, but he used them often to encourage his students to learn a foreign language.

After opening activities, Jeff dismissed Jonathan to go to his mainstreamed class; sent Hau, Demetri, and David to do their independent math worksheets at their work-stations; and instructed Justin, Jimmie, Sid, and Buddie to prepare for their math lesson in long division. All four students were excited because Jonathan was doing long division in his inclusion class, and they wanted desperately to keep up with him. Jeff started the lesson by giving them their instructions in French.

"*Ecrivez votre nom et la date sur le papier*," instructed Jeff, "*et tournez a la page 243 dans les livres*. Now, can anyone tell me what I just said?" he asked.

"Piece o'cake, easy," said Justin. Others chimed in, indicating they knew the answer as well. Hands flying high and shouts of "I know, I know" signaled to Jeff that his students were engaged.

Jeff was elated! This response sent little tingles up and down his spine. This is why he had become a teacher. It was amazing! His little learning disabled kids were learning French. "OK, Justin," he said. "You haven't translated this week, so I'll let you give it a shot. Now what did I say?"

Justin replied in a confident voice, "You said write your name and date on your paper and turn to page 243 in your books."

"*Excellent, Monsieur, Jordon, tres bon!*" replied Jeff. He heard David say to Hau and Demetri from his workstation, "He just said, 'excellent, Mr. Jordon, very good.'" Even David was catching on. "If only they could do this for everything," Jeff thought. He then began his introductory lesson for long division. On the board in a column he wrote the words *divide*, *multiply*, *subtract*, and *bring down*. Then he began his lecture.

"OK, guys, today I'm going to start teaching you how to do long division. The trick to long division is to learn the sequence. You guys already know your facts, and for those who forget, you can use the chart hanging from the wall here or your calculators. Now, it's really easy. All you have to do is follow the steps I just wrote on the board. First you divide, then you multiply, next you subtract, bring down, and then start the process all over again." After modeling how to use the steps a few times, Jeff told the students to begin working on some of the problems on the worksheet he'd given them. Then things started to fall apart. The excitement he felt during opening activities and his French mini-lesson quickly faded as he realized that, once again, they weren't getting it.

How can they not get this? he thought as he went from one to the other, observing them complete problem after problem incorrectly. Justin wasn't following the sequence, and when Jeff told him his first three problems were wrong, he ripped up his paper and put his head on his desk and started sulking. "I can't do this. It's too hard. I'm too stupid."

Jimmie was spaced out, as usual. He was following the sequence pretty well, but he was aligning his numbers incorrectly and making careless calculation errors. Jeff started feeling tension in his temples, the beginning signs of a headache. He couldn't help it. He tried to hold back, but he lit into Jimmie.

"Jimmie, why can't you follow the simplest instructions? I told you and showed you what to do, and you're not following the steps. You're putting your numbers in the wrong place. And look at this! What's seven times five? If you don't know the answers, why don't you use the calculator or the chart like I told you? Honestly! Why do you have to make things so hard? Do number one again."

Jimmie appeared oblivious to the fact that Jeff was angry. "OK," he said nonchalantly. He erased his answer and started again.

Before he could finish with Jimmie, Jeff heard a book slam and Buddie scream, "I hate it, Mr. H! I can't do this! Who cares about stupid long division anyway?!" Buddie stood, knocked his math book and worksheet to the floor, ran into the bathroom, and slammed the door behind him.

Demetri, Hau, and David thought the entire scene was hilarious. They were having a field day sniggering at the older boys. Jeff raised his right hand and said, "Chill out, guys." Then he consoled Justin, praised Jimmie for concentrating through Buddie's outburst, and went into the bathroom to reassure Buddie that he'd eventually learn how to do the problems. He told Buddie to calm down, wash his face, and return to his seat. Jeff returned to his math students to learn that Sid was the only one in the group who knew what he was doing. In the midst of all the outbursts, he had completed all the problems on the worksheet correctly. Jeff praised him for a job well done.

By this time, Jeff was beside himself with anxiety and frustration. He felt awful for lambasting Jimmie—even though the space cadet hadn't been fazed by his scolding. He told the students to pass in their worksheets, that they would continue to work on this new skill tomorrow and try a new approach. He then pulled out a multiplication bingo game and had this group play it together while he called David, Hau, and Demetri over to work on subtraction with regrouping. They worked nicely together and completed their work early. Jeff then let them join the others in their game of multiplication bingo until Jonathan reappeared. Jonathan's presence signaled that it was 10:00 and time to begin reading. Jeff dismissed Sid to go to his inclusion classroom for language arts.

Alone in the Dark

ALAN STEAN

I was sitting in my classroom waiting to see if any of my students' parents would appear for the October parent-teacher conferences. This was my first year at Junction High and I wasn't sure what to expect from either the parents or the faculty. My classroom phone rang. It was Steve Lopez, the assistant principal.

"Is a Thelma Crabtree one of your students?"

"Yes, I have her for social studies and geography."

"I just got a call that someone saw her biting her mother out by the road. Does that make any sense to you?" He asked.

"I have never met Mrs. Crabtree," I answered. "Thelma is always cooperative but very quiet in my class. Biting her mother seems very out of character."

"I don't know either Thelma or her mother. Would you mind taking care of it?" Steve asked.

I stepped outside to a rather strange sight. Two women, both looking dishevelled and agitated, were standing by the road at the corner of the school lot. I recognized one as Thelma, my quiet, conscientious 15-year-old student, and I assumed the other was her mother. As I approached, Thelma was holding tightly to the corner of Mrs. Crabtree's sweater, appearing for all the world like a little girl desperately clutching her mother's apron strings to save herself from a threatening world.

"Hello, Thelma," I said as calmly I could, approaching the silent pair. I looked at her mother and said, "I'm Alan Stean, one of Thelma's teachers. Would you like to come to my class?"

"I wanted to, but Thelma wouldn't let me," Mrs. Crabtree explained in a bewildered voice. "It took me 30 minutes to get from the car to the corner of the school, one step at a time. When we got here, Thelma refused to move and started biting me."

I turned to the quiet, frightened girl and asked, "Did you bite your mother?"

Thelma explained, "Carrie (one of the school psychologists) told us both that Mother wasn't to come in the school and talk to the teachers. I can't let her in there."

Mrs. Crabtree turned to Thelma and pleaded, "I just want to ask the teachers if there is anything that I need to do for you. I need to know how much material to buy for your home economics project. It's alright."

Without speaking, Thelma bent down and started biting her mother on the upper arm through her sweater. As Mrs. Crabtree tried to turn away, she cried out, "Ow! Ow! Ow! Thelma, stop! Why are you doing this? OK! OK! We won't go into school."

Thelma stopped biting her mother and started sobbing, "You know you can't go in there."

It became clear to me that Thelma was holding her mother's sweater for support and also to keep her from getting any closer to the school. I was shocked. I had never seen Thelma do anything remotely aggressive. This seemed more a desperate attempt to satisfy the conflicting instructions she had received from the important adults in her life than aggression toward her mother. I watched Mrs. Crabtree try to reorient herself and regain her composure. I started to realize that this was a bigger problem than it appeared to be.

As Thelma continued to sob, I told her, "Your mother has a right to know how well you are doing in school. Have you told her that you are getting *A*s and *B*s in my classes?"

Thelma's trembling became more noticeable as she answered, "No. You aren't supposed to be talking to her either."

Mrs. Crabtree, trying to be positive, said, "I know that you are good in school. If you won't tell me what is happening in school, the only way I can find out is to come here and talk to the teachers."

Thelma bit her mother again. I moved toward them but I was afraid to intervene for fear that I might make the situation worse. I told Thelma to stop but I don't think either of them heard me as they engaged in a curious dance around each other.

Finally, the dance stopped.

"You can't go on biting your mother. We need to talk and find a way to work this out."

Thelma did not reply.

Mrs. Crabtree thought aloud: "High school can be scary. I guess there are a lot of things that are different here than at the middle school. I don't want to upset Thelma but I need to know if she is doing OK."

"Thelma's teachers say that she is very quiet in class," I told Mrs. Crabtree. "As of last week when I talked to them, she was getting good grades in all of her classes. Do you know what Thelma means when she says you aren't supposed to go in the school?"

Mrs. Crabtree asked her daughter, "If you are doing so well in school, what harm would it do if I went in for a minute to ask your home economics teacher how much material I need to buy?"

Thelma's only answer was to bite and pinch her mother again. Thelma stopped long enough to say, "I have to pee."

Mrs. Crabtree rubbed her arm and explained.

"Whenever Thelma gets upset, I worry that she will pee in the car before we get home. It's a half an hour drive back home, and we left home two hours ago."

"Thelma, do you need to go into the school to use the rest room?" I asked.

"She'll go into the school if I leave her," Thelma answered, pointing to Mrs. Crabtree while looking down at the ground. "Even though she knows she shouldn't."

"Well," I said, playing for time, "we can stay out here and talk until you get back."

Thelma turned and wouldn't face me again. She was becoming more distressed and confused by our inability or unwillingness to follow the simple instructions she had received from Carrie. "No! You aren't supposed to talk to him either. Let's go home!" She pleaded.

"I guess we should go," Mrs. Crabtree said. I knew further efforts were unlikely to be successful. I asked Thelma, "Can you wait to use the bathroom until you get home?"

Thelma nodded yes.

"Are we still friends?" I asked.

Thelma stared at the ground and shook her head.

"Maybe by the time we get back to class tomorrow we will be able to talk about this," I said hopefully.

Thelma shook her head and started pulling her mother's sweater toward the car.

"I guess we should go. You won't pee will you? You promised," Mrs. Crabtree pleaded.

Thelma shook her head from side to side.

As they turned to leave I said, "It was nice meeting you, Mrs. Crabtree. I hope we can talk and be friends again tomorrow, Thelma. Being your friend is important to me."

The pair shuffled away.

Returning to the building, I was worried that I had unintentionally violated Thelma's trust. She was a quiet girl who only talked when spoken to and then always in a monotone. She never interacted with other students in my class. At lunch time each day I could count on seeing her standing alone in the hall five minutes after being dismissed from my class. I had worked hard to develop a friendly, supportive relationship with Thelma.

Steve Lopez stopped me in the hall. "Well, was your student really biting her mother?"

I briefly related what had happened.

"It doesn't make sense," said Steve, "I don't think there's any constraint keeping Mrs. Crabtree out of the school—she has custody of Thelma, so she should have the right to talk with us."

"Carrie's not here right now," said Steve, "but check with Doris Dexter. I think she has had some dealings with Thelma in the past."

Doris was in her office.

"I remember Thelma. She's the big dumpy girl with old dirty clothes that just hang on her. I've seen her shuffling down the hall. The first time I met her was when she came back to school after a year on a psychiatric ward. It seems that she drove a spike through her foot and then wouldn't let anyone touch her foot to treat it."

"Until this morning Thelma has always been really quiet and cooperative," I said. "This morning I felt that she must have been feeling the same way she did when she drove the spike through her foot. I'd hate to think of her doing anything drastic like that again."

"The first time I met with Thelma's father," Doris continued, "was the only time I have ever been afraid for my personal safety in dealing with parents. Mr. Crabtree acted so irrationally that I was sure I was going to be beaten up at any moment. In fact,

I remember removing my watch and glasses—at least they would be safe even if something happened! But back to today. I can't imagine what Carrie might have meant or said to Thelma to give her the impression that we weren't allowed to talk to her mother."

I talked with Carrie a few weeks later, and the picture of the day in the parking lot became a little clearer.

"I asked Thelma's mother to wait in the car on Thursdays when she picks Thelma up after school and brings her to counseling. They need to work on separation. In a few years, Thelma will be out on her own, and they need to start working on that. Mrs. Crabtree insists on meeting Thelma at the school door or even at the classroom door. She claims that Thelma won't be able to find the car on her own. Mrs. Crabtree always arrives at our meeting scratched and bruised, so we haven't been very successful yet. The rule wasn't intended to restrict the mother's access to the high school staff."

When Thelma returned to class, she refused to talk to me or do any work. She sat quietly at her desk waiting for the class to end. When I tried to discuss the incident by the road she would only say, in reference to what Carrie had told her, that I had lied, that I had broken "the rules" and her trust. Nothing seemed to help.

I felt as if I was in a room with the lights off—as if in my dealings with Thelma I would unwittingly destroy something. At the same time, I desperately needed to get to a door and let some light in.

In spite of my best efforts, I never did.

Caught in the Middle

LEANN GROSSLEY

Louise Jones's sixth-grade class seemed to take longer than usual to come in and settle down after their morning break. With the warm sunny weather and the playground right outside the classroom window, they were reluctant to resume the joys of math.

This was my second year as a substitute teacher in the Geneva City school system. Being a substitute teacher gave me valuable learning experiences in a wide variety of classes and schools while I attended East State University where I was working on my master's degree in education. I had been in the system long enough that most of the principals knew me by name and often called me when a teacher or aide was absent.

As the children filed in, I recalled the first time that I had worked with this class three weeks earlier. Shaun Haley, the principal of Church Street Elementary, had called to get me to fill in for Julia Bell, Louise's classroom aide. I remembered leaving Louise's class that day with a renewed excitement about my chosen profession. When Shaun called again, this time to substitute for Louise, I looked forward to working with the sixth-graders again. I recalled that the class was not that large—18 students. They were a lively bunch whose enthusiasm knew no bounds. They were curious, funny, and motivated.

On this second visit, I arrived a little early to get the "feel" of the classroom. I had learned long ago that most teachers who knew they would be absent would leave instructions and materials in plain view on their desks. I checked Louise's desk. Sure enough, there were several pages of detailed notes and directions. As I carefully read Louise's messages, I made a mental note of what I needed to do and jotted down several reminders on a pad. Deep in concentration, I became somewhat puzzled by several inserts in the morning activities where Louise had added post-it notes, all saying the same thing: "Check with Julia for details of what to do here." I felt a little uncomfortable with these mysterious directives—11 in all. I liked to know exactly the way the morning would go. I had had enough unpleasant experiences desperately trying to improvise with children to whom I was a relative stranger!

Activity in the hallways increased, and I made a quick trip to the staff lounge for a fresh cup of coffee before the day began. On the way, I pondered my situation: I was acutely aware that the introduction of a substitute teacher was, at best, unsettling for the students, who almost always perceived that I was "not their real teacher." I had always managed to overcome these perceptions by being well prepared by the start of the day. At least I had worked with this class once before. Louise's little notes meant that I couldn't possibly be as prepared as I wanted to be. Another nagging thought arose: Was I to be the aide to Julia or a replacement teacher for Louise, with Julia acting as my aide? By the time I returned to the classroom, Julia was already there.

Louise had told me that Julia was a competent aide. She had had no prior teacher training except an in-service that the city schools required of all aides working in elementary classrooms. She had been an aide since the in-service several months earlier. A rather large, imposing figure, Julia's long, straggly hair framed her pale face. She wore very thick, smudged spectacles that enlarged her dark brown eyes. She seemed to move quite slowly but with great deliberation. My initial impression was that she appeared very cautious and very tentative. Our conversation went like this:

> **ME:** Hi, I'm Leann Grossley. Shaun Haley asked me to substitute for Louise. You must be Julia Bell?
>
> **JULIA:** Good morning, Leann. Nice to meet you.
>
> **ME:** I've already looked over Louise's instructions, so . . .
>
> **JULIA:** Yes, I know. I'll get things started as soon as the bell rings. In the meantime, would you mind checking over these math sheets? The answer key is right here.

Julia, it appeared, liked to be in charge, and I didn't feel like arguing. I moved to Louise's desk and began grading the sheets.

Class began at 8:00 sharp. The tardy bell rang at 8:05 and was followed by a series of school announcements over the public address system. A bell signalling the beginning of the academic day rang at 8:10. Julia's teaching style became quickly apparent. She delivered instructions in a booming voice, her ample arms flailing the air to emphasize her point. Her directions were constantly punctured by admonitions to various students who were not complying with her wishes:

> **JULIA:** Now, we're going to begin. Phil, get a move on! We're going to begin our math. Mary, what's the matter with you? Can't you sit still even for a few minutes? Let's begin by opening our math books to page . . . Manuel, are you quite finished with your little private conversation now? Thank you so much. Turn to page 231. Quickly now!

After several more minutes, Julia finally succeeded in getting the class focused. Several students looked somewhat anxious. It was clear that Julia was revelling in her role of "teacher for a day." The math lesson swiftly became a macabre game of Julia doing her level best to catch students in wrong answers. When she did, her punishment was a diatribe that left the offending student mortified:

> **JULIA:** Conchita, what's the answer to number seven?

CONCHITA: Thirteen ... um, no, twelve, ... wait ...

JULIA: Can't you make up your mind? If you'd been listening to what we did in class yesterday, you'd know! Are you sure you're supposed to be in this class? Doesn't seem like you should be from what you're saying. That's the easiest math problem in the whole exercise!

Conchita turned bright red and remained silent for the rest of the lesson. Julia was relentless, but not everyone got the same treatment.

JULIA: Jonathan, number eight.

JONATHAN: Thirty-seven.

JULIA: Exactly! Jonathan, it's so nice to have people in this class who have brains and use them. Why don't you try number nine as well?

JONATHAN: Sixteen.

JULIA: Of course! Conchita, are you getting the picture now?

I felt so sorry for Conchita and several others who failed to escape Julia's wrath, and who never had a chance, it seemed, to redeem themselves. As the unswerving barrage continued, I became increasingly angry. What had children like Conchita done to deserve this? It was clear that they didn't understand the work, but Julia's little game did not involve teaching. Julia changed her focus to Chris, a reedy, sandy-haired boy who, it seemed to me, wore a permanently baffled look. I had noticed that look the last time I had worked with the class. I also remembered that Chris appeared to be one of the weakest students in the class. When Julia called his name, I knew things would go from bad to worse.

JULIA: Chris, number fifteen, now!

Chris was visibly startled. His brow deeply furrowed, he stared at his book. The room was absolutely silent. By this point, nobody was looking up from their books. It seemed that the other students were simply glad that Chris had been chosen and not themselves. Their bowed heads betrayed their wish to hide as much as was possible while sitting in a desk facing Julia's stony gaze. Chris began to squirm in his seat, his left leg trembling slightly.

CHRIS: Number fifteen?

Chris was playing for time, hoping to delay the inevitable.

JULIA: What's the matter with you? Are you deaf? If you're deaf, you shouldn't be in here! Deaf people don't belong here. We move too fast! Chris, are you *really* deaf, or as *usual*, just not paying attention? You should, you know, your grades are the worst in this class!

CHRIS: I'm sorry, I thought you said . . .

Julia: Number *fifteen*. What's the answer?

CHRIS: Twenty-three?

JULIA: Twenty-three? How on earth did you get twenty-three? Are you on the planet here with us? Twenty-three? Twenty-three? Puhhhhleeeease!

Chris looked like a stunned animal. As Julia turned her gaze to another victim, I couldn't stand it any more. I got up and went over to Chris's desk. As I crouched down beside him to help him find his place, Julia turned on me.

JULIA: Ms. Grossley, I'd appreciate your waiting to help Chris until I've finished the exercise. He'd do a lot better if he'd listen and get his homework done. It's really not your problem.

Against my better judgment, I retreated to my seat, just as humiliated as some of the students had been. I felt my cheeks getting hot, and my knuckles were white in my clenched fists. Several students, risking Julia's unwanted attention, looked sympathetically in my direction. By the time the mid-morning break arrived, I was more than ready to escape the oppressive atmosphere.

The children straggled reluctantly in from their break. Julia positioned herself at the classroom door, and, as usual, was yelling at the kids.

JULIA: Move it! We don't have all day you know! Josh, sit down NOW! Felicity, what's your problem? Do you need me to come over there and solve it for you? You'll be really sorry! If you people won't settle down, I'll begin writing down names! You know what that means—name down, then the office! I'll bet you don't want that to happen!

Everyone quickly settled down and looked at Julia—everyone, that is, except Chris, who had his head down on his desk.

JULIA: Chris, get your head up this minute! What do you think this is, your bedroom?

Chris didn't respond. But Jonathan did.

JONATHAN: Ms. Bell, I think Chris is sick. I think he threw up on the playground . . .

JULIA: Nonsense—he was fine before the break, he should be fine now. Chris—up, NOW!

Chris didn't respond. Julia was furious.

JULIA: Get you head up NOW, get with the program, or you can get out and go
    to the office!

Chris had had enough. Looking up for the first time since entering the class, he
gave as good as he had gotten.

CHRIS: I will do anything I want to and YOU can't make me do anything!

JULIA: I CAN send you to the office!

CHRIS: SO?

The entire class was watching, blow by blow. Julia was trembling as she walked
over to Chris's desk.

JULIA: How DARE YOU?

Without warning, Julia turned to me. She turned so swiftly that I jumped.

JULIA: It's either Chris leaves or me. YOU take him to the office and write the
    referral when you get there.

Reluctantly, I walked to the door, opened it, and waited for Chris to join me.
Slowly, he pulled himself up out of his seat, tears streaming down his cheeks. Every pair
of eyes tracked us through the door on our way to the office.

   There was so much I wanted to say to Chris. I wanted to tell him that it wasn't all
his fault. Julia had been awful. It had all happened so fast. One minute we were coming
in from break, and the next minute there was this ugly confrontation.

   There I was caught between Julia and Chris. I very much wanted to side with
Chris, and yet, what example would I be setting for Chris or the other students by taking
one side against the other? After all, Julia worked with these students every day and
Louise had given no hint to what I had just witnessed. As we slowly walked to the office,
I agonized over what Chris must have been feeling.

   I filled out the referral to Shaun with a heavy heart. Chris, seated in the office,
looked so dejected. He was pale, sweaty, and breathing rapidly. I sent him to the nurse.

   As I turned to leave, I made a decision. Returning to the office counter, I attached
a note to the referral:

Mr. Haley: I really must talk to you about this referral. If you don't get this
before I leave at the end of the day, please give me a call at home.

Teaching for me would never be the same.

My Son Is Not Average!

HARRIET KARR

"My son is NOT average!" I screamed to myself as I read Roger's kindergarten report card. "Any child who can build a space shuttle complete with launching pad out of DUPLOs at age 3 is not average. He's got some kind of problem." I told the special resources teacher the first week of school that I suspected Roger should be tested. "Why hasn't anything been done?" I asked.

This was just the beginning of my education about the school system.

I arranged a meeting with Roger's teacher. I told her about the DUPLOs. I also explained to her that I had a language specialist test Roger when he was 4 years old because I was worried about his slow development of speech, our difficulty in understanding him, and his intermittent difficulty in putting his ideas into words. The language specialist had reported that Roger had "high average to above average receptive language scores, and low average to below average expressive language scores." He continued, "This, combined with numerous articulation and semantic errors, reduces Roger's intelligibility so that he can be understood only about 65 percent of the time." The specialist had not recommended direct intervention at the time, but had given Roger's preschool teacher and me exercises and instructions about how to work with Roger.

I also explained to Roger's teacher that this was his second year of kindergarten. To give him time to work on his speech, I had put him in a private kindergarten the previous year. As a kindergarten teacher of many years, Roger's new teacher kindly assured me that I shouldn't worry—my son was within the average performance for kindergartners. She went on to say that she expected his behavior to improve once he got used to the other children and her routine. I told her that I thought he should be tested again. She told me to give him a little more time to "settle in."

I spoke to the special resources teacher again. I told her about Roger's average report card, his history, and asked if she could retest him. But two more reporting periods came and went—"Average to Below Average." Roger and I were working hard to bring home "Happy Faces" instead of "Sad Faces" every day. I was more than a little frustrated that there had been no mention of testing my son. Finally, someone at my workplace told me, "Put your request in writing. They have to respond if you put it in writing. And keep a copy."

May 27
Dear Ms. A.,

I would like you to test and evaluate the language and speech of my son, Roger, who is currently in Mrs. B's kindergarten class. He was tested at the age of 4 and found to have quite a number of speech and language problems. I have asked her to send you a copy of her report.

My son was reevaluated casually a year later. His speech had improved considerably, but he was still having a great deal of trouble with the correct use of pronouns.

I would like a second formal test for the purpose of comparison and to catch any lingering problems while we can still easily correct them. In my opinion, he still has some speech problems—difficulty with certain sounds, "l" for instance, and he tends to stutter. However, I feel the bigger problem is in his expressive language, particularly word finding.

> Sincerely,
> Harriet Karr
> Cc: Mrs. B.

July 5
Dear Ms. A.,

In response to my May 27 letter requesting that you test my son's speech, you suggested that we do it in August. I was wondering when you would like Roger to come in. We are planning a vacation the week before school starts (August 18-21). Since we will miss the Open House, I am trying to arrange to bring him by Monday afternoon to find his room and meet his teacher. That day might be a possibility. Please let me know what is convenient for you.

> Sincerely
> Harriet Karr

School started at the end of August. Roger and I met his new startlingly young first-grade teacher. I found out that my son was in the lowest reading and math groups. After a couple of weeks of school, I arranged to meet Roger's teacher. I asked her about Roger's placement, explained about the DUPLOs and my concern that he has a problem. The meeting did not go well. I sensed that she felt—incorrectly—that I was trying to intimidate her. She told me that they do not "track" students, but they grouped students with others who were at the same point instructionally, which enabled the teacher to make most efficient use of her time.

Mid-September. Still no word about testing my son. I was getting extremely frustrated. All the research I had done indicated that many language problems could be remediated if addressed early enough—while the brain was still forming—but that once a child got older there was not much that could be done. I felt I was racing the clock, particularly since Roger was already a year older than most of the other first-graders.

Finally, a form letter came by "backpack express," setting a meeting date on September 14th. I wrote again.

September 11
Dear Ms. A.,

I am looking forward to meeting with you on Monday, September 14, regarding my son Roger. I am very concerned about his speech, specifically his expressive language ability.

In May I requested that you test my son's speech, and you suggested that since it was so close to the end of school and because children change so much over the summer that we should test him in August. I appreciate you setting up this meeting with yourself, my son's teacher, and us. My primary concern is if the large discrepancy still exists between his receptive language scores and his expressive language scores that it might not go away without some therapy. I know that the older a child is, the less therapy is able to effect significant change.

Sincerely,
Harriet Karr

We met on the 14th. I was glad to see his teacher was there. I thought she needed to know what we were doing. I signed some papers allowing the speech teacher to give Roger some tests. What I did not realize until this meeting was just how formalized it all was. School services and testing were not something that could be requested or used à la carte. My letter in May had started the "evaluation process to determine whether or not your child qualifies for speech and/or language services." The "Eligibility Committee" would review the results of the evaluation in November. All I wanted was a test!

November finally arrived. I took leave from work and went to the school to meet with the Eligibility Committee, which turned out to consist of the speech teacher, my son's classroom teacher, and the assistant principal. The speech teacher presented the results of her tests.

Hearing: Pass

Voice Evaluation: WNL

Fluency Evaluation: WNL

Examination of Oral Mobility Coordination: Reduced

Syllable Repetition: Reduced

Articulation Evaluation: WNL-Dev.

Comments: *Goldman-Fristoe Test of Articulation*

   w/l I in word, f/o I, M,F

   w/l in blends /bl, fl, kl, pl/

Progress from K screenings

Language Evaluation: WNL *Peabody Picture Vocabulary Test*: S.S. 120
  (M = 100) CELF3

Receptive: S.S. 98

Sentence Structure: S.S. 10

Concepts and Directions: S.S. 10

Word Classes: S.S. 9

Expressive: S.S. 96

Word Structure: S.S. 9

Formulated Sentences: S.S. 10

Recalling Sentences: S.S. 9

Total Language: S.S. 96

Recommendation: Therapy is not recommended at this time.

I realized shortly into the presentation that I was like an ill-prepared tourist who had embarked on a tour of a foreign county without knowing a word of the language. My first question demonstrated my ignorance. "What is WNL?" "Within Normal Limits," came the reply. Of course! So, basically, they were saying that my son had no problems—or that they couldn't find one. I found myself wishing I had paid closer attention in statistics class: S.S. turned out to mean "Standard Score," with Mean (M) generally being 100 or 10. So, why was my son testing 20 points above the mean on one test (Peabody) and 4 points below the mean on another (CELF3)? Knowing that this evaluation was a "process" and a well-choreographed one at that, I asked, "What is the next step?" They explained that I could either stop here or ask for a "full evaluation." Based on the point differences on the two tests and my intuition, I asked for more testing.

More papers to sign. I found out that a "full evaluation" included sociocultural, educational, developmental, speech/hearing/language/auditory processing, and psychological testing. What had I gotten my son into?

In December, I got a form letter by "Backpack Express" setting the next meeting of the "Eligibility Committee" for 2:30 on February 1 in the conference room. More than a year had past since my first conference with my son's kindergarten teacher!

Report cards came out in January. My son was classified as a "Late Emergent" reader and was in the "Early Letter Name" stage of spelling. His teacher told me that at this point in the year, she would have liked him to be at least one stage higher in both areas. She also said that she was having a hard time getting him to write more than one sentence. "He loves to tell the class about his pictures, but he doesn't write about them." She went on to say that he still was having a hard time following directions.

February finally came. Since I had felt so overwhelmed at the last meeting of the Eligibility Committee, I asked a teacher friend of mine if she could come with me to translate. She graciously agreed. When we had found the very small room that served as a conference room and all of the participants had arrived, eight people were in the room; four specialists to report on their findings, my son's teacher, the assistant principal, my friend, and me. Without my friend, I would have been outnumbered six to one!

The social worker went first, reporting her findings on the sociocultural aspects of my son's life—based on a 45-minute interview with me in December. In summary, she saw a happy child with no medical problems other than glasses for far-sightedness; development of speech had been slow; highly enriched learning environment at home. My translation: Nice child; no problems.

Next was the *educational report*, which concluded much the same: The student appears to function within an appropriate range for a beginning first-grade student. Reading and mathematics do not show significant discrepancies at this time. Therefore, it is not felt that Roger needs educational support at present. The report listed the tests administered:

> *Wechsler Individual Achievement Test—Reading* = 86, Math = 84, Spelling = 89, Listening comprehension = 111
>
> *Beery-Buktenica Developmental Test of Visual-Motor Integration* = 108
>
> *The Test of Early Mathematics Ability* = 95
>
> My translation: Average child; no problems.
>
> *Speech/Language/Hearing*: The student has a wide range of language scores, all of which are in the average to above-average range. Other discipline test scores should be compared to determine if Speech/Language Services are warranted. Hearing within normal limits; articulation—developmentally appropriate errors noted.
>
> *Peabody Picture Vocabulary Test* = 120
>
> *Test of Auditory Perceptual Skills*: Subtests ranged from 2nd percentile to 99th percentile, with difficulty in short-term auditory memory of words and numbers, and reasoning skills very high.
>
> CELF3 Expressive Language = 96, Receptive Language = 96, Total language score = 96
>
> My translation: Average child; no problems.
>
> Finally, the *psychological evaluation*:
>
> *WISC-III: Verbal* = 112, *Performance* = 133, and *Full Scale* = 123. Performance score significantly higher than Verbal score; above-average to superior cognitive functioning; significant relative weakness in short-term auditory memory; well-developed perceptual organization and spatial skills. VADS—difficulties with short-term memory, with overall score below 10th percentile; suggests difficulties with memory for symbols as well as sequencing and recall of information. *Woodcock-Johnson-R*: Visual processing = 121, Short-term memory = 81, Auditory processing = 86. *Bender*: age equivalent of 9-0 to 9-11. In summary: The student demonstrated well above-average cognitive functioning. Processing deficits were noted in the areas of short-term memory and auditory processing; visual processing is a significant strength.

I admit that by the time the psychologist spoke in the warm, stuffy room my head was swimming with numbers and acronyms. However, I noticed that all the teachers sat up in their chairs. One of them asked, "What was the score on the WISC Performance?" When the psychologist got to the summary, I did catch the phrases "well above-average cognitive functioning" and "processing deficits." I thought to myself, "YES! YES, YES, YES!!! At last!!" The mood in the room shifted from, "See, this is just another pushy mom who thinks her baby is a genius and we professionals don't understand him" to "Whoa! She was right!"

Then I had to figure out what exactly was "auditory processing" and what exactly was my son's problem and how to fix it . . . but that's another story.

The One That Got Away

CHARLES ALLEN

Part A

Yesterday, I had lunch with Polly, a retired teacher I used to work with. During our gabfest about family and friends, what Polly calls, our "catch-up" session, she asked, "Did you know that Calvin is in the penitentiary?"

I had not heard this, but I was not surprised. In my 29 years of teaching physical education to elementary students, Calvin stands out as the most frightening child I have ever taught. He was the only child who could make my blood feel icy when he walked into the gym, and I've taught some pretty tough cases. Over the years, I've had every kind of special education child that administrators can think up labels for, but none of them can hold a candle to Calvin.

Calvin had always been a problem, even in kindergarten, but when he entered third grade a combination of things sent him spiraling into serious behavior problems. Before Calvin started school, his mother and father were incarcerated for selling drugs, and so his aunt took care of him. Around third grade, his mother and father were released from jail, and resumed caring for him. I never did hear the whole story, but it seemed that his mother and father did not live together, and both lived with other partners. Neither parent seemed real excited to have Calvin, but the dad did try to deal with this little boy, and Calvin lived with his Dad and his girlfriend.

Polly said, "Well, yes, the dad did seem to care more for Calvin than the mother, from what I heard. Then one night, he and Calvin came back home from somewhere, and found that dad's girlfriend had thrown the dad's and Calvin's belongings in the yard. She wouldn't let them back in, even to get Calvin's schoolbooks."

"I never heard that story," I said. "That's really sad."

Polly continued, "This child's whole life was so sad. When Calvin was in the third grade, right after the dad's girlfriend threw them out, Calvin's father lost his job. Social services provided the necessities, but the dad didn't have any money for Christmas. The special education supervisor told me that when she was observing another child in Mary Anderson's class, she became interested in Calvin and his situation, and begged some money from her church to give to the dad to buy presents for Calvin. She also thought

228

that Calvin should have some money to buy his dad a gift. She even helped Calvin pick out a gift for his dad."

I said, "Poor fella. He did have a tough life for a young boy."

"He had a tough life for anybody."

Around this time, Calvin experienced a growth spurt and was as large as some of our fourth-graders, our BIG fourth-graders. He was angry, probably frightened, and he had the size and strength to make his anger a real threat.

Polly said, "I don't how Mary Anderson dealt with that child for a whole year. She had to instruct her class what to do if Calvin 'went off.' I mean, one afternoon when he was absent, Mary told the children where to evacuate the room if he exploded by the side door. Or by her desk. Or by the hall door. I can't believe that parents in that class didn't scream bloody murder, but they didn't."

I said, "The kids might have been too frightened of Calvin to tell anybody anything. You know he extorted money from other children, but no one would tell on him. You had to catch him in the act, which was not always possible."

"Well, yes, I know about that because I caught him in the act, but he promptly told me to mind my own business if I didn't want to get hurt. I left him in the hall with his victims and got the principal to deal with him. Unfortunately, I didn't know the names of the smaller children he was victimizing, and by the time she arrived, the kids were gone. I'm not sure what happened with that situation."

I talked to Polly for about an hour and reconstructed some of the major episodes in our relationship with Calvin. Calvin had always been noncompliant, but my issuing a bottom line consequence was usually sufficient to keep him from pummeling other students. My calm statement, "Either sit by the wall for a few minutes, or go to the office," had worked before his third-grade year. Sometimes he went to the office, and sometimes he sat out for a few minutes. But he usually complied.

The first time I was aware of his defiance was one afternoon when all the students had left. Mary Anderson, Calvin's teacher, had gotten permission from Calvin's dad and school administrators to keep Calvin after school. Apparently he decided that he was not going to stay. I had the misfortune to be in the office, to look out the window, and to see Calvin dragging Mary Anderson, down the sidewalk. Actually, she was holding on to one of his arms with both her hands while he walked steadily down the sidewalk. Her feet were planted firmly, but he was so strong that he was able to drag her along as if she were a wagon he was casually pulling. I asked if she needed some help, she replied that she did, and when I approached Calvin and asked that he return to the classroom, he became a tornado, a whirling machine of flailing body parts. I restrained him, took him to the office where the principal, Mrs. Robertson, Mary, and I tried to deal with him. I don't know exactly how it happened, but Calvin and I ended up in the principal's swiveling chair, my legs around his body, my arms holding his arms in the straightjacket hold while he rammed his head backward into my head.

I remember angrily saying to Mrs. Robertson, the principal, "I'm not getting paid enough to do this."

She said, "Let him go."

I did, and he began to destroy the office. He cleared the shelves, the desk, and turned over furniture. He had a wild look on his face, and frankly, he scared me, but when he had pretty much trashed the room, he began to calm. Then he picked up a pair of scissors, opened the blades, put one blade on his wrist, and threatened to slice his wrist. I was afraid to breathe, but the principal talked quietly and calmly, and after what seemed like a lifetime, got him to put down the scissors. Mrs. Robertson then decided that she would call a cab and send Calvin home.

When the cab came, the three of us escorted him to the cab, put him in the back seat, and watched him leap out the door on the other side, and bolt across the schoolyard. Mrs. Robertson said, "Leave him alone. Don't chase him. I'll call the police." Even though I was too exhausted to chase him, I was also worried about him. I wondered how Calvin, who was already frightened and angry, would react to the police.

Before I left school that afternoon, I told Mrs. Robertson, "Calvin needs help. He's gotten worse this year."

Polly said, "You're not the only one who thought that Calvin needed help. His poor teacher must have come to the child study committee every week. She was so good about implementing our strategies, but Calvin needed so much more than any strategies we could offer. And he consumed most of Mary's time and energy."

Polly went on to tell me about the time she had met a parent for an IEP meeting in the office area, and had difficulty conducting the meeting because Calvin was destroying one of the offices on the hall. She said, "He never left the office, but he turned over a heavy bookshelf, one of those that reach from floor to ceiling and was full of books. He then threw the books against the wall one by one, and finally punched a large hole in the drywall with his fist. Even though I closed both the door to the conference room, and the door to the office he was systematically destroying, the noise level was distracting. The parents kept asking me, 'What is that racket?' We managed to sign the IEP, but whew!"

I said, "I never could understand why no one saw fit to test Calvin for possible placement in special education."

Polly said, "I have wondered that myself. Some of us on the child study committee pushed for testing, but our concerns always got overruled. Thought you might know why he was never referred."

"Not me. We support folks are out of the loop. We just teach our nine classes a day, do our lunch duty, our bus duty, and try not to complain. Not many folks think to ask us how we see the children. But Mrs. Robertson did try to help me out. Because I don't have an intercom in the gym, Mrs. Robertson put a phone in the gym office so that I could call her when Calvin went off. I did appreciate that. It was frightening to be at the end of the hall, in the basement, not close to any other classrooms, with no intercom, and no way to get help. I certainly couldn't leave the class with him acting out like that. I did carry him a couple of times to the office, but it never looks good for a teacher to subdue a child like that. And besides, I may be an average-sized male, but Calvin was big, and he was becoming more than I could handle. Particularly when he was flailing around."

I told Polly, "I finally learned to 'read' Calvin. I knew when he walked in the gym door if he was on edge, and I would do all I could to keep him from going off. But sometimes he still exploded. I never knew what would provoke him, and because he was bigger than the other kids, I was nervous the whole time he was in gym. One day, I knew what had set him off. After we had talked a lot about his controlling himself, another student insisted that he have the same gym scooter that Calvin wanted. Can't figure out what the other boy was thinking, most kids were afraid of Calvin, but the other boy did finally back off and let Calvin have the scooter. I was proud of Calvin that he didn't loose it with this other boy, but by the time he finally got possession of the scooter, he didn't want it. And you should have seen him. His eyes got a wild look in them, he walked to the end of the gym away from the rest of us and paced up and down, up and down, real fast. I asked him if he wanted to go back to his classroom, but he refused to answer. When it was time for his class to leave the gym, he refused to go with them. It was one of those rare days when I didn't have a class after his, so I just let him pace the gym until he was ready to go. After about 15 minutes, he calmed down and went back to class."

Polly said, "I'm glad that you had the good sense not to touch him. Do you remember what happened to Mr. Wheeler, the custodian who befriended Calvin? One morning when Calvin had trashed the classroom, and was out in the hall threatening to run away, Mr. Wheeler walked up to Calvin, and said, 'Come on, Calvin. Let's you and me go for a walk.' When Calvin just stood there trembling and clenching his fists, Mr. Wheeler placed his hands on Calvin's shoulders. Before Mr. Wheeler could utter a word, Calvin clawed both Mr. Wheeler's arms with his fingernails. Calvin left deep wounds on Mr. Wheeler's arms. Poor man had to go to the doctor, and he missed a couple days of work. He said that Calvin looked like a wild animal when he scratched him."

"I know the look. I thought he looked more like a frightened animal. I guess he was frightened. But you know, when he was calm, and when you had him one on one, he was a friendly, funny kid. And smart too."

I told Polly about my plan for Calvin in the fourth grade that was partially successful. That particular year, I was blessed as never before and had the last class free on Fridays. So I talked with his teacher, and told her that if Calvin had a good week, he could come shoot baskets with me at that time. His teacher, Betty, devised some kind of behavior management plan, I don't remember what it was, and this seemed to help control him. All during the week, I'd remind him to hold it together so we could shoot some baskets. His teacher would remind him also. She would say, 'Calvin, don't spoil it. You're doing great. Try to hold it together so you can shoot some baskets.' He usually did. I don't know. I reckon that helped some. His teacher seemed to think that it did. And you know what, I really enjoyed our time together his last year at our school."

James's Uncertain Future

DAN PARKER

James Judson was enrolled in my third-grade special education class from the beginning of the school year. James lived with his mother and an older brother, Kenny. Kenny was a tenth-grade straight-A student and an athlete—an all out, good kid. I was not surprised that James idolized Kenny. As was so often the case with my students, Kenny took the place of James's father. James knew where his father lived, but he hadn't had any contact with his father for about a year.

James's mother, Anna, did her best to support the family but had a history of frequently changing jobs. She was very big and tall, an intimidating figure complimented by a generally belligerent attitude. She had a very deep, raspy voice, and when she talked her comments were so pointed and harsh that they often left me breathless. In our many interactions over the year, she often appeared angry and usually claimed that everyone was picking on James or criticizing her parenting skills. However, Anna was highly verbal and always seemed very interested in James's academic progress. If he took work home, she usually tried to help him.

The family lived in a run-down part of town comprised of mostly Mexican American and African American low SES families. The area had a reputation for gang activity, and children commonly witnessed violence in the neighborhood. The school reflected the neighborhood. West Side Elementary housed 1,200 students with multiple classes for each grade. Official school statistics reported the ethnic mix as 50 percent Hispanic, 45 percent African American, and 5 percent Caucasian and Asian American students.

When I first met James, he seemed nice enough. However, I didn't see James every day—he would only come to me for extra help or re-teaching as needed. At first, James would come to my class only once in a while. Even in those early days he was very distractible and talked out of turn all the time. If the class were answering questions from the textbook, for example, he would burst out with "Oh! Oh! Oh! Mr. Parker! Mr. Parker! I know that! Oh! Oh! Oh!" and then, nine times out of ten, he'd give the wrong answer.

What I was seeing in my classroom was soon mirrored by what Jill was experiencing in hers. James had begun picking on other kids. He'd been hitting, pinching, scratching, kicking, and tripping. Students would walk by to go to the pencil sharpener and James would whack them on the back of the head. Soon, Jill started sending James to me much more often—as much for his inappropriate behavior as his schoolwork, I thought.

Although James was labeled learning disabled (LD), he was academically up to par. If his inappropriate behaviors hadn't been so obvious, he never would have been in my room. Everyone knew James's behavior was the problem. Even his mother acknowledged that: "Well, he's active, that's all there is to it." His activity, however, wore people out. Jill would go home crying almost every day. He just overwhelmed her.

By mid-year, James was acting out all the time. We tried a wide variety of behavioral approaches, but none of them worked. The school psychologist tried, the general education teachers tried, the LD teachers tried, and the principal had ideas that she tried, all to no avail. By the middle of the year, we had had four conferences with Anna. In spite of our strenuous urging, Anna would only help with the homework, and not much else.

In the fifth conference we repeated the now growing litany to Anna. She refused to believe that James was misbehaving in class.

"He's not really doing that," she said.

By this point we had all had enough, so we invited Anna to see for herself. We put up some dark paper on my windows with small viewing slits into the classroom so that Anna could observe James in my class without being seen. After witnessing James's behavior for a two-week period, Anna seemed completely overwhelmed.

At our next meeting we saw a different Anna. She broke down, saying she couldn't believe this was her James. We were all touched by her outpouring of frustration as she told us how hard it was for her to hold the family together, her helplessness at not being better able to provide for her children, and her bewilderment that James was "not more like Kenny." I was concerned, though, that she seemed to leave the meeting with a fiercely determined look on her face. Her parting comment that she'd "take care of things" didn't help, either.

Whatever Anna had meant by "taking care of things" appeared to work. James was quiet and compliant for about a week and actually attended to academic tasks. We soon realized, though, that this was not necessarily progress when, one day, he came to school but couldn't sit down at his desk in Jill's class. Jill insisted he explain what the problem was. James reluctantly showed her switch marks from the middle of his back to the middle of his thigh where Anna had "whipped" him. Besides being unable to sit down at all, he was scared to go home without having done his work.

Even beatings didn't help for long, though. Anna was soon "whipping" him at night quite regularly, but the effects of this harsh punishment wore off swiftly and the misbehavior reappeared as troublesome as it had been before.

County child protective services intervened quickly. When they spoke with Anna, she was defensive. All she said was, "This is *my* child, and he gets a spanking." That's all that ever came out of it. Inexplicably, child protective services never followed up on the incident. I think James slipped through the cracks or the report was simply put under a pile of others somewhere and forgotten. All that came of the report was that our action didn't endear us to Anna. Her growing suspicion that we were all conspiring against her only intensified.

In desperation, I reviewed James's records carefully once more and found that he had been diagnosed as having a severe attention deficit-hyperactivity disorder (ADHD) almost 18 months previously. In spite of the physician's recommendation that James receive medication for his disorder, no further action was noted in the record. I began to wonder. Why hadn't James received the recommended medication? I raised the issue with Jill, and then I learned another piece of the puzzle.

After school and over the weekends, James spent a great deal of time at church. Anna was a devout follower of her faith, part of which frowned on reliance on medical science, including medical treatment for James's hyperactivity. Any mention of medication drew vehement protests from Anna.

With this additional information, I called yet another meeting with Anna and insisted that James be retested for ADHD. Reluctantly, she agreed. The physician's report was the same as it was before. James had severe ADHD, but Anna refused to allow medication. She would not budge. Her perception that we were all ganging up on her increased to the point that she demanded the appointment of a mediator to serve as a buffer between her and the school. In the last two months of the school year, Anna would communicate only with the mediator, so all our recommendations had to be relayed through him. We were desperate. Medication was not an option, and nothing had worked with James except, at least for a while, Anna's physical abuse.

Eventually, Anna suggested that she spend a good part of each school day in the building in the hopes that her presence would keep him on track. She began appearing at school for several hours each day. James only knew that she was physically somewhere in the building. Sometimes she would be watching through the peephole. At other times she spent time in the office or walking around the playground.

James's behavior improved, but as with the beatings he received at home, the effect of Anna's presence soon wore off. By the last month of school, Anna's appearances dwindled, although she remained available by phone. Two or three days a week we would call Anna to come and get James by noon. It was the only strategy we had left—to get him out of the way. It stayed that way until the end of school.

The following year, James's home was rezoned for construction of a new school several blocks away. I heard that Anna was very excited that he was going to a new school. She thought he would get a fresh start.

I saw James yesterday. Still energetic, still impulsive, still unmedicated. My thoughts were not positive. He's going to get into trouble not only with authority figures but also with his peers, who will understand even less about him than we did. Soon he'll get to high school, where there are more guns, knives, and aggressive behavior. He's going to upset someone so seriously that that'll be the end.

As I tried to look on the sunny side, I couldn't help but remember Anna's parting words to me the year before: "I don't want the teachers spanking him, and I'm tired of having to get James from school when he misbehaves. I'll just have to take care of his sorry attitude at home."

Carmela's Predicament

CARMELA HINES

Royce Burrows, age 16, comes from a troubled family residing in a small rural town in a largely agricultural state. He lives with his mother, Monica Lake, his stepfather, Larry Lake, his brother, Mike Burrows, and a younger half-brother, George Lake. Royce also has two older sisters. Karen Burrows, 17, lives in permanent foster care and has a history of suicide attempts. Prior to her permanent foster care arrangement, Karen had been placed in temporary foster care three times during her adolescence. Janice Burrows, the older sister, lives on her own in another part of the state and rarely has any contact with the family. Larry Lake is self-employed and has a long history of alcoholism and other substance abuse. Larry and Royce are careful to avoid each other at home, and when they don't, bitter fighting ensues.

John Peavy, the school counselor reports:

> Larry is self-employed so he is home at odd times during the day if he happens to be working in the area. He's in and out a lot and there's generally friction when he and Royce are home together. Royce will usually go to his room and stay there and will not come out as long as Larry is in the house.

Monica Lake, Royce's mother, appears to revel in her role as the family advocate to the school system, especially when Royce is involved. She worked hard to obtain an education degree but did not obtain a teaching license. Monica has a reputation in the county for being aggressive, persistent, and threatening.

Jeremy Lyons, an assistant principal, recalls:

> Monica . . . knows all about education and special education law. She knows all kinds of things that the normal run-of-the-mill parent usually has to be told by teachers or the district. Monica *certainly* doesn't have to be told. She's very involved with every advocacy program and committee in the county and several at the state level.

Royce attends Willow High, where he has just completed tenth grade. His school records report long-term learning and motivational problems. The domestic turbulence is reflected in all the children's school attendance.

Teacher Carmela Hines takes up the story:

The family has gone through school districts like water. I think they get tired of fighting battles in one district or something happens to make them move on. I think Royce was failing in the other schools, and the school was after her to get Royce help, so she wanted to get out of there. That's their history.

Royce has been in our school district for three years. During his first year he spent most of his school time at a day treatment center because of what had happened the previous year at his old school. Apparently, he would not go to class and would run away and hide under the bleachers at the football field. He also assaulted a teacher. The previous district supplied a one-on-one teacher for Royce for a while, but when that didn't work they put him in day treatment, where there's much more structure. It was only in April of his first year here that he started to be reintegrated back into Willow High again. Since then, we've all worked hard with Royce and done our best to cope with Monica. Royce's behavior isn't unmanageable, but he does nothing, just nothing—he's oppositionally defiant. He also has an anxiety disorder, so he is very nervous—new unpredictable situations are quite problematic for him.

Our even keel didn't last long. Monica thinks he's good with his hands (he's not) so she wanted him to take a bunch of vocational classes. When we asked him if he wanted to do a metal class, because he's Royce, naturally, he said 'Yeah, I'll try it, whatever."

Soon he started having problems with the vocational teacher. Unless the teacher stood right over him, Royce did nothing. Finally Royce told me that he was afraid of the welder: "I'm afraid I'm going to get burned," he said, "Or I'm going to do something wrong and I'm going to burn somebody else." So I talked to the voc. ed. teacher and got that straightened out.

When Royce got back to school, he was hell on wheels. He wouldn't go to class, and he refused to do any of his make-up work even though it was right at the end of the quarter. Nothing that we did worked, so we practically had to start over with him to get him going to classes again. He ran away from school twice. We decided that we were getting nowhere fast and decided to have a team meeting. Monica was there, of course (Larry never attends). I was there, as well as the welding teacher, another vocational education teacher with whom Royce had a class, his social service manager from the day treatment center, the paraprofessional, and Jeremy, the assistant principal.

Throughout the meeting Royce would not talk directly to Monica. Instead, he talked through me. Keeping him in the meeting was difficult, though. He'd start out OK, and then he would get frustrated as Monica attacked him. She kept at him right from the beginning of the meeting: "Royce, you can do this, this is what you have to do. You are 17 years old, and it's either this or you're out." It went on and on: "You have to do this work. You need to be in this class—you're doing work with your hands, you can do that. I'll help you, your stepfather will help, you have to do this." She'd say all this while half turned away from him. His body language was very tense and tight as he listened. I tried to stem the flow by pointing out that Royce really didn't like the class and that there were several alternatives that might be less threatening. She just went right on. She wanted him to stay in the class no matter what.

While this barrage was going on, Royce left the room several times. I would go out after him and talk him into coming back in. I remember saying to him, "Royce, tell me what you want, and I'll tell them. If you feel like coming back, come back." When he did, Monica would weigh right in again. He just couldn't handle that kind of pressure.

Monica finally agreed that he should quit the class, but she stipulated that he had to fail it. The shop teacher was willing to give Royce the option of making up the work after school, but Monica wouldn't hear of it. Instead, she said, "No, he can fail the class—he needs to fail." It almost seemed her way of proving a point—that if we were going to say he didn't need to take this class, then he should fail it.

As soon as we took him out of the metal-working class there was a general improvement in Royce's performance and attitude. He didn't have to face that class anymore. He liked the teacher in his other vocational class. He took the tests independently; he did the work, and in fact ended up with a *B* at the end of the semester. His other classes were also coming along, although English was very difficult for him, mainly because he could not write cursively at all and because his grammar skills were very poor.

But it wasn't all bad. I remember that in English they did a unit on Shakespeare's *Julius Caesar*. You would have thought any kid would have said "Yuck!" Not Royce. He took my audiotaped version of the play home and listened to it day after day. He would go to English fully prepared and participate in class. The English teacher came over and said, "You're not going to believe this!" This was the same kid who previously wouldn't participate even when he knew the answer. He ended up with a *B* in English—quite phenomenal for Royce.

We finally had Royce back on track. Everything was going along just fine until just before the end of school, when Royce told me that Monica was insisting that he apply for a summer job in our county job training program, Job Success (JS). JS is a job training program for adolescents and adults who qualify either because they have disabilities or are below the poverty line. Royce had been part of the JS program the previous summer, where, after two weeks, he quit because he "didn't like it." We suspected Monica's renewed insistence that he try JS again had more to do with keeping him out of the house for the summer rather than any good JS might be able to do for him. Monica knew that having Royce at home in the summer just doing nothing created problems—especially with Larry.

Suddenly, during the last week of school, Monica called and insisted that Royce needed to have an extended school year through the summer. "He's going to regress," she said. "He's going to be terrible. He's not going to want to go back to school in the fall if we don't do the extended school year. You have to do it!" I was completely floored. I made a couple of phone calls and discovered the reason for Monica's urgency—the Department of Rehabilitation and JS didn't have any vacancies for Royce. Apparently, Monica had been calling everyone on the face of the earth trying to get Royce accepted, but given his poor performance in JS in the past and her belligerence, she ran into a stone wall. The extended school year seemed like a last resort. The district coordinator also indicated that the extended school year idea was inappropriate.

I called Monica on the last day of school to let her know. She was angry, to say the least. I tried to deflect some of her anger by offering to have the team meet with her to discuss the matter. "Please call me if you are willing to have this meeting," I said, "We need to have it at nine o'clock on Friday morning, which is my last duty day for the year." She never responded, so I thought that she'd given up on that idea, too.

Three weeks later, I got a call from Jeremy saying that Monica had called him and demanded a meeting to discuss the extended school idea again. By this point, we were getting beaten down. School was over for the year and both of us were busy with other things. We discussed it for a while. Eventually, I said, "Jerry, let's just do it. It will take two hours out of our day. So what? Perhaps we'll make her happy, and perhaps we can go from there . . . "

I knew that Jeremy was reluctant to meet with Monica. They've had a history of conflict, mostly at Monica's instigation. I knew, for example, that Monica had accosted Jeremy out in public a couple of times, insisting that he discuss some problem or the other right there in public.

Jeremy set up a meeting for that Thursday morning, two days later, at 10:00. He called everybody else on the team, but with little success. The case manager was away at a workshop, Royce's other teachers were not available, and the district coordinator was out of town.

By the time I arrived for the meeting, Jeremy was furious. Monica had called him half an hour earlier and said she just couldn't make the meeting at 10:00 and also that she wanted Royce's case manager from the day treatment center to be there. Jeremy managed to hold firm and explained that I was already on my way and that the meeting would proceed whether she was there or not.

When I arrived for the meeting, I realized that we didn't have a general education teacher there, and we needed one in order for the meeting to be legal. Two teachers just happened to be in the building at that time, both of whom knew Royce quite well. We begged them to help us out. Luckily, they agreed.

Monica finally showed up a little after 10:00, and I decided that we needed to really lay down the law that the extended school year idea was not appropriate for Royce. I knew that what Monica really wanted was day care. Monica was her usual self, but Jerry and I were persistent and focused. As soon as she realized that we weren't going to budge, she appealed to the two commandeered teachers, but they knew Royce well enough to know that Jeremy and I were right. I could see Monica getting nervous, and she soon switched tactics: "Well, if we can't do extended school year, then I want Royce in summer school because he failed the metal class," she said. We nixed that idea, too. Monica, however, was relentless, and her next remark pushed Jerry over the edge.

"Well," she said, "we have to do something. You people aren't being any help. I wanted something done about this, and you won't do anything." I tried to head Jeremy off by interrupting Monica by going through my record book, reciting all of the meetings, phone calls, discussions, and other efforts we had made through the year. Jeremy was just livid. His face reddened even further when Monica said, "Well, obviously you're not going to help me. I'll just have to do this on my own." Monica rose abruptly and left the room. We all just sat there looking at each other.

Jerry was the first to speak: "I'm sorry. I probably shouldn't have gotten so mad, but it just makes me angry that we have bent over backwards for her all year but as soon as she doesn't get what she wants, then we're the bad guys." Before any of us could respond, Monica reentered the room and started right in with her "poor me" theme. We tried our best to brainstorm some alternatives, but Monica kept coming back to the extended school year, and we kept rebuffing it.

By this point, Jeremy was a little ashamed of letting Monica get the better of him. He tried his level best to make up for it with a number of viable suggestions, but to no avail. She had excuses for everything he suggested:

"How about an in-home family therapist?"

"We're on a waiting list."

"A support group for parents of children with oppositional defiance?"

"I already started one."

"How about letting Royce work at odd jobs around the neighborhood?"

"There are none."

Suddenly, Monica showed her hand. "You're just not going to help me—I can see that. What am I supposed to do when Larry comes home and yells at Royce because Royce has been lying around all day doing nothing?"

With that, she left, slamming the door behind her.

That was a month ago. I stopped at my usual convenience store last week, and there was Monica, working behind the counter. She was quite friendly, although our pleasantries studiously avoided any talk of Royce. I'll bet she solved the summer problem with Royce by getting herself out of the house instead.

What's Inclusion Got to Do with It?

ANITA ATKINSON

Anita Atkinson walked from her third-period U.S. History class in a daze. "I've been teaching for 27 years," she thought, "27 years and I've never had a class of students who were so needy. I don't know, maybe I'm just getting too old for this. Maybe it's just time for me to retire."

There were so many changes at McGinnis High School this year, all in the name of educational reform and improved outcomes for students. Anita's classroom was no longer in the main building, but in a mobile unit. She and her students had been displaced to make room for a computer lab. Most of her students returned to McGinnis from early morning classes at the county's vocational and technical center, and they were finding it difficult to get from the building to her class on time. She frequently found herself interrupting lessons to check in tardy students and redo her attendance sheets.

For the first time in 20 years, the school administrators had abolished ability grouping. The district superintendent's cry for higher standards was now trickling down to the school and classroom level. "We have to become more competitive with other developed nations," Anita had heard her principal say time and time again at faculty meetings. "All students need to be exposed to a more rigorous and comprehensive curriculum." So now all students were placed without consideration of their achievement levels. Well, almost all students. The classes for average to above-average and advanced placement students were now combined; however, X-level classes were maintained for students who were functioning below grade level. Anita's class, for example, was supposed to be an inclusion classroom where students with disabilities were mainstreamed with nonlabeled students. For the past three years, special education teachers had been assigned to coteach with general education teachers who had large numbers of students with disabilities enrolled in their classes. This year, Anita was assigned to work with Jennifer, a second-year teacher of students with behavioral disorders.

Anita made her way to a study room in the library for her planning period. She had every intention of planning for next week's lessons, but she couldn't get her mind off her motley crew. She made it to the study room, closed the door, and just sat, reflecting about her students and what had just transpired in her class. In her mind's eye, she pictured her students sitting in their assigned seats at the beginning of class. Before her sat 20 students—15 males and 5 females, 16 white and 4 black. Most were from low-income families. Of the male students, 10 were labeled as having learning disabilities, and 2 were diagnosed as BD (behaviorally disordered). All 5 female students and 1 male student were labeled as at risk for dropping out of school. "What a bunch," she said aloud as she opened her NEA tote bag and pulled out her planner, teacher's manual, and supplementary materials for the Revolutionary War. She ran down the list of her most needy students.

Floyd, a 19-year-old white male, was severely learning disabled. Anita couldn't remember when she had worked with another student as low-functioning as Floyd. He was basically a nonreader who required someone to read everything for him. He hated writing anything because of his poor writing skills. The school psychologist told her at the beginning of the year that Floyd had a very low IQ and had come very close to being placed in a class for the mentally retarded.

Greg, an 18-year-old African American student, was bright but unmotivated. He had failed every class for the marking period and was chronically absent from school. He was either sound asleep or on top of things, contributing intelligently to class discussions. Unfortunately, he worked a 3:00 to 11:00 shift at the Mr. Joe's Sub Shop down the street and always complained of not getting enough rest. He could've made it in one of the heterogeneous sections, but he'd opted to remain in X-level.

Kendell, another African American student, had a severe learning disability. He read at the second-grade level, was chronically absent from school, and was just barely passing. Kendell had one thing going for him, though. He was a star on the football team, so every marking period he managed to get grades high enough to keep him on the squad. He wasn't concerned about passing the competency exam, earning a high school diploma, or playing football in college. "Um just coasting, Mrs. A.," he told Anita once when she was pushing him to try harder. "I can't read, can't write, ain't nobody gonna accept me into no college. Umma just be satisfied with my certificate of attendance."

Mitch, a 17-year-old white male, was diagnosed with a behavior disorder. Mitch had a lot of potential, but he was always getting into trouble with the law. At the end of one class, he had come up to Anita and volunteered: "Mrs. A., I might not be here next year. This might be my last day. I haven't told anybody else, but I got in trouble again and the judge said if I got in trouble again, I was a goner. I was driving without a license and got caught." Prior to this incident, Mitch had gotten busted on school property for selling drugs.

Thinking about these and other students, Anita wondered how she was supposed to get them interested in U.S. History when many of them were just trying to survive from one day to the next. Was she kidding herself, or what!

Anita awoke from her daydream but jumped right back into it as her mind switched to another problem—working with Jennifer, her special education coteacher. At the beginning of the year, Jennifer had asked if she could coteach with Anita, as her BD students and several LD students had been placed in Anita's so-called inclusion classroom. Anita had been involved in a very successful and mutually satisfying relationship with Carol—another special education teacher—two years before, so she was thrilled when Jennifer requested to work with her. She missed having that extra pair of hands to deal with all the unique needs present in her classroom.

Unfortunately, though, things hadn't gone as smoothly with Jennifer as they had gone with Carol. "It's just not the same," Anita told Carol one night during a telephone conversation. "You and I talked, we shared, we planned together on a regular basis. You were always in my room on time and you were always willing to modify worksheets, group assignments, tests, and stuff like that. You got all those kids on track when it came to being organized. You did more than just walk around and keep them awake and on task. It was like a 50/50 split, a 50/50 partnership. But this one . . . Well, I don't know, she just doesn't take the lead, and even when I ask her to do something, she doesn't follow through. Now she's missing at least two to three days a week from my class even though I have two of her BD students. It won't surprise me if by the end of the year she's not coming at all."

Anita was startled by the sound of sledgehammers and bulldozers outside the library. A crew of construction workers were building a new addition to the library that would be equipped with state-of-the-art instructional technology. She smiled as she thought about the messiness that accompanies new construction and compared it to the messiness of school reform. "I've seen the pendulum swing from one end of the spectrum to the other so many times over the past 27 years," she thought as she bit into a big, red, juicy apple. "I've always managed to survive the changes and even grow as a result of them. But this time, for some reason, I can't see my way through the messiness. What will be the end result? When it's all said and done, what difference will it all make?"

Anita now turned her attention to what had transpired in class today. If she concentrated, maybe she could come up with some problem-solving strategies that might help her reach the kids and deal more effectively with Jennifer. Her mind raced back to the beginning of class. It was 10:27 and the tardy bell had just sounded. Jennifer was nowhere to be found. She was supposed to have constructed a study guide for the midterm exam and begin going over it in class. Anticipating a no-show, Anita had developed the study guide herself and was preparing to review with the students.

Jennifer burst through the door at 10:35, apologizing that she was late and hadn't done the guide because she'd had to call several parents to arrange IEPs for newly labeled BD students. Anita couldn't believe her ears. "Carol would never have done this," she thought. "I would never have done this. I would've been here at 5:00 in the morning or called after school or at night." Still, she wasn't one to make waves, so she maintained her composure and acted as if Jennifer's tardiness hadn't fazed her.

"That's OK, hon," Anita replied. She wanted to kick herself for not telling Jennifer what she was really thinking. "I already did the study guide, and now I'm going to put them in cooperative learning groups and have them search for the answers to the questions. You can help me monitor them and make sure they're finding the correct answers." She handed Jennifer a copy of the study guide with the correct answers written in red ink.

"Cool," Jennifer responded, impressed by the organization of the guide. "Wow! This is a really neat study guide with page numbers where they can find the answers!

And I see you divided stuff up so they won't have such a large bank of words to choose from for the fill-in-the-blank questions."

"Oh, I learned that from my other coteacher a couple of years ago. Yeah, it really helps the kids stay focused and makes them feel like they don't have so much to do at one time. They can break it down into chunks." Anita stopped talking, thinking to herself, "Duh, Jennifer, it would be nice if you would do something like this every once in a while!"

They then quickly got the students into five groups of four students. Unfortunately, the students weren't interested in completing the sheet even though it would help them prepare for their midterm exam. Anita had just attended a workshop on cooperative learning and had spent last week talking to students about how it works. Today, she'd started out by videotaping the cooperative learning groups so students could assess the quality of their teamwork and performance. Around 10:38, Jennifer approached a group that wasn't working and urged them to complete the assignment. As Anita walked around videotaping, she discovered that only one group was following instructions. Disappointed, she turned off the camcorder, put it away, and tried to come up with a way to get the students on task.

"I'll give three points extra on the exam to the group that gets the right answer to the first three questions on the study guide," she called out, thinking that this announcement might spark some enthusiasm. Unfortunately, there were no takers. At this point, spitballs were flying, attackers were being cursed by the attacked, and no one seemed to care that the mid-term exam was next Wednesday.

At 10:42, Anita was experiencing serious stress. She decided to refocus, to try another approach. She called "time" and told the students to prepare for a whole-class activity. "Yeah, that's it," she speculated silently. "Maybe I can get more out of them if I pull everyone together in one large group." She called on students from each group and asked for answers to the questions. Jennifer was standing next to her at the front of the room, looking on in silence.

As Anita continued her reflection, she still couldn't believe what had gone down in her classroom. She'd lost all control. All around her, students were engrossed in private conversations. Kendell threw a spitball at Lakeesha from across the room. Lakeesha turned around in her seat, looked Kendell in the eye, spotted a smirk on his face, and shouted, "Go to hell!" as loud as she could. Needless to say, no one responded to Anita's question about the Revolutionary War.

In desperation, Anita had shouted out to the class. "Now wait just a minute! I'm not going to stand here and try to talk when everyone else is talking, so knock it off right now!" She was furious, and the students knew it. Jennifer continued to stand beside her with a blank look on her face.

The students sensed Anita's anger and decided to comply with her demand for their undivided attention, at least for a few minutes. Anita asked her question again, and a few students raised their hands and answered correctly. Some of them even seemed a little interested in the discussion about events that led up to the Revolutionary War. After several students responded correctly to questions on the guide, Anita attempted a discussion about excise taxes, but noticed she was once again losing the students. At this point, Jennifer must have noticed her frustration, for she walked around the room awakening sleeping students, breaking up private conversations, and telling students to raise their hands if they wanted to speak.

Anita called on Kendell to answer a question, trying to get his mind off harassing Lakeesha. "Kendell, can you give us an example of how the colonists protested the excise taxes placed on them by England?"

All eyes were now on Kendell, and he saw this as an opportunity to disrupt the class further. With that infamous smirk on his face, he responded, "This is what happened when those colony guys threw a bunch of whiskey in the ocean and everybody got drunk and had a big PARTAY. Even the fish!" The class broke up in laughter. Students were holding their stomachs. "I'm through, I'm finished!" screamed Lakeesha. Floyd reached over and gave Kendell a high five. Anita looked at Jennifer and saw the tiniest of smiles on her face.

Anita was at her wit's end. "You know, Kendell, you're really getting on my nerves. Now, what did you tell me just yesterday when I asked you to stop goofing off and get serious about school?"

No response.

"I want an answer from you now, Kendell!"

In a terse and apathetic tone, Kendell uttered, "Sorry, teach, that's the way I am. When I work, I work. When I don't, I don't."

"Well you need to work, then; get in your working mood. You need to get it together so you can stay on the football team."

This statement jolted Kendell into reality. He sat up in his seat, thumbing through the pages in the book to find the answer. "OK, OK," he responded. He found a picture depicting the Boston Tea Party and tried to read the caption underneath it. "This is a . . . um . . . this is a um. Damn! Mrs. A., you know I can't read this crap!" Several students giggled and teased Kendell because he couldn't read such a simple sentence. Floyd proceeded to imitate Kendell's attempt to read the caption, being careful to capture the puzzled and frustrated look on his face. Kendell was furious.

"If I was you, I wouldn't be makin' fun of nobody's readin', boy, cause you can't even read 'I see the cat.' You need to shut up before I come over there and bust you in yo mouth!"

"Come on, then. I ain't scared of you just cause you the big man on the football team. Come on over here and try to bust me in my mouth and see what you get."

The bell rang, ending the period just as the two boys were rising from their seats to attack each other. Anita quickly told the rest of the students to go to their fourth-period classes, and she and Jennifer escorted Floyd and Kendell to the office. "Yes, there is a God," Anita thought as she realized that the bell had saved her from having to deal with a fight.

When the bell rang signaling the start of fifth period, Anita still had thought of no solutions, no answers to her questions. She packed her tote bag and headed for her class full of above-average and AP students. Right now, she had to shift gears and think about the planning for the reenactment of the Yorktown surrender with this talented group. She would grapple with the messiness of inclusion later. She needed help desperately, but she didn't know where to turn.

Finding the Mesh: A Conversation with Collaborative High School Teachers

BRUCE SULLIVAN

Part A

Good evening to all of you in our studio audience and to those of you at home. I'm Bruce Sullivan, and I'll be your host tonight as we explore the experiences of educators who are implementing partial inclusive education programs in the Haverford County Public School District. *Inclusive education*, a term that emanated from the word *mainstreaming* from the 1970s and 80s, is one of several special education service delivery options, all of which must be provided as mandated by the Individuals with Disabilities Education Act, better known as IDEA.

With inclusion, students with disabilities are taught in general education classrooms with their nonlabeled peers to the fullest extent possible. However, some school districts have moved to full inclusion models in which *all* students with disabilities, including those with severe disabilities, are served in general education classes 100 percent of the time. Instead of teaching these students in pull-out settings, special educators serve as consultants to general educators or teach collaboratively with them in general education classrooms. This is a very controversial issue in special education today. Some educators argue that within the next 10 years, parent advocacy and litigation will result in a renewed emphasis on improving all special education service delivery options. For the time being, though, the push for full inclusion is on the rise.

As a part of its initiative to increase the number of "inclusive schools," Haverford has been implementing a collaborative, or co-teaching, model for almost three years and has decided to assess the efficacy of the model. The district wishes to identify strengths and weaknesses, and to determine whether the program should be continued and expanded. If the school district decides to continue the model, teachers and administrators want to identify changes that need to take place to sustain successful implementation. They also want to identify what markers and measures constitute success. To do this, the school system administrators and board members wish to include all voices in the discourse about inclusion and co-teaching. This is why we are here tonight. Just look around you. This audience is made up of parents, students with and without disabilities, general and special education teachers who are involved with inclusion, as well as those who aren't. Also, some building and central office administrators are present. Tonight's program, aired on public access channel WPAT, is the first in a series of programs designed to allow all concerned citizens to raise questions and provide input about the inclusive education programs.

To kick off our series, we are happy to have with us tonight two teachers from Johnson High School who have co-taught in the county since the first year the program began. Yvonne Parsons is a teacher of students with learning disabilities, or LD, and Terri Carter is an eleventh-grade English teacher. They co-taught with other teachers during the first two years of implementation, but are now co-teaching a group of 19 students who are classified as having LD, LD with emotional or behavioral disorders, sometimes referred to as *LD/BD* or *at risk*. Yvonne and Terri videotaped most of their classes and have graciously agreed to show some segments from them tonight. To be more efficient, we provided index cards and pencils to all studio audience members and asked them to jot down questions, concerns, and recommendations they have about co-teaching. Unfortunately, we don't have enough time to field all the questions, but we have categorized them into themes that will be addressed tonight. For those of you at home, you can email your issues to Hav1@include.edu. If you don't have access to the Internet, simply call us at INC-LUDE, or 762-5833. To the left, you can see that we have several operators here to take your calls. So, sit back, relax, and get ready for a very informative hour with some very special teachers. Let's give them a warm welcome as they come forward to share their experiences with us.

(The audience applauds vigorously. Yvonne and Terri wave, bow, and mouth "thank you" as they enter from stage right and sit on a long beige sofa in the center of the stage. Bruce takes his seat next to them in a dark brown, leather swivel chair behind a mahogany stained desk. There is a coffee table in front of the teachers with mugs of water, coffee, and soft drinks. In the background are large posters showing Yvonne and Terri working with students in their inclusive classroom. The audience stops applauding after the "applause" light goes off. At this point, Bruce begins the dialogue.)

BRUCE: Good evening, ladies, it is so nice to have you on our very first show this evening.

YVONNE: Why thanks, Bruce, we feel very honored to be here.

TERRI: Yes, and we hope that this will be a learning experience for everyone here, including the two of us who are sitting here on the hot seat. *(Laughter from the audience.)*

BRUCE: Well let's get started then, shall we? Several audience members want to know how you got started co-teaching and if there is a system in place to sustain effective co-teaching practices. Now, tell me again, ladies, how did you get into co-teaching? You co-taught with two other teachers during the first two years of implementation, correct?

YVONNE: Yes, that's correct. This is my third year of co-teaching. The first year I co-taught in a science class, and I felt uncomfortable because it was something that I didn't have a lot of experience with, and the other teacher and I didn't work together real well. Um, you know, it just wasn't a good mesh. The second year I worked with an English teacher, and it was wonderful. It was the greatest thing I'd done, and I was able to work with a much larger population of students than I ever had before. I got to see what the general education teacher has to do and then back that up with things that I know about teaching kids with LD. This year, the administration told me I had to move up with this class because they would need me even more for eleventh-grade English. I really had no choice, but luckily I ended up with Terri. From the very minute we saw each other we just, you know, we just *knew* that we were going to hit it off. Unfortunately, that doesn't always happen.

BRUCE: Hmmm . . . Sounds kinda like love at first sight to me. *(Laughter from audience and the teachers.)*

TERRI: *(still laughing)* Oh, wow, funny you should mention that, Bruce! So many of us refer to co-teaching as a marriage. Sometimes things turn out great, sometimes you have to temporarily separate, and sometimes you just have to call it quits and get a divorce. *(A few chuckles from the audience.)*

BRUCE: How interesting! Terri, can you tell us more about this, um, the marriage, and what do you call it, the mesh?

TERRI: For sure. When you are in a good marriage or when you reach the mesh, you've gotten to a point where you *want* to be in here, you *want* to participate, you *want* to be loyal, and you *want* to be a part of everything that goes on in here. And you've got to be in here every day, or at least as much as you possibly can . . .

YVONNE: Yeah, and you know what, even though we had gut reactions that we would hit it off, we still spent some time talking and observing each other before we actually started teaching together. We realized that our philosophies are very much the same, and even though we may do things differently, we can put our differences together and make them work to our advantage.

BRUCE: Makes sense to me. Terri, is this the way things started out for you in your first year?

TERRI: *(throwing arms and hands in the air)* Lord have mercy! You don't know how much I wish I could say that, Bruce, but in all honesty, I really can't. It really depends on that mesh that you have with the other teacher. That first year the girl seemed to feel like it was a time when she could get her IEPs done, a time when she could meet with students one on one. And a lot of times I got a note that read, "I'm going to work in my room," even when at least half the kids in my room were LD or EBD. When she *was* in the room, it ended up with her sitting in my rocking chair like a bump on a log, and the kids never even knew her name. They would ask, "Why is that lady in here?" I got along better with the girl I had last year, but this year has been even better. The kids really do treat us like we are both their teachers. At this point, it's not "Miss Carter and that lady" or "that lady and Miss Carter." You know what I mean? At first they looked more to me as the "last word" person in charge, but now we have gotten them to a point where they're very comfortable calling on either of us.

You better believe it! If this were not the case, our kids would play us one against the other, and all kinds of behavior problems would just pop up out of nowhere. In fact, they have tried. We have proof of that.

BRUCE: Thank you so much, ladies. Now, audience, this looks like a topic where these teachers as well as the district could use some suggestions and recommendations. Seems like I'm hearing that pairs of teachers who co-teach might have incompatible beliefs and approaches. What are some things that administrators and teachers can do to make better decisions about pairing teachers? What can be done to increase the likelihood that there will be a good fit between co-teachers? Please let us hear from you on this.

Now, let's turn our attention to an area that is directly related to this one. You mentioned that you were compatible in many ways, but you did have some differences in the way you operate. Many audience members want to know your answer to this question: What differences have caused problems for you to date? Also, they want to know how you go about resolving conflicts and disagreements.

(Terri and Yvonne give each other a glance and smirk that evolves into laughter. Bruce and several audience members look puzzled.)

BRUCE: Sorry ladies, but did we miss something?

TERRI: Oh, Bruce, please forgive us! Your question just brought back memories of one of our first, shall we say, dilemmas. Boy did we learn a thing or two from this experience! Funny, we anticipated these questions, so we brought a clip of a specific class session to let everyone see how, early on, things got out of hand, not because of the kids, but because of us. We call this segment "The Infamous MacBeth Test."

BRUCE: *(pointing to cameraman)* OK, Mike, roll it!

The Infamous MacBeth Test (November 4ᵗʰ)

It is 8:38 A.M. All 19 students are present. Terri is taking the roll and finishing other morning clerical work. The tardy bell rings. Most students are sitting in their seats, talking quietly to neighbors. One student is selling candy bars for a school fund-raising project. At 8:40, Terri calls the students to order and tells them that she is about to hand back the last *MacBeth* test. Many students begin to slump down in their seats at the mere mention of one of Mr. Shakespeare's most intriguing protagonists. Terri then tells students to get out their notebooks and textbooks in preparation for the class discussion. Some students comply with this request, but others focus undivided attention on the tests she is passing back. At 8:42, Yvonne comes in and helps Terri pass back the tests.

At 8:44, Jon, a tall African American male student, comes up to Terri who is sitting on a stool in the front of the classroom. He shows Terri his test and asks her about a vocabulary word that has been marked incorrect. Terri looks at the word and tells Jon to circle the mistake and she will look at it again. Jon says, "OK" and returns to his seat. Then, Tonya, sitting at her desk, asks Terri a question about how the test was graded. Terri tells Tonya to hand her the paper so that she can look at it. Terri looks at the paper and says, "Mrs. Parsons graded this, and if I had graded it I would have marked it wrong also. You must really try to write letters distinctly so we can make them out."

Between 8:46 and 8:49, several students approach Terri with questions about the test. Many see discrepancies between what she taught them when they were covering the material and the actual scores on the test.

It is 8:50. Yvonne has been working with a student at his desk for several minutes and has not responded to any of the complaints about the test. She asks the student she is helping to step out in the hall so that she can retest him orally. At 8:56, Tonya and April discreetly share their feelings about the test and co-teaching.

Says Tonya, "You know I am really pissed off. See, this is why we shouldn't have two teachers."

"For real, girl," replies April, "One tells you one thing and the other one tells you something else, and then you get the test back and you get a damn *F*. Don't make no damn sense."

"Yeah, I hate this damn class, girl, and I ain't takin' no more of this s___. I know I did better than this on this test." Quickly, Tonya's voice goes from a whisper to a roar. One hand on her hip and the other pointing in the direction of the door, she belts out, "So why you let *her* grade them?" *(Other students respond in support of her inquiry.)*

Calm and poised, Terri assures the students that she will go over the tests and tells them not to be so hard on Yvonne. "She doesn't know the play as well as I do. She did the best she could. I was swamped, and she was trying to help me out." At 9:10, Yvonne returns to the room with her student only to hear Jon complaining about another question. She is standing in the back of the room. She nervously shares with the class, "I marked a lot of the questions wrong because the answers on the key were real vague. So don't get upset, Tonya, we'll take care of this." Tonya, apparently appeased, sits down in her seat and says, "OK, but y'all need to make sure y'all tellin' us the same thing."

It is 9:22, nearly time for the bell to ring. Dealing with the test has taken up the entire class period. There was no instruction today. As the students prepare to leave, Terri calls out to them, "Let me have your attention again, class. I take full responsibility for this. It's my fault. Please don't blame Mrs. Parsons. We apologize. *(Yvonne nods her head in the affirmative.)* We promise to do a better job next time." The two teachers stand in front of Terri's desk and begin talking about what just happened. As the bell rings and the students leave, tears begin to run down both their faces.

(The clip ends and the camera zooms back to Yvonne and Terri. They both have tissues and are wiping tears from their eyes. Bruce gives them a few seconds to compose themselves. Then he resumes the discussion.)

BRUCE: Wow! You know, before we move on, I must say that it takes a lot of courage to share yourselves and your classroom with so many people. This must really make you feel vulnerable. OK audience; let's hear it for these brave ladies!

(The audience applauds, some rising to their feet in support of Yvonne and Terri.)

BRUCE: Oh, before we go on, the parents and the students themselves gave written permission for us to use these clips. So what happened, Terri,? Um . . . how did you deal with this problem?

TERRI: Well, it's a long story, but we'll try to make it brief. I felt like it was my fault because I gave her a really shoddy key. Now, I am not the most organized person in the world. Sometimes I can be all over the place. I think I used a key from a previous quiz from last year, and it was a key that I made up for my own purposes, and I knew what I wanted in my head. What Yvonne did was write down to the letter what was on the key, and then I gave them back without looking over them and the kids asked, "Who graded this?" and "Why did you mark this wrong?" I didn't want to blame her because I felt like it was my fault.

YVONNE: And I was a little angry with myself because I didn't know enough about *Macbeth* to accept the broad answers that she was accepting and, I was also a little angry with partner here because that key was prreeetty bad! Most of the time I'm real right-brained, but when it comes to grading tests and that type of thing, I'm left-brained and I want specifics down to the letter. And it caused me some frustration, and she knew it did. So, after class, we sat down and we talked it out, and I shed some tears, and she shed some tears—and we said, "OK, how are we going to solve it?"

BRUCE: Sounds like a real learning experience. So what did you end up doing?

YVONNE: Now we meet and design the tests together. We are also very honest with each other now and we realize that problems can sometimes lead to growth if you are open. If something aggravates me, I let her know it right away, and vice-versa. That's the only way to go, but some co-teachers I know just hold it all in because they don't want to hurt anybody's feelings, and they make little if any progress. They are the ones who end up separating and divorcing. We've made lots of progress in this area, but we still have a ways to go. We could definitely use any advice anyone has to offer. For starters, I need someone to help me be more organized!

BRUCE: Great! And that is a great lead-in to another question we have from our audience. You've already touched on this a bit. What roles do each of you take when co-teaching? But before we shift to this topic, let's pause for an announcement from the Executive Director of WPAT. Remember, they provide a wonderful service to us, and we need to help keep them on the air. We'll be back in about 60 seconds. *(Screen fades to black.)*

INDEX